Highlights of Jewish History

VOLUME FOUR

FROM THE MIDDLE AGES
TO MODERN TIMES

HIGHLIGHTS OF JEWISH HISTORY

VOLUME FOUR

From the Middle Ages to Modern Times

WITH MAPS,
EXERCISES AND PROJECTS

By

MORDECAI H. LEWITTES

Illustrations by

SAM NISENSON

HEBREW PUBLISHING COMPANY
NEW YORK

To Judith Marcia Lewittes, beloved daughter
of her people, whose nobility of spirit will ever
remain a cherished memory

Preface

This is the fourth volume in a series of books dealing with Jewish history. Other titles in the series are:

a. *Heroes of Jewish History: Abraham to Moses*
b. *Heroes of Jewish History: Joshua to Jeremiah*
c. *Highlights of Jewish History: Daniel to the Rambam*

The present volume covers eight centuries of Jewish history. The author has sought throughout to stress abiding Jewish values. Among the major themes are courage in the face of persecution, the participation of the Jew in the struggle for emancipation and for human rights, his steadfast devotion to his faith as he builds new centers of Jewish life, the primacy of the synagogue and of Torah, Jewish contributions to America and to modern civilization and the redemption of the Land of Israel.

In keeping with the expanding intellectual horizons of the Junior High School pupil, the author has devoted increased attention to discussion of political, economic and social changes in the life of the Jew. Sources are quoted fully and frequently to give the student a sense of history in the making. Nonetheless, the direct, dramatic style of the earlier volumes is retained to assure the interest of the reader.

The last two units, entitled "The Jew in America" and "Israel," are intended merely as an introduction to these vital centers of contemporary Jewish life, since space is necessarily limited. The author believes that Jewish secondary schools should make provision subsequently for an entire semester of studies devoted to each of these countries.

The varied exercises, review tests, topics for discussion, suggestions for supplementary reading, projects, maps, illustrations and charts will be an aid to teacher and student provided they are not followed slavishly. The extent of their use will depend on the needs and nature of the class.

During the composition of this series of books the author was ever mindful of the Biblical injunction, *V'hig-gad'ta l'vin'cha* ("and thou shalt tell unto thy son"). Just as the retelling of the story of the Exodus has helped to keep alive the flame of freedom, so too it is hoped that the retelling of the long and dramatic story of the Jew will serve to inspire our youth with a love for the great ideals that characterize the Jewish way of life.

Contents

PAGE

UNIT ONE

The Staff of the Wanderer

1. Rabbi Meir of Rothenburg   17
2. Persecution   25
3. Expulsion from Spain   34
4. In the Days of the Marranos   45

UNIT TWO

Lands of Refuge

5. Italy and Turkey   61
6. The Holy Land   71
7. Holland   80
8. The New World   91

UNIT THREE

Eastern Europe

9. Poland   111
10. "Out of the Depths of Despair"   123
11. The Baal Shem Tov—Founder of *Hasidism*   132
12. The Vilna Gaon   144

UNIT FOUR

The Dawn of Emancipation

13. Moses Mendelssohn—Father of Jewish Emancipation   155
14. The French Revolution and Jewish Emancipation   169
15. Moses Montefiore—Defender of Jewish Rights   180
16. Russian Jewry   194

9

UNIT FIVE

Jews in America

17. Citizens of a New Country 207
18. Proud Jews and Patriotic Americans 219
19. Growth and Conflict 231
20. "Your Huddled Masses Yearning to Breathe Free" 244

UNIT SIX

Israel

21. Zionism 259
22. Rebirth 275
23. Under the Mandate 284
24. War and Resistance 293
25. An Independent Jewish State 302

Appendix 311

Index 317

Illustrations

	PAGE
Israel (*Map*)	*Frontispiece*
In the Middle Ages (*Map*)	33
A Marrano Secret Seder	48
Rembrandt and Menasseh ben Israel	83
Asser Levy and Peter Stuyvesant	98
Eastern Europe (*Map*)	121
A Hasidic Dance of Joy	143
Western Europe (*Map*)	170
The Newport Synagogue—A National American Shrine	223
Emma Lazarus and the Statue of Liberty	246
Herzl on the Way to the Land of Israel	270
Colonists in Israel	298

TO THE STUDENT

"Every Jew must feel that he himself was freed from Egypt and was present at Sinai." Thus say the Rabbis. Indeed all of Jewish history is almost like a living memory to us because we feel that we were there. Each Jew identifies himself with his people.

It is just as if we were with Abraham, Isaac and Jacob as they wandered in Canaan, and began to teach mankind the belief in One God. Each Passover we relive the inspiring story of freedom from Egyptian bondage. On *Shavuot* we recall the granting of the 10 commandments, and on *Sukkot* when we enter the *Sukkah* we are reminded of the wandering of the Israelites in the desert for 40 years.

And now we are crossing the Jordan with Joshua as we enter the promised land. With Deborah, Gideon, Samson and Samuel we seek to lead the 12 tribes in time of war and peace.

For a brief period we feel the strength that comes from unity during the reigns of Saul, David and Solomon. But, alas, soon we are in a house divided as the 10 tribes of Israel break away from the leadership of Judah. We hear the immortal words of Elijah, Isaiah and Jeremiah as the prophets condemn evil and preach justice, peace and righteousness.

We weep with the captives by the waters of Babylon, but sing with joy as the exiles return to Zion. We pledge our renewed loyalty to the Torah with Ezra, and rebuild the walls of Jerusalem, tool in one hand and sword in the other, as Nehemiah teaches us to build and to defend what we have built.

On Purim we recall the victory of Mordecai and Esther over wicked Haman in Persia, and on Chanukah we kindle the lights to commemorate the triumph of the Maccabees over Syrian tyranny and of light over darkness. Lag B'Omer reminds us of the heroic but futile attempt of Bar Kochba to free Judea from the deadly talons of the Roman eagle.

But as we read the teachings of Hillel, Johanan ben Zakkai, Akiva and Judah the Prince we see how defeat is turned into victory. Bible and Mishnah, written law and oral law, unite the Jews, scattered though they were, into one nation.

With Rav and Samuel we watch the growth of academies of learning in Babylon. Centuries of study and discussion live again as we turn the pages of the Talmud.

We see how new religions, claiming Judaism as their source, spread throughout the world. But forgotten are the words of Moses, "Love your neighbor as yourself"; the sword of hatred is turned against the Jew who staunchly remains true to the faith of his fathers.

We follow the Jew as he builds new centers in Arabia, in the land of the Khazars, in France and Germany and as he reaches new heights during the Golden Age of Spain. We admire the wisdom of Saadia Gaon, the sage comments of Rashi, the poetry of Judah Halevi and the great teachings of the Rambam.

And now we are ready for further adventures.

What new happenings befell the Jewish people in Europe and Asia? How did the Bible and Talmud continue to guide the Jew? Who were the heroes and leaders that arose in modern times? How did the Jew find refuge in the New World? What contributions did the Jewish people make to modern civilization?

As we seek to find the answers to these questions we know that the story of the Jew cannot fail to be vital. We read it not as strangers but as members of the Jewish people. It is almost as if it happened to us.

Even though separated by time and space we march with our people through Jewish history; in spirit we are there. We are part of one nation united under God.

UNIT ONE

The Staff of the Wanderer

CHAPTER I

RABBI MEIR OF ROTHENBURG

THE JEWS of France and Germany had lived in peace for hundreds of years. Only the Crusades were a sad omen of the cruel days that were to come.

One of the greatest of the German scholars was Rabbi Meir ben Baruch. He was born around 1215, ten years after the death of the Rambam, in the city of Worms. It was here that the great Rashi, prince of commentators, had once studied.

As a young man Meir decided to continue his studies in France.

"I have heard that there are great scholars in Paris," said Meir to his family. "With their help I can master the study of Talmud."

Meir made excellent progress in his studies. In Paris, however, Meir was witness to a sad event.

A renegade named Nicholas Donin, a convert from Judaism, resolved to vent his hatred on his former religion by destroying all copies of the Talmud. Donin presented his plan to the highest officials of church and state in Rome and in Paris.

"It is only because of the Talmud that the Jews refuse to convert," argued Donin. "Destroy the Talmud, and Jews will soon enter the church."

King Louis IX of France decided to arrange a debate between the Rabbis and Donin. Four of the leading Rabbis of France were ordered to appear before the king. Meanwhile, all copies of the Talmud were confiscated. The Rabbis were informed that the charge against the Talmud was that it blasphemed the founder of the Christian religion. They knew how unfounded was the accusation, but they feared that the king merely sought an excuse for destroying the Talmud.

The debate began on June 12, 1240 in the presence of the royal court. The queen-mother, who was present, insisted that every courtesy be shown the Rabbis. The debate continued for many days.

The Rabbis showed how false Donin's charge was. They stressed the greatness of the Talmud which applied the Biblical ideal of justice to every aspect of life. Their cause was hope-less from the start. A biased court decided that all copies of the Talmud were to be burnt.

Every effort was made to avert the evil decree. A friendly archbishop succeeded in postponing the day when the sentence would be executed.

After two years the dreaded day came. On Friday, June 17, 1242 twenty-four carts were filled with priceless manuscripts. The carts rumbled through the narrow streets of Paris to a public square. Here the tomes of the Talmud were consigned to the flames.

Meir ben Baruch and his fellow-students watched the flames as they leaped higher and higher. They wept to see their most precious treasure destroyed. They knew that this meant the end of the great French academies of Talmud. It was a spirit-ual death-blow for all of French Jewry.

As Meir watched the bonfire of books he recalled the Tal-mudic story of Hanina ben Teradyon who was tortured by the Romans. The captors had wrapped a scroll of the law around Hanina and consigned man and scroll to the flames.

"Our Rabbi, what do you see?" called out the pupils of Hanina in anguish.

"I see the parchment being consumed, but the letters are flying in the air," replied Hanina.

So too it seemed to Meir as he watched the flames in the streets of Paris. Only the parchment was destroyed. The let-ters, the words, the teachings, the ideals of the Talmud—these were deathless and could never be destroyed. They would free themselves and fly to some other land where they would find sanctuary. The Talmud would live again wherever Jews were free!

Sadly Meir returned to the Academy. With heavy heart he sat down and poured his sorrow into a bitter dirge:

"Ask, O thou who wast consumed in fire,
Can there be peace for those who mourn thy loss?
I see the light of day which shines for all
Yet cannot lift the cloud from me and thee!"

The lament of Meir is still recited in the synagogues on *Tisha B'Av* when we mourn the loss of the Temple.

French Jews continued to study the Talmud in secret. Louis IX, however, never relented. His zeal in persecuting members of other religions was so great that he, ironically enough, was called "Saint Louis." He once recommended as the most persuasive way of converting men to his religion, forcing the sword into the body as far as it will enter. Before setting out on a Crusade in 1249 he ordered all Jews to be expelled from his kingdom, but fortunately the order was never carried out.

Meir ben Baruch, his student days completed, returned to Germany where somewhat better conditions prevailed.

2. A GREAT JUDGE

Meir settled in the city of Rothenburg where he established a school of Talmud. He lived in a large house containing 21 rooms, most of which were occupied by his students.

Meir's fame soon spread far and wide. His students observed his every act and made it the model for their own religious conduct. The Rabbis and courts of the German, French and English communities turned to Meir for advice in all legal and religious matters. His decisions were accepted as binding; he became, in a way, the Supreme Court for all German Jewry.

"Abraham cannot repay his debts," wrote one inquirer. "May his creditors collect by seizing the jewelry his wife brought with her upon marriage?"

"The garments and jewels a woman brings with her upon marriage belong to her exclusively," replied Meir. "The jewelry may not be touched."

"May Reuben break into his neighbor's house and forcibly take valuables in payment of a debt?" inquired the court of the community of Speyer.

"This is a direct violation of the Biblical law," replied Meir. "The Bible states: When you lend your neighbor anything as a loan, you may not go into his house to take his pledge. In the street you must stand, and the man to whom you made a loan shall bring out unto you the pledge into the street." Meir added that under no circumstances may a man take the law into his own hands; he may not touch an object belonging to another person unless accompanied by an official of the court.

One community inquired whether a teacher who had become ill must be paid for the entire season. Rabbi Meir ruled that he was entitled to full payment.

Another Rabbi inquired concerning the right of a new settler to move into a community. "Isaac claims that Samuel should not be permitted to settle here since he is engaged in the same business and will compete with him."

"Jews may settle wherever they wish," replied Meir, "without asking permission of the residents, unless there is a local law prohibiting the entry of new settlers. Jews enjoy personal liberty, and this freedom cannot be taken from them."

Rabbi Meir's main purpose was to strengthen the Jewish courts. Each Jewish community enjoyed almost complete self-government, except for the heavy taxes it paid to the dukes and local rulers. All matters pertaining to religious, business or family problems were settled by the Jewish court in keeping with the law of the Talmud. A Jew who appealed to a Gentile court was considered almost a renegade.

Rabbi Meir was also eager to maintain the high moral

standards of the Jewish community. The Jewish home was marked by an atmosphere of peace and harmony. Rabbi Meir praised the tenderness between husband and wife in Jewish families; such kindness was so different from the brutality he often observed in other homes.

3. MEIR'S IMPRISONMENT

Meanwhile, life in Germany became more and more difficult for the Jews. Several communities were ruined by riots and massacres. Germany, however, was divided into many small duchies and governments. Whenever one ruler treated the Jews harshly, they would flee to a nearby community where they were welcomed by a more tolerant prince or duke.

In 1273 Rudolph I became emperor of Germany.

"Jews are servants of the crown," said Rudolph, "and will enjoy our protection provided they serve us."

Meir opposed Rudolph. Formerly Jews paid taxes to the local rulers only and not to the emperor. He was afraid that Rudolph would seek to extort large sums of money from the Jewish people. He did not trust Rudolph's promise of protection. The emperor might try to use his power to deprive Jews of their personal liberty and prevent them from settling where they pleased.

Meir's fears were more than justified. Rudolph demanded ruinous taxes from the Jews of Germany. He confiscated much Jewish property. When riots took place he did almost nothing to protect the Jews or to punish the rioters.

Meir sought escape from Germany. Now was the time to carry out his lifelong ambition to settle in Palestine. Traveling incognito Meir and his family began to make the long journey in 1286. Many other Jews, also seeking to escape, arranged to meet Meir in Italy from whence they would set sail for Palestine.

In Italy, however, Rabbi Meir was recognized by a renegade. He was arrested and delivered to Rudolph who imprisoned him in the tower of Ensisheim.

The Jews of Germany pleaded with the emperor to release their beloved Rabbi.

"We are willing to pay ransom to secure his release," they said.

Rudolph wanted more than ransom. He demanded a large annual tax which Jews must pay as servants of the crown.

Rabbi Meir sent word to his friends:

"I refuse to be set free under these conditions. Who knows whether Emperor Rudolph will keep his word and free me after receiving the ransom? Will he not imprison other Rabbis and demand further ransom? Jews will be ruined by the large annual tax which they will be required to pay."

Meir's friends made every effort to secure the release of their beloved Rabbi. Even the Pope in Rome appealed in his behalf. All to no avail!

For seven long years Meir remained in the prison tower. He continued to write legal opinions which were carefully followed. Here he received word of the sad fate of English Jewry.

At last in 1293 he passed away in prison. He was mourned as "the father of all Israel," as the great judge of Talmudic law and as a martyr in the cause of liberty.

EXERCISES

I. Fill in the missing name. (Review the section called "To the Student," pages 13 to 14.)

1. _____, Isaac and Jacob began to believe in One God.
2. On _____ we recall the granting of the 10 commandments.
3. _____ crossed the Jordan and brought the Israelites to the promised land.
4. The Hebrew nation was united during the reigns of Saul, David and _____.
5. Three great prophets who taught the ideals of justice and righteousness were Elijah, Isaiah and _____.
6. _____ helped rebuild the walls of Jerusalem.

7. _____ commemorates the victory of Esther and Mordecai over Haman.

8. On Chanukah we celebrate the victory of the _____ over Syrian tyranny.

9. Rav and Samuel inspired the growth of academies of learning in _____.

10. Jews celebrated a Golden Age in the land of _____.

II. Who? (Review section 1, pages 17 to 19.)

1. Who decided to study the Talmud in France?

2. Who planned to destroy the Talmud?

3. Who arranged for a debate concerning the Talmud?

4. Who argued that the Talmud was a great book which applied the Biblical ideal of justice to every aspect of life?

5. Who said, "I see the parchment being consumed, but the letters are flying in the air"?

III. What was Meir's decision in each of the following cases? (Review section 2, pages 19 to 21.)

1. May a creditor collect by claiming the jewelry that the debtor's wife brought with her upon marriage?

2. May a creditor enter a debtor's house and seize security for an unpaid debt?

3. Must a teacher be paid for the time that he was ill?

4. May a resident prevent a new settler from entering the community because he will compete with him in business?

IV. Choose the correct word or phrase. (Review section 3, pages 21 to 22.)

1. Rudolph I became emperor of _____. (Germany, Spain)

2. Formerly Jews paid taxes to the _____. (emperor, local ruler)

3. Meir opposed Rudolph because he deprived the Jews of _____. (personal liberty, religious liberty)

4. Meir was arrested in _____ while trying to escape to Palestine. (England, Italy)

5. _____ appealed to Rudolph to free Meir. (The
   Pope, Louis IX)

V. Questions for discussion:

   1. Why is the study of Jewish history of special importance
      to us?
   2. What were the chief contributions of each of the follow-
      ing to the Jewish people: Abraham, Moses, David,
      Isaiah, Judah the Maccabee, Hillel, Rashi, the Rambam?
   3. Compare the conditions of the Jews in France and in
      Germany during the days of Rabbi Meir?
   4. Why was Rabbi Meir of Rothenburg mourned as "the
      father of all Israel"?

THINGS TO DO

1. *Trial*—Book-burners are among the greatest enemies of
civilization. What happened under Louis IX in 1242 was repeated
under Hitler on May 10, 1933 when the works of many great
authors were burned.

Bring up the book-burners on trial. Let there be a judge, a
prosecuting attorney, a defense attorney, a jury etc. Books that
have been burned or their authors might be called upon as witnesses. The judge must pass final sentence.

2. *A Play for Jewish Book Month*—Prepare an original script
for Jewish Book Month based on the idea that books can never
be destroyed. Among the books from which excerpts might be
included are the Bible, Talmud, *Siddur*, *Haggadah*, poetry such as
Judah Halevi's poems, commentaries such as Rashi's commentary
on the Bible etc.

CHAPTER II

PERSECUTION

THE FIRST JEWS came to England with the Roman armies. A Bar Kochba coin recently found in England indicates that refugees may have fled to England after Bar Kochba's defeat.

When William the Conqueror crossed from France to England in 1066 many Jews followed him. This was during the period of Rashi when French Jewry flourished. Other Jews fled to England in 1096 to escape the fury of the Crusaders who cruelly exterminated thousands of Jews in France and in Germany.

Prosperous communities sprang up in England, Wales and Ireland. The Jewish section of London came to be known as "The Street of the Jews." Jews in York, Lincoln, Norwich, Cambridge, Oxford, Gloucester and other towns became well known as financiers, merchants and doctors. Others worked as weavers, smiths, teachers, carpenters, peddlers and wine-merchants.

Jews were regarded as servants of the king and were protected by him. One king proclaimed, "No Jew shall remain in England unless he perform the service of the king; and immediately any Jew shall be born, male or female, he shall serve us in some manner."

The kings granted a charter to the Jews and extended many privileges to them. They could settle where they pleased; they were allowed to travel without interference. They followed the royal court and did business in the royal ante-chamber. They were protected from violence by the royal sheriffs. They could sue in the royal courts for recovery of debts.

Kings often conversed and jested with their Jewish subjects. One king who knew that *hayim* meant life joked about
this to a financier with that name. "The King wishes to
Hayim," he said, "a better state of life."

Jews performed a vital function as bankers and financiers.
The kings found it impossible to finance the government without their Jewish treasurers. The great buildings and monas-
teries of England were put up with the help of Jewish financiers. Barons, merchants, students—all sought the help of the
Jewish banker when credit was needed.

Contracts drawn up between Jews and Christians—often
recorded in Hebrew—were registered in a special chest
guarded by royal officials. When a loan was repaid the Jew
would draw up a document called a *shtar* in Hebrew. This
term became generally known and probably gave its name to
the famous Star Chamber where the documents were kept.

Jews were allowed to conduct their religious life undis-
turbed. The synagogue was the center of religious and community activity. Jewish courts settled all legal matters pertaining to Jews. As we have already seen, the Jews of England
turned to Rabbi Meir of Rothenburg for advice in Talmudic
law. Most Jews could read and write although the general
population was ignorant and illiterate. England boasted several
great scholars; the torch of learning was held high.

For more than a century English Jewry enjoyed freedom
and prosperity.

2. THE CUP OF SORROWS

The Third Crusade, which began in 1189, marked the
turning-point in the history of the Jews of England. Such
hatred was aroused by the fanatical spirit of the Crusades that
peaceful citizens were turned into rioters and murderers.

The first episode occurred at the coronation of Richard
the Lion-Hearted on September 3, 1189. A delegation of Jews
came to Westminster Hall bearing rich gifts to the new king.
The doorkeeper drove them away declaring that women and

Jews were not allowed to disturb the solemn proceedings. The mob at the palace gates turned against the Jews, brutally beating them and trampling several to death.

False rumors spread to London that the king had ordered the extermination of the Jews. The mob attacked "The Street of the Jews" and the stone houses in which the Jews lived. One of the mob threw a lighted torch which set fire to a thatched roof. The flames spread quickly and soon the entire section was in flames. Some Jews were protected by friendly neighbors; others found refuge in the Tower of London. Many perished in the flames or at the hands of the cruel mob.

The news reached the king as he sat banqueting. Richard immediately ordered the punishment of the ringleaders. As soon, however, as Richard left England in December, 1189 to complete his preparations for the Third Crusade, the rioting was renewed. The entire community of York was wiped out; other communities suffered heavy losses.

Richard was distressed by the news, but there was little he could do since he was engaged in fighting the Mohammedans. While in Palestine, it is reported, he sent word to Cairo inviting Moses ben Maimon to become his physician, but the great Jewish doctor refused.

Richard fought brilliantly in Palestine. He succeeded in arranging a truce with Saladin which assured Christian pilgrims the right to visit Jerusalem. On his return Richard was captured by the Duke of Austria. A tremendous ransom was demanded. The Jews of England were taxed heavily, paying an amount far out of proportion to their numbers to secure the release of Richard the Lion-Hearted.

After Richard's death English Jewry drank deeply of the cup of sorrows.

One of the reasons for the suffering of the Jews was political. The people regarded Jews as servants of the king. Whenever the nobles fought the tyranny of the king they turned against the Jews. Even the great Magna Carta of 1215 which protected the people against abuses by the king, contained anti-

Jewish clauses. The king, on the other hand, regarded the Jews as a milch-cow to be milked whenever necessary. He extorted large sums of money from his Jewish subjects to carry on his wars and often confiscated their property.

A second reason for Jewish persecution was economic. Christians were not permitted to lend money at interest. Jews often resorted to money-lending since most other occupations were closed to them. The results were most unfortunate. Debtors frequently turned against the money-lenders. Whenever there was a riot attempts were made to burn all records of debt.

Ignorance and religious prejudice added fuel to the fires of hatred. In 1218 Jews were ordered to wear a special badge to set them apart from the rest of the population.

The most horrible expression of prejudice was the ritual murder charge. If a child was found to be missing Jews were falsely accused of taking the child's life for ritual purposes. Such false charges were often followed by riots and massacre.

At last, after 100 years of suffering, English Jewry was reduced to misery and poverty. Even as money-lenders they were no longer needed since the Lombards and other Christians disregarded the laws of the church and began to engage in banking.

Finding that there was no more money for him to extort from the Jews and that nearly all means of livelihood were closed to them, Edward I resolved to expel them from England.

According to the Hebrew chroniclers of that period, Edward himself did not hate his Jewish subjects. He was influenced by the Dominican friars who were especially incensed because one of the members of their order, a certain Robert of Reading, had converted to Judaism.

The decree of expulsion was issued in 1290 on the fateful 9th of Av. Jews were ordered to leave the country within three months.

The king warned his subjects not to harm the exiles physically. Jews wearily returned with their meager belongings to the lands from which their ancestors had come.

Despite the king's warning there were many tragic incidents. One ship grounded on a sandbank at the mouth of the Thames River. The captain invited the Jewish passengers to disembark with him for a brief walk on shore. When the tide began to rise the captain climbed back on deck, but refused to allow the Jews to return to the boat.

When the Jews pleaded for their lives the captain replied mockingly, "Pray to Moses. He will split the sea for you just as he did with the Red Sea so that you can cross over on dry land." Leaving them to their fate the captain sailed away in his boat. The captain was later sentenced to death because of this cruel deed.

About 16,000 Jews succeeded in reaching France, Germany or Spain. Thus ended, for the time being, Jewish life in England. When Shakespeare wrote his great plays 300 years later, not a single professing Jew lived in England.

3. PERSECUTION IN FRANCE AND GERMANY

In the Middle Ages society was organized on a feudal basis. Peasants were serfs of the lord of the manor; he in turn owed loyalty to the baron or noble who served the king. Jews were excluded since the whole feudal organization was based on a common, religious faith. Jews were also excluded from the town guilds to which skilled artisans belonged.

Jews found their place as merchants or as money-lenders. Jewish merchants made their way through Egypt and the Red Sea to India and China bringing back with them spices and the rare products of the East. Jewish traders are credited with introducing many new products to Europe such as oranges, sugar, and rice.

The Crusades, however, had helped create a merchant class of Christians. Jews were again excluded. Even as money-lenders they were no longer essential. Loss of economic status made the Jews an easy target for those who preached hatred and intolerance.

France soon followed England's unhappy example. Finding his treasury empty King Philip the Fair decided to confiscate the property of the Jews. On July 22, 1306 all Jews were thrown into prison and then condemned to exile. One month later 100,000 Jews took up the wanderer's staff and sadly made their way into Spain, Italy or Germany.

Nine years later Philip's brother, Louis X, finding the treasury still empty invited the Jews to return, hoping they would help to finance his government. Those who did return soon became the victims of a new Crusade. In 1321 a report spread that Jews and lepers, in league with the king of Granada, were poisoning the wells. After a century of persecution the final order of expulsion from France was signed by the mad Charles VI in 1394.

In Germany the ritual murder charge, which had originated in England, spread like wildfire. In one community after another Jews were accused of using Christian blood for Passover or for other religious ceremonies. The Popes in Rome denounced this horrible lie, but all to no avail.

The height of persecution was reached during the Black Plague in 1348. One-third of the population of Europe was swept away by this dread disease. Many Jews died during the plague, but because of their hygienic way of life there seemed to be fewer deaths among the Jews. Ignorant people soon placed the blame for the plague on the Jews.

"The Jews are guilty," declared one peasant.

"Their Rabbi has confessed," said a second.

"They have made a potion of frogs, lizards and the hearts of Christians with which to poison the water," added another.

"The Jews have poisoned the wells! Death to the Jews!" shouted the mob. "Death to the Jews!"

The Pope condemned the new libel, but again his words fell on deaf ears. Sixty large communities and 150 small ones were exterminated before the madness subsided.

Despite these horrible persecutions the morale of the Jew never wavered. The badge of shame which he was forced to wear on his outer clothing became a red badge of courage. On Sabbaths and holidays the Jew forgot the outside world and devoted himself to prayer and to Torah. The Sabbath was like a queen and the Jew like a prince with none to disturb his peace.

Bravely the Jew clung to the faith of his fathers and prayed for the coming of a better day when hatred and persecution would cease.

EXERCISES

I. True or false? (Review section 1, pages 25 to 26.)
   1. Jews came from France to England after William the Conqueror's victory in 1066.
   2. The kings of England refused to protect the Jews.
   3. Jews enjoyed many privileges such as the right to travel without interference.
   4. Contracts were often drawn up in Hebrew.
   5. The Jews of England had no contacts with the Jews of France and Germany.

II. Answer each question in a complete sentence. (Review section 2, pages 26 to 29.)
   1. What sad event occurred during the coronation of Richard the Lion-Hearted?
   2. What proof do we have that Richard was friendly to the Jews?
   3. What disadvantages were there for the Jews in being declared "servants of the king"?
   4. Mention examples of religious prejudice in England.
   5. What effect did the conversion of Robert of Reading have on the Jews of England?

III. What important event occurred in each of the following years? (Review section 3, pages 29 to 31.)
   1. 1290
   2. 1306

3. 1321
4. 1348
5. 1393

IV. Questions for discussion:
1. What were some of the causes of persecution of the Jews in England?
2. What contributions did Jews make as merchants and as financiers?
3. "The badge of shame became a red badge of courage." What is meant by this statement? Show how it is true.
4. Jewish persecution reached great heights during the 13th and 14th centuries. Show how this is true.

THINGS TO DO

1. *Supplementary Reading*—Read *Ivanhoe* by Sir Walter Scott. This is a historical romance which takes place during the reign of Richard the Lion-Hearted. The heroine of the story is the beautiful Jewess, Rebecca, daughter of a Jew of York named Isaac.

2. *Unit Work*—The "Jews of Medieval Europe" could serve as the basis for an extended unit of study. Committees might be formed to gather added information concerning the Jews of England, France, Germany and Spain. Other committees might consider topics such as social conditions, home life, education, religious activities etc. After each committee has presented its report to the class, there might be an evaluation to consider what the class has gained as a result of the unit study.

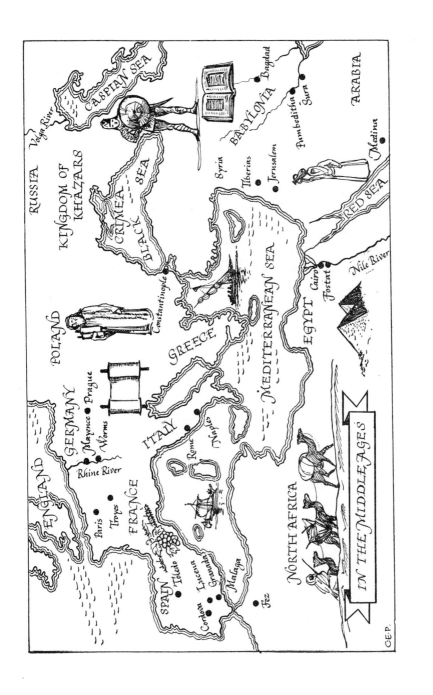

IN THE MIDDLE AGES

CHAPTER III

EXPULSION FROM SPAIN

I. JEWISH CONTRIBUTIONS TO CIVILIZATION

THE SPANISH PENINSULA remained the home of the largest Jewish community of the Middle Ages. The Jews of Spain and Portugal were called Sefardim, while those of Germany and the continent of Europe were called Ashkenazim. The Ashkenazic Jews excelled in Talmud; Sefardic Jews mastered both science and Hebraic scholarship.

The Sefardic Jews were prominent as doctors, poets, astronomers, philosophers, statesmen and financiers. Unlike the Jews of Germany they were not restricted to money-lending and commerce. Handicrafts were very popular among the Jews. There were Jewish guilds of goldsmiths, weavers, tanners, cutlers, shoemakers, dyers and saddlemakers. There were Jewish landowners and farmers. Jews were even prominent as jugglers and lion-tamers; for many generations Jews were lion-tamers for the king of Aragon in Spain.

Jews made important contributions to every field of learning. The so-called Arabic numerals which we use today were brought to Europe from India by Jewish merchants and scholars. Our entire system of numbers is based on the use of zero and decimals which were part of the Indian arithmetic.

On the basis of various sources historians have come to the conclusion that Jews brought the Arabic numerals to Europe. Their views are confirmed by the words of a great Jewish scholar and poet named Abraham Ibn Ezra who lived at the time of Judah Halevi.

This is what Ibn Ezra wrote:

"In olden times there was neither science nor religion among the sons of Ishmael till the great king, by name Es-Saffah, arose who heard that there were many sciences to be found in India. And there came men saying that there was in India a very mighty book on the secrets of government in the form of a fable. Thereupon he sent for a Jew who knew both languages, and ordered him to translate this book. And when he saw that the contents of the book were extraordinary he desired to know the science of the Indians, and he accordingly sent the Jew to Arin, whence he brought back one who knew the Indian numerals, and besides many astronomical writings."

Jews brought from India not only the numerals but also the game of chess, a game in which Jews have always been prominent. They also translated the Indian fables of Bidpai, the source of many of our most popular fables and fairy-tales.

We have already seen how scholars like Judah Halevi and Moses ben Maimon were famous doctors. Moses ben Maimon's work in the field of diet and nutrition was especially influential. Many of the Popes in Rome and kings throughout Europe employed Jewish physicians.

Jewish translators were busily engaged translating Greek and Arabic works into Latin. Often the books were translated first into Hebrew and then into Latin. Thus, again, Jews brought the wisdom of the East to the West.

Jewish scientists made substantial contributions to the fields of geography, navigation and astronomy. There was an entire school of Jewish map-makers on Mallorca, an island in the Mediterranean off the coast of Spain. A Jew named Cresques who lived on this island drew a famous map which was the first to include the discoveries of Marco Polo. The king of Aragon in Spain proudly sent this map as a present to his brother in France. When Prince Henry of Portugal established a nautical observatory in 1423, he appointed Cresques as its leader. This marked the beginning of the modern era of geographical discovery. Portugal became a world power.

The Toledo astronomical tables were compiled in Toledo

by Jewish astronomers. These were revised at the request of
Alfonso X of Castile by a Jewish astronomer named Isaac Ibn
Sid. Further revisions were made by other Jewish astronomers.
The most important of these tables were those composed by
Abraham Zacuto, astronomer to the king of Portugal. His
Perpetual Almanac published in Hebrew was translated into
Latin, and was used by Christopher Columbus in his expedi-
tions to the New World. The copy used by Columbus with
notes in his handwriting is still in existence.

Jews helped invent nautical instruments to aid the navigators. Levi ben Gershon perfected the quadrant, an instrument
which measured the altitude of the sun and stars. He described
his invention in a Hebrew book called *Wars of the Lord*, fin-
ished about 1340. Pope Clement VI immediately ordered the
book translated into Latin. The quadrant perfected by Levi
ben Gershon became popularly known as Jacob's Staff. It was
used by Christopher Columbus, Vasco da Gama, Magellan and
other mariners for hundreds of years. Another quadrant, introduced by Jacob ben Makir, was generally known as "The
Jewish Quadrant."

Thus, nearly every field of learning was enriched by Jewish
scholars.

2. SPANISH PERSECUTION

But Spain, alas, was not free of the hatred and cruelty
which are such a blot on the history of mankind. Here again
political disturbances, economic greed and religious fanati-
cism combined to undermine the safety of the Jewish communities.

The leader in the crusade of hate was Ferrand Martinez,
confessor to Queen Leonora of Castile. Week after week he
thundered from his pulpit, "Destroy the synagogues of Seville!
Death to the Jews!"

In dismay the Jews of Seville tried to silence Martinez. The
leader of the Jewish community, Don Samuel Abravanel accused Martinez before a judicial court of inciting to riot and

to murder. Martinez was condemned by the bishop and by the king, and was forced to remain silent.

But Ferrand Martinez waited for the opportune moment to wreak vengeance on the Jews. In 1390, both the king and the bishop died. The new king, a lad of eleven, had no real power. Queen Leonora permitted Martinez to do as he pleased.

Martinez resumed his harangues in 1391 with even greater hatred and bitterness. Passions aroused to fever-heat, the masses could no longer be controlled. They broke into the Jewish quarter pillaging, destroying and murdering wherever they went. The 23 synagogues were either burnt to the ground or converted into churches. Only a few Jews escaped the fury of the mob; thousands were forced to accept baptism at the point of the sword.

The cry "Death or baptism!" spread throughout Spain. Toledo, Cordova, Barcelona, Madrid and hundreds of smaller communities soon drank from the cup of sorrows. Only in the Moorish kingdom of Granada and in Portugal were the Jews spared these horrors.

When the terror subsided Spanish Jewry was but a skeleton of its former self. Those who had succeeded in escaping death or baptism became the victims of many oppressive laws. They were forced to wear the badge of shame; they were confined to special quarters; they were excluded from the professions; they were not allowed to engage in handicrafts. Jewish courts were deprived of all power.

"How long, O Lord? How long?" wailed the Jews of Spain in despair. And yet their suffering was not at an end.

3. DON ISAAC ABRAVANEL

Among those who were forced, at the point of the sword, to accept baptism was Samuel Abravanel. He retained his high office at the royal court but secretly yearned for the day when he could practice Judaism again. For a convert to return to Judaism was a crime punishable by death. At last, in 1397, he quietly fled to Portugal sacrificing all the wealth he had amassed in Spain.

In Portugal, Samuel was allowed to worship as a Jew without interference. The Abravanel family rose to prominence and was looked upon with favor by the court.

Isaac, grandson of Samuel, was born in Lisbon in 1437. He was brought up from childhood in wealth and honor, receiving an excellent Hebrew and secular education.

Although Isaac's childhood was a happy one there were many reminders of the suffering of his people. Each evening when the church bells rang there was an enforced curfew for the Jews. The lad, Isaac, knew that Jews were compelled to remain at night behind the gates of the Jewish quarter, or else suffer severe punishment. When Isaac was twelve years old, an anti-Jewish riot swept the city.

After completing his education, Isaac divided his time between financial and literary activities. He became a favorite of King Alfonso V who recognized his financial genius. Isaac also served as the representative of the Jewish community at the court.

In 1471 a village of 250 Jews in North Africa was captured during a military expedition, and the members of the community sold as slaves to Portuguese nobles. Don Isaac did not rest until all of the North African Jews were ransomed. For six full months he traveled throughout Portugal negotiating with the harsh masters for the release of the slaves. After the slaves had been freed he cared for them until they found a means of livelihood.

Alfonso V was an enlightened king who treated all of his subjects fairly. Once during a debate between a Christian and a Jew he stated, "Jews are destined to receive divine reward, since their religious motives are pure."

Alfonso admired Isaac Abravanel's learning and diplomatic ability. Isaac rendered excellent service especially during the war between Portugal and the Spanish kingdom of Castile.

But all that changed when Alfonso died in 1481. He was

succeeded by his son Don Juan II who suspected all of his father's favorites of conspiracy. Isaac Abravanel served the new king faithfully, but he refused to help Don Juan uproot the innocent advisers of the former king.

Don Juan used every flimsy excuse to destroy his opponents.

"All of you are worthy of death," he said. "You have conspired to surrender me and my country to the kings of Spain." He then seized one of the princes, second in rank to the king, and put him to death.

In the midst of the turmoil couriers brought this message to Don Isaac Abravanel, "King Juan commands you to appear before him at once."

Don Isaac innocently proceeded to the appointed place of meeting. On the way, while stopping at an inn, Don Isaac was approached by an agent of the murdered prince.

"Go not near the place of meeting," he warned. "These are evil times. Your enemies seek your death. Escape and save your life."

Fearing the worst Don Isaac arose at night and fled toward the Spanish border. The king's soldiers pursued him for an entire day, but Isaac reached the border in safety.

Isaac sent letters to the king pleading his innocence. The plea fell on deaf ears. Don Juan confiscated Isaac's rich estate, but he allowed his wife and children to join him in Spain.

4. FERDINAND AND ISABELLA

Don Isaac now devoted himself to the writing of a commentary on the Bible. Unlike Rashi whose comments were terse and pithy, Abravanel wrote long explanations for each passage. His views concerning political problems in early Israel were especially interesting since he had the experience of a statesman. In particular, Don Isaac confirmed the words of Samuel the Prophet who had warned against the cruelty and tyranny of kings.

When Ferdinand and Isabella, rulers of Spain, heard that Abravanel was in their kingdom they invited him to become their agent. Isaac, who was hard at work on his commentary, accepted reluctantly.

"I abandoned my inheritance from the kings of Israel and Judah," complained Abravanel, "for the king of Aragon and Castile."

Little did Abravanel realize how much hatred there was in the hearts of the king and queen for all members of different faiths. Torquemada, confessor to Isabella, had made her swear that if she ever became queen she would devote her life to uprooting heresy.

In 1480 Isabella had introduced the Inquisition. This court, however, had authority over the converts but not over the Jews. The Inquisition brought up on trial converts and other Christians who were accused of not observing the laws of the church.

Thus far Isabella had not persecuted the Jews. She felt she needed their help in the war against Granada. Jews occupied important positions at court; in fact, Isabella's own marriage had been arranged by Jewish agents at the court.

Isaac Abravanel served Ferdinand and Isabella faithfully for eight years. He raised large sums of money and helped finance the long, drawn-out war against the Moorish kingdom of Granada.

At last after a long siege Granada fell on January 2, 1492. For the first time in almost eight centuries all of Spain was in Christian hands.

Torquemada now brought pressure on Ferdinand and Isabella to expel all non-Christians from Spain. How could the converts be persuaded to follow the laws of the church, he argued, when they saw so many Jews and Mohammedans practicing their own religion without interference?

Ferdinand and Isabella readily agreed that this was the time to rid Spain of all those with different religious beliefs. They no longer needed the support of the Jews since all of Spain was now in their hands. Let those who feared exile, convert to Christianity. Besides, they thought, the property of the exiles would fall to the crown; their riches would help fill the empty treasury.

On March 30, 1492, sitting in the captured Alhambra palace in Granada, Ferdinand and Isabella signed a decree expelling all Jews and Mohammedans from their dominions within a period of four months.

5. THE EXPULSION

Abravanel and the Jews were stunned by the tragic news. Little did they expect such a blow from a king who had been helped so faithfully by his Jewish subjects.

Don Isaac and another Jewish official quickly sought an audience with Ferdinand.

"O King," pleaded Abravanel, "save your loyal subjects. Why do you act so cruelly toward us?"

Ferdinand promised to think the matter over, but soon sent word that nothing could change his mind.

Abravanel would not rest in his endeavors to save his people. He pleaded with many of the nobles to intercede with the king.

"But his ears were closed," wrote Abravanel in one of his books, "as though he were stone deaf."

Don Isaac obtained a second interview. Turning to Ferdinand he said, "We have prospered in this land and we would gladly give all we possess for our country."

Abravanel offered 300,000 ducats if the king would revoke the evil decree. This was a tremendous sum of money. At this moment, it is reported, Torquemada stormed into the room, and threw down a crucifix in front of the king warning him not to break his religious vows.

It is possible that Ferdinand would have yielded to Abravanel were it not for the evil influence of Isabella. The Inquisition which she had established had already shed much innocent blood. Claiming to believe in a religion of love, she did not hesitate to perform the cruelest act if it helped win souls for the church.

In the third and last interview Don Isaac turned to Isabella. He spoke proudly as the descendant of King David and as the representative of an eternal people.

"Do not think you can destroy us," he warned. "Israel has always survived even though our enemies were strong and powerful. God will surely punish you and your country for this wicked act."

Panic struck when the people learned that Abravanel's offer had been rejected by the king and queen. A feeling of hopelessness seized all Jews. Whither could they turn?

At this crucial moment Abravanel proved how great a leader he was. He warned the people to be firm in their faith. Not even the greatest suffering would cause the Jews to weaken in their loyalty to their religion.

Ferdinand and Isabella made strenuous efforts to convert Abravanel and his family. If they changed their religion, surely all Jews would follow suit. But Abravanel spurned these attempts to make him betray his faith and his people.

According to Abravanel 300,000 Jews sadly left the land in which they had been born. Many went to Portugal. Thousands of others set sail for North Africa, Italy, Palestine or Turkey. The exodus from Spain took place on August 2, 1492 which fell on the fateful 9th of Av. Nearby in the port of Seville lay Columbus' fleet ready to set sail the following day—an expedition which Don Isaac had helped to finance.

Abravanel succeeded in keeping alive the hopes of the exiles. The Rabbis ordered musicians to play lively melodies for the wanderers as they trudged along the roads of Spain.

Don Isaac Abravanel wrote that the exiles bravely encouraged each other with these words: "Let us cling unflinchingly to our faith, holding our heads with pride before the voice of the enemy that taunts and blasphemes. If they let us live, we will live; if they kill us, we will perish. But we will not break our divine covenant nor shall we turn back. We will go forth in the name of the Lord our God."

Don Isaac, along with many other Jews, succeeded in

reaching the shores of sunny Italy. An Italian historian who saw the refugees wrote, "One might have taken them for spectres, so emaciated were they, and with eyes so sunken." The king of Naples, whom Don Isaac called "a prince of mercy and righteousness," allowed the refugees to settle in his land.

Abravanel's warning to Spain ultimately came true. Spain, having expelled many of its finest citizens, began to lose its power and greatness. The Inquisition and the expulsion of the Jews were the beginning of Spain's decline and ruin.

Don Isaac Abravanel will always be remembered because of his faith and courage. At one of the darkest moments in Jewish history he inspired his nation to face tragedy with the brave words, "We will go forth in the name of the Lord our God."

EXERCISES

I. Match. (Review section 1, pages 34 to 36.)

Column A	Column B
Ashkenazim	1. Quadrant
India	2. Astronomical tables
Mallorca	3. German Jews
Abraham Zacuto	4. Jewish map-makers
Levi ben Gershon	5. Numerals

II. Choose the correct name or phrase. (Review section 2, pages 36 to 37.)

1. Ferrand Martinez was confessor to _____. (Queen Isabella, Queen Leonora)
2. The leader in the struggle against Martinez was _____. (Isaac Abravanel, Samuel Abravanel)
3. The riots in 1391 began in _____. (Cordova, Seville)
4. The Jews of Spain accepted baptism _____. (at the point of the sword, willingly)
5. Jews were not persecuted in _____. (Castile, Granada)

III. Complete each sentence. (Review sections 3 and 4, pages 37 to 41.)

Alfonso V, Ferdinand, Isaac Abravanel, Don Juan II, Samuel Abravanel

1. _____ escaped from Spain to Portugal in order to practice Judaism openly.

2. _____ said, "Jews are destined to receive divine reward, since their religious motives are pure."

3. _____ was famous as financial adviser to the kings of Portugal and Spain and as author of a Bible commentary.

4. Isaac Abravanel ran away from Portugal to Spain to escape the tyranny of _____.

5. _____ conquered Granada from the Moors.

IV. Why? (Review section 5, pages 41 to 43.)

1. Why were the Jews of Spain surprised that Ferdinand signed an anti-Jewish decree?

2. Why did Abravanel offer Ferdinand 300,000 ducats?

3. Why did Torquemada warn Ferdinand not to break his vows?

4. Why were Ferdinand and Isabella eager to convert Abravanel?

5. Why did the Rabbis order musicians to play as Jews left Spain?

V. Questions for discussion:

1. What contributions did the Jews in the Middle Ages make to world civilization?

2. How did religious prejudice bring suffering to Spanish Jewry?

3. What, in your opinion, was Abravanel's greatest achievement?

THINGS TO DO

1. *Research*—The conquest of Granada was an exciting event. Bring in a report concerning the victory of Ferdinand over the Moors.

2. *Letter*—Pretend you were a student in Seville in 1492, and that you and your family were forced to leave Spain. Write a letter to a cousin in Lisbon, Portugal describing the events leading up to the exile, and the exodus from Spain.

CHAPTER IV

IN THE DAYS OF THE MARRANOS

MOST OF the Jews who were forcibly converted in 1391 secretly remained Jews. Outwardly they professed Christianity, but in reality they remained Jews in belief and, as far as possible, in practice. These secret Jews, who were called Marranos, have written one of the most romantic and courageous chapters in Jewish history.

Chief among the enemies of the Marranos was Torquemada, confessor to Queen Isabella. He knew that in their heart of hearts the Marranos were still Jewish. Many of them even attended synagogue on occasion, or contributed oil for the illumination of Jewish houses of worship. He made Isabella swear, even before she became queen, that she would devote her life to uprooting heresy. (Heresy referred to the failure of Christians to observe the laws of the church; thus, converts could be guilty of heresy if they practiced Judaism. The Inquisition had no power over those who remained Jews without converting.)

Under the influence of Torquemada, the queen in 1480 introduced the Inquisition, whose purpose it was to punish those guilty of heresy. The first *auto-da-fé*, or act of faith, was held in Seville in 1481, at which time six men and women were burned alive. Before the end of the year no less than 298 persons had been consigned to the flames.

Later, Torquemada himself was appointed one of the chief inquisitors. One of the reasons he demanded the expulsion of the Jews in 1492 was that there was little hope of the Marranos

45

ever becoming observing Christians as long as Jews remained their neighbors.

The numbers of the Marranos increased because of the tragic turn of events in Portugal. The Spanish exiles in 1492 were allowed to remain in Portugal for eight months until they could arrange for passage to another country. Many of the refugees, finding it impossible to obtain shipping, remained longer.

In 1496 young King Manuel of Portugal married Isabella, daughter of Ferdinand and Isabella. One of the conditions of the marriage was that Portugal treat the Jews as Spain had done. Jews were given 10 months in which to leave the country.

Long before that, during the Passover of 1497, all young Jewish children were snatched from their parents and forcibly baptised. Scenes of horror took place as parents tried to protect their precious young ones. The grandson of Isaac Abravanel was among those seized. We do not know whether he was ever again seen by his family.

Meanwhile, twenty thousand Jews who passed through the capital on their way to a port were arrested and accused of not leaving the country in time. With the exception of the Chief Rabbi, who was imprisoned and tortured to death, they were not even given the choice of conversion or death. They were dragged to the baptismal font and pronounced Christians. The captors declared that this was done only as an act of mercy to save the souls of the victims.

The Marranos were horrified by their sad fate. In their hearts they remained true to Judaism. At the risk of their lives each Friday night they descended into the cellars and lit the Sabbath candles, or as they called them, "the candles of the Lord." On Passover they baked unleavened bread, met in secret passages for a festive *Seder* and, staff in hand, retold the story of the freeing of the Israelites by Moses. On Yom Kippur they fasted and spent the day in prayer, pouring out their tears as they prayed that their sins would be forgiven and that the day when they would be free would soon come.

2. A VISITOR TO THE MARRANOS

It is no wonder that strange tales reached the ears of Jews in other countries concerning the faith and courage of the secret Jews.

One legend, which seems to have a historical basis, tells of the visit of the famous Joseph of Rosheim. He was the leader of German Jews and their representative at the court of Emperor Maximilian.

Maximilian was head of the Holy Roman Empire which included Germany, Holland, Austria, Bohemia and part of Italy. Joseph who once saved the emperor's life by warning him about a conspiracy, was one of Maximilian's favorites. He obtained a charter for Jewish merchants, defended Jews against charges of ritual murder and fought successfully against enemies of the Jewish people.

In 1519, King Charles of Spain, was elected head of the Holy Roman Empire. Charles V was a grandson of Emperor Maximilian.

Joseph of Rosheim was greatly concerned about the fate of the Jews of Germany. Would Charles V seek to extend the wicked anti-Jewish laws of Spain to Germany? Joseph decided to seek an immediate interview in Madrid. Disguised as knights, Joseph and a companion named Moses Cohen, entered Spain. They arrived in Madrid just before Passover.

"Where can we spend the Passover?" asked Moses Cohen.

"I have heard that there are many secret Jews in Spain," replied Joseph. "Perhaps we can find one of the Marranos."

At that moment Joseph and his companion stood near the market-place. Just then a Spanish noble drew up in a beautiful coach. The Spaniard descended from the coach and purchased lettuce, parsley and horse-radish from a vegetable vendor.

A MARRANO SECRET SEDER

"Have you noticed what he bought?" asked Joseph. "Perhaps he needs these vegetables for the *Seder.*"

Joseph of Rosheim then drew near to the noble and whispered in Hebrew, "*Yehudi atah?*" ("Are you a Jew?")

The Spaniard looked in all directions to see whether anybody was listening. He beckoned to Joseph and his companion to enter his carriage.

On the way to his palace the noble revealed the truth.

"I am a Marrano," he said. "The secret Jews are meeting in the cellar of my house tonight for a *Seder.* You may join us if you wish."

Joseph thanked the Marrano and explained the purpose of his mission.

At night a trap-door was opened, and the Spaniard beckoned to the members of his household and to Joseph and Moses Cohen to follow him.

Joseph was amazed by the scene before him. The tables were beautifully set with white linen. Candles illuminated the entire passage. On the table were cakes of unleavened bread, cups of wine and the vegetables needed for the *Seder.*

"This year we are slaves, next year may we be free men!" recited the Marranos with tears in their eyes.

When the *Seder* was over Joseph of Rosheim spoke to the noble about his mission.

"I am an adviser of Charles V," said the Spaniard, "and shall try to arrange an interview for you."

Within a few days a meeting was arranged. It was not a moment too soon, for the Dominican friars had already approached Charles V with a petition to expel the Jews from Germany.

Joseph of Rosheim showed the letter which he had received from the former emperor. In this letter Maximilian not only praised Joseph for his outstanding services but ordered his successor to renew the privileges granted to the Jews.

Charles V promised to carry out his grandfather's orders. The Jews of Germany were permitted to retain their ancient privileges.

Joseph of Rosheim thanked his Marrano host and returned with his companion to Germany. The Jews of Germany rejoiced when they heard that Joseph's mission had succeeded.

Although many of the details of this account are legendary, historians believe that it may have a historical basis. It is very possible that Joseph did cooperate with the secret Jews of Spain.

For hundreds of years the Marranos preserved their belief in Judaism and sought to maintain some contact with Jews of the free world.

3. DAVID REUBENI

The hopes of the Marranos were revived when a strange Jewish adventurer named David Reubeni appeared in Rome in 1524.

"I am the brother of the king of one of the lost ten tribes," said David Reubeni. "My brother Joseph is king of the tribe of Reuben in the wilderness of Habor. I come requesting help from the Pope in Rome and from the king of Portugal against the Moslems who seek to conquer my nation."

David Reubeni related a marvelous tale of adventure in Arabia, Egypt and Palestine. He had fasted in Hebron near the graves of Abraham, Isaac and Jacob, and had prayed near the ruins of the Temple in Jerusalem. He spoke in Hebrew.

Was Reubeni telling the truth or was he just imagining a romantic story? To this day we do not know. It is possible that semi-independent Jewish tribes remained in existence in the Arabian desert or along the coast of India, and that David Reubeni was sent as their ambassador to obtain aid against their enemies.

The Pope wrote to the king of Portugal whose explorers confirmed Reubeni's story. The Pope then received David Reubeni with great honor, and promised him assistance. Reubeni was provided with a guard of honor and rode, clothed in princely garments, on a white horse through the streets of Rome.

Later, David Reubeni received an invitation to visit the king of Portugal, John III, in Lisbon. The boat on which Reubeni sailed flew a Jewish flag on which was inscribed in Hebrew the motto of the Maccabees, "Who is like unto Thee, among the mighty, O Lord?"

The Marranos of Portugal hailed the Jewish ambassador of a Jewish kingdom who flew a Jewish flag. Some even whispered, "Maybe he is the Messiah, who will redeem us from captivity."

The king of Portugal promised to help Reubeni. He offered him 8 ships, ammunition and soldiers to fight against the Moslems. Meanwhile he relaxed his persecution of the Marranos who began to breathe more freely.

4. SOLOMON MOLCHO

Among those whose imagination was stirred by David Reubeni was a young Marrano, an official at the court, named Diogo Pires. He had been born in 1501, just four years after the forced conversion of the Jews of Portugal. Secretly he had been given excellent training in Hebrew and in Judaism. To his family he was known by his Hebrew name, Solomon Molcho.

Diogo Pires came to Reubeni, announced that he was returning to Judaism, and that he had dreamed dreams concerning the redemption of the Jews. Reubeni advised him to leave Portugal.

Diogo fled to Turkey, openly professed Judaism and was known henceforth by his Hebrew name Solomon Molcho. He studied in Salonika, Turkey and then later in Palestine with some of the great Rabbis of that day. All were impressed by his brilliance, his fiery devotion to Judaism and his visions of redemption.

Meanwhile news of Molcho's return to Judaism reached Portugal. The king's advisers accused David Reubeni of responsibility for this act.

The king called Reubeni before him and said, "I have

changed my mind about equipping you with boats and weapons. I see that you have really come to encourage the new Christians to return to Judaism."

Reubeni denied responsibility, but was ordered to leave Portugal. Unfortunately his boat was shipwrecked in the Mediterranean and Reubeni was forced to seek shelter in a Spanish port. Here he was thrown into prison, but later released by Charles V who knew that Reubeni was favored by the Pope. At last Reubeni reached Italy in safety. There he was treated with great honor by the Italian Jews.

Molcho and Reubeni were reunited in Italy in 1530 after several years of separation. Molcho wrote to one of his friends in Turkey, "I was constantly with him, even as a servant is with his master."

Molcho now appeared in the synagogues of Italy and preached eloquent sermons about the coming of the Messiah. He intimated that David Reubeni was the forerunner of the Messiah.

Molcho sought an interview with the Pope who was fascinated by the visions of this young prophet. Molcho warned the Pope that soon the Tiber would overflow its banks and that Rome would be flooded. He also predicted that Lisbon would be partly ruined by an earthquake. Both predictions came true.

The Pope became Molcho's staunch friend and protector. When the king of Portugal asked for permission to introduce the Inquisition into Portugal, the Pope refused, partly because of Molcho's protests.

Meanwhile the Inquisition in Italy made every attempt to destroy Molcho. Was he not guilty of heresy since he was formerly a member of the church?

Molcho was imprisoned and condemned to die. But his life was saved by the Pope. According to Molcho the Pope's servants seized a condemned prisoner, dressed him like Molcho and sent him to the stake in place of Molcho.

David Reubeni and Solomon Molcho now resolved to place

their plans for a war against the Moslems before Charles V. They were convinced that thousands of Marranos seeking freedom would join them in their adventure if only they received aid in the form of ships and ammunition.

Charles V was then in Ratisbon, Germany. Flying the Jewish flag, Reubeni and Molcho traveled to Ratisbon in 1532. There Molcho met Joseph of Rosheim whose brilliant and tireless efforts had saved the Jews of Germany from many disasters.

Joseph of Rosheim was impressed by the fiery zealot, but knew that his plans would come to naught.

"I warn you not to stir up the anger of Charles V," warned Joseph. "You are playing with fire."

"I am not afraid of death," was Molcho's reply.

Just as Joseph had warned, Charles V decided to imprison the two adventurers. Molcho was sent to Mantua, Italy in chains. There he was consigned to the flames.

Just before his execution a messenger approached Molcho with these words: "Charles V will pardon you if you repent."

Molcho replied, "My only regret is that I did not serve God openly as a Jew during the early years of my life. You cannot harm me, for now my soul will return in purity to God." He died with the *Shma Yisrael* on his lips.

Reubeni was allowed to languish in prison in Spain where he probably died five or six years later.

Despite the death of their two heroes the Marranos still waited hopefully for the coming of the Messiah.

5. THE TERRORS OF THE INQUISITION

Reubeni and Molcho had succeeded in postponing the introduction of the Inquistion into Portugal. In 1536, however, the court of the Inquisition was set up in Lisbon and in other cities of Portugal. The Portuguese Inquisition outdid in terror even that of Spain.

Suspects were arrested on the basis of the flimsiest evidence.

Changing linen before the Sabbath was enough to bring down the wrath of the Inquisition upon some unfortunate victim.

The most inhuman tortures were used to make a person confess heresy, or to force him to reveal the names of others who observed some of the practices of Judaism. One of the most common methods of torture was the *strappado* in which the victim was dropped from the beam to which he was attached by a short rope, being brought up with a violent jerk before he reached the ground. Another was the water torment.

It is estimated that 400,000 people were tried by the Inquisition in Spain and Portugal. Of these about 30,000 were put to death for observance of Jewish customs. It was a special act of mercy when the victim was strangled to death before being burnt. Those who repented were given lighter sentences.

Yet such is the courage of the human spirit that many braved the terrors of the Inquisition rather than betray the religion in which they believed. People from every walk of life were involved—doctors, professors, students, artisans, merchants, housewives and peasants.

Many who studied for the priesthood secretly retained their belief in Judaism. In some cases men and women who were not descended from Jews began to believe in Judaism as a reaction to the cruelty of the Inquisition. In a period of eight years, 44 nuns and 15 members of the clergy were forced to appear at *autos-da-fé* in Portugal because of their practice of Judaism.

A notable believer in Judaism was Don Lope de Vera. He was the child of Spanish Christians who had no Jewish blood in their veins. In preparing for the priesthood he became an excellent Hebrew scholar. His study of the Bible convinced him of the truth of Judaism. He converted to Judaism changing his name to Judah the Believer.

For 5 years the Inquisition tried to make him change his mind. Judah the Believer's constant reply was, "Long live the law of Moses."

He was finally condemned to death in 1644. While being

led through the streets he recited Hebrew prayers. From the midst of the flames he was heard to recite with his very last breath the words of the Psalmist, "Unto thee, O Lord, do I lift up my soul."

Although Marranos were not allowed to leave the country, many succeeded in escaping. The Nunez family, for example, after practicing Judaism secretly for over 200 years decided to escape from Portugal. In 1733, Dr. Samuel Nunez, a court physician in Lisbon, was warned that the Inquisition intended to arrest him.

Dr. Nunez gave a great banquet on his estate which was on the banks of the Tagus River. In the midst of the festivities, while all the guests were eating, drinking and making merry, Dr. Nunez and his family boarded an English brig which stood in the bay. The members of the family took with them as much silver and jewelry as they could carry.

The English captain of the brig, who was well paid for his assistance, quickly sailed to London. After several months in England, Dr. Nunez brought his family to Georgia which had just been settled by Oglethorpe. Dr. Nunez' daughter, shortly thereafter, married Rabbi David Machado who was invited in 1737 to become the Rabbi of the *Shearith Israel* Congregation in New York.

In similar manner Marranos were the pioneers of modern Jewish communities in England, Holland, France, Turkey and other countries. By their courage and loyalty they helped to preserve and strengthen Judaism throughout the world.

EXERCISES

I. Answer each question in a complete sentence. (Review section 1, pages 45 to 47.)

1. What were the secret Jews called?
2. What was the purpose of the Inquisition?
3. Why did Manuel introduce the Inquisition into Portugal?
4. What happened to the Jews of Portugal in 1497?
5. How did the Marranos show loyalty to Judaism?

II. Who said to whom? (Review section 2, pages 47 to 50.)

1. "Where can we spend the Passover?"
2. "I have heard that there are many secret Jews in Spain."
3. "Perhaps he bought these vegetables for the *Seder*."
4. "*Yehudi atah?*" ("Are you a Jew?")
5. "I am an adviser of Charles V, and shall try to arrange an interview for you."

III. Indicate which are correctly paired and which are incorrectly paired. (Review sections 3 and 4, pages 50 to 53.)

1. Marranos—Secret Jews
2. David Reubeni—Representative of tribe of Reuben
3. Hebron—Grave of Moses
4. Jerusalem—Ruins of Temple
5. John III—King of Spain
6. Lisbon—Capital of France
7. Solomon Molcho—Marrano who helped Reubeni
8. Tiber—River in Spain
9. Charles V—Emperor of Holy Roman Empire
10. Joseph of Rosheim—Leader of German Jews

IV. Write a sentence about each of the following. (Review section 5, pages 53 to 55.)

1. *strappado*
2. *auto-da-fé*
3. Judah the Believer
4. Dr. Samuel Nunez
5. Rabbi David Machado

V. Questions for discussion:

1. Why are the Marranos important in Jewish history?
2. Do you regard David Reubeni as one of the heroes of Jewish history?
3. Compare Solomon Molcho and Joseph of Rosheim.
4. The Inquisition is one of the most shameful chapters in human history. Why?
5. What can we learn from the lives of Solomon Molcho, Judah the Believer and Samuel Nunez about the Marranos?

THINGS TO DO

1. *Story*—Write an original story about a Marrano who is suspected by the Inquisition of secretly practicing Judaism. Let the story end happily.

2. *Library Hour*—Take out a book from the library dealing with the Marranos or the Inquisition. Report to the class about incidents showing courage in the face of persecution.

UNIT TWO

Lands of Refuge

CHAPTER V

ITALY AND TURKEY

1. ISAAC ABRAVANEL IN ITALY

AT THE TIME of the expulsion of the Jews from Spain in 1492, Italy was divided into many little independent states. The largest of these states, Naples, included the southern part of Italy. After knocking wearily at the gates of the northern ports only to be rejected, Isaac Abravanel and his fellow-refugees were finally accepted by the king of Naples.

Ferrante, king of Naples, was a cousin of Ferdinand of Spain. Unlike his cousin, Ferrante was tolerant to the Jews. He welcomed Isaac Abravanel with open arms, knowing full well how brilliantly Don Isaac had served both Spain and Portugal. He soon invited Isaac to serve the court.

Abravanel became the king's most trusted adviser. When a plague broke out in Naples, Don Isaac helped to organize relief work among the victims. Many of the refugees called upon him for aid.

Ferrante died in 1494 and was succeeded by his son, Alfonso. Don Isaac remained close to the throne. Unfortunately, however, France thought this a good opportunity to invade Naples. Realizing that he was too weak to resist French arms, Alfonso decided to abdicate the throne and to retire to Sicily.

Alfonso communicated his plan to Don Isaac who resolved to accompany his king. Again the wanderer took up the wanderer's staff! He helped Alfonso escape. When the king entered a monastery, Don Isaac found refuge in a seaport belonging to Venice. Later, he moved to Venice itself where he joined his son, one of the prominent physicians of Venice.

Even here his public service did not end. In 1503, the

Venetian Council of Ten which ruled the republic called on Don Isaac to arrange a treaty with Portugal regulating the trade in spices. Although the efforts to draw up a treaty were not successful, Venice appreciated the loyalty of the diplomat who had already served so many countries.

Isaac Abravanel now devoted most of his time to his writings. He continued his excellent commentary on the Bible. The introductions contained a description of his flight from Portugal, the tragic exile from Spain and the escape from Naples.

Of special interest is Abravanel's attack on monarchy as a form of government. He reminds the reader of the Biblical verse, "The wrath of a king is as messengers of death."

"Behold and see," wrote Abravanel, "the countries where the administration is in the hands of kings, and you will observe their corruptions; for the earth is filled with wickedness through them."

In contrast, the Republic of Venice was a model of justice. "Even today," wrote Don Isaac, "Venice rules as mistress, great among nations, princess among states. If the leaders are good, it is better that they should be many and not one; if they are bad, one left free to his lusts is more dangerous than many."

The great statesman who had seen the tyranny of kings raised his voice in behalf of democracy over 450 years ago!

Abravanel wrote 3 books about the coming of the Messiah. Thus he helped to keep alive in the hearts of the people the belief in a better day when justice would prevail and when Israel would be redeemed.

The great leader passed away in Venice in 1508 at the age of 71 mourned by both Jew and Gentile.

2. JEWS AND THE RENAISSANCE

Abravanel's three sons became the leaders of Italian Jewry. Two were distinguished physicians; the third was a financier who inherited his father's financial genius. Rabbis, authors and men of learning gathered in their homes and were encouraged by the Abravanels.

Italy now enjoyed a rebirth of learning known as the Renaissance. Jewish scholars played a prominent part in this revival as translators, philosophers, scientists, inventors, musicians and actors. In Mantua, which was the center of the theater, the entire Jewish community would be called upon when a dramatic spectacle was presented. On Friday afternoons the performance would be held earlier in order not to interfere with the Jewish Sabbath.

Popes, cardinals and princes seemed to favor Jewish doctors. One reason given is that the fear of poisoning was so great that it was necessary to employ physicians who had no contacts with rival princes. Many Jews studied medicine at the medical school of Padua in Italy.

One of the greatest physicians of the Renaissance was the Marrano doctor, Amatus Lusitanus, who fled from Portugal to Italy where he openly professed Judaism. Lusitanus became the personal physician of Pope Julius III.

Lusitanus was author of the famous Physician's Oath in which he stated:

"I swear by God the Almighty and Eternal and by his most holy ten commandments given on Mount Sinai by the hand of Moses the lawgiver that I have never in my medical practice departed from what has been handed down in good faith to us and posterity; that I have never practiced deception; I have never overstated or made changes for the sake of gain; that I have ever striven that benefit might accrue to mankind. I have treated many without accepting any fee, but with none the less care. I have given my services in equal manner to all, to Hebrews, Christians and Moslems. Loftiness of station has never influenced me and I have accorded the same care to the poor as to those of exalted rank."

The censor would not allow this oath to be published in full. He struck out the reference to the ten commandments and to treating Hebrews and Moslems with equality!

Jews were among the pioneers of printing in Italy as well as in Spain, Africa and Asia. The first dated, printed Hebrew book was Rashi's commentary on the 5 Books of Moses. Venice became the center of Hebrew printing which was called "a holy art" since it helped to spread a knowledge of the sacred writings.

Rome boasted the oldest Jewish community in Europe. The Popes treated Jews in a more kindly manner than did the kings of Europe.

The community of Venice, in particular, rose to prominence. It is no accident that Shakespeare, writing about a Jew, picked Venice as his home. Over the main canal of Venice stretches a bridge called the Rialto. It is here, according to Shakespeare in "The Merchant of Venice," that Shylock maintained his shop. Venice, mistress of the seas, traded with all parts of the world and many Jews were active in this trade.

But conditions were far from ideal in Italy. The first ghetto, as the separate Jewish section was called, was set up in Venice. Jews were made to wear the badge of shame. The Popes, becoming worried about the growth of Protestantism in Europe, became harsher in their treatment of the Jews.

It is no wonder that Shakespeare makes Shylock say in bitterness about his opponent:

"He hath disgraced me, and . . . scorned my nation . . . and what's his reason? I am a Jew. Hath not a Jew eyes? Hath not a Jew hands, organs, dimensions, senses, affections, passions? Fed with the same food, hurt with the same weapons, subject to the same diseases, healed by the same means, warmed and cooled by the same winter and summer as a Christian is? If you prick us, do we not bleed? . . . If you tickle us, do we not laugh? If you poison us, do we not die?"

Fortunately, since Italy was divided into small independent states, Jews who were oppressed in one city could move into a nearby city where the ruler was more tolerant. Thus Italy always remained a small but important center of Jewish life.

3. GRACIA NASI

At this time there rose to fame a great Jewish woman named Gracia Nasi who eased the suffering of her people.

Gracia Nasi was a member of a prominent Marrano family in Portugal. Her husband was a wealthy banker whose firm had branches throughout Europe. He traded especially in precious stones, some of which had been brought back by explorers from the New World.

Donna Gracia Nasi's husband died in 1536, the year in which the Inquisition was established in Portugal. A faithful adherent of Judaism, Gracia Nasi feared imprisonment by the Inquisition. She and her family fled to Antwerp. Although controlled by Spain, Antwerp and the Netherlands had not yet become terrorized by the Inquisition. Using her vast wealth to aid her people, Lady Gracia Nasi helped many Marranos escape from Portugal.

Gracia Nasi was greatly honored by the royal court. The Queen Regent of Holland asked her to give her daughter, Reyna, in marriage to one of the court favorites.

It is reported that Donna Gracia Nasi replied, "I would rather see my daughter dead."

Meanwhile, Gracia Nasi was warned that Emperor Charles V, aware of her secret practice of Judaism, intended to confiscate her property. Again she fled—this time to Venice. The Venetian Council of Ten, hoping to rob her of her wealth, threw Gracia Nasi into prison accusing her of heresy.

At this point the Sultan of Turkey came to her aid. Thousands of refugees had found sanctuary in Turkey. Here they were able to profess Judaism openly. When the Jews were expelled from Spain in 1492 the Sultan had said, "How can you call King Ferdinand wise, when he drives out people from his country in order to enrich mine?"

Gracia Nasi appealed to the Sultan for protection by means of his Jewish physician. She announced her intention of traveling to Turkey to become a subject of the Sultan. He immediately sent a special messenger to Venice warning the Council of Ten to release Gracia Nasi.

Fearing the wrath of the powerful Sultan, Venice freed Donna Gracia. The brave woman settled temporarily in Ferrara, Italy openly declaring her adherence to Judaism. Several years later she sailed to Constantinople. Here she celebrated the marriage of her daughter, Reyna, to her brilliant nephew, Joseph Nasi.

The wealthy Donna Gracia now devoted her fortune to aiding her people. She established an underground system which helped many Marranos escape from the hated Inquisition. She built synagogues in Turkey and in Palestine, organized schools for the study of Torah and supported Rabbis and scholars. She even maintained a printing press which published holy books. Frequently she appealed to the Sultan who protected many Jews from their enemies.

"She is like Rachel our mother," wrote one famous Rabbi, "shedding tears at the tragic plight of her children. Hers is the great heart which feels all pain and all sorrow. She has comforted her people through her good works, and has shown the piety of Miriam, the wisdom of Deborah and the devotion of Queen Esther."

4. DON JOSEPH NASI

Joseph Nasi, nephew of Gracia Nasi, was born in Portugal in 1520. His father was a Marrano physician at the royal court who never faltered in his loyalty to Judaism.

Joseph received an excellent education. At the age of 13 he was probably called up to the Torah, and acquainted with the secret practices of the Marrano Jews. He was a master of many languages, a skilled swordsman and rider. He was a friend of princes and nobles and was knighted by Emperor Charles V.

Joseph fled from Portugal with his aunt in 1536, living first in Antwerp and then in Venice. Although outwardly still a member of the church, Joseph Nasi proposed a plan whereby Venice would set aside one of its island possessions as a place of refuge for persecuted Jews. Venice rejected the suggestion, but Joseph Nasi never lost sight of this bold plan.

Joseph helped to secure the protection of the Sultan when his aunt was imprisoned in Venice. In 1554, shortly after Donna Gracia had traveled to Turkey, Joseph came to join her, accompanied by 500 Marranos who had found a temporary resting-place in Italy.

Don Joseph immediately declared his belief in Judaism. Soon thereafter he married his beautiful cousin, Reyna. For months before and after the marriage there was festivity, and lavish gifts were distributed to the poor. Reyna Nasi was as virtuous and as charitable as her distinguished mother.

Joseph was overjoyed to discover how prosperous Jews were in Constantinople, in Salonika and in other Turkish cities. One met many Jews in the picturesque Oriental bazaars such as the Street of the Weavers, the Street of the Goldsmiths, the Street of the Copper-Workers or the Street of the Dyers. Everywhere could be heard Ladino, the language combining Spanish and Hebrew, which Jews had brought with them from Spain.

A year after his arrival in Turkey news reached Don Joseph that Pope Paul IV had arrested all Marranos in Ancona, Italy accusing them of observing Judaism. Gracia and Joseph appealed to the Sultan for aid, especially since some of the Marranos regarded themselves as subjects of the Sultan. The Turkish Sultan sent a warning note to the Pope demanding the immediate release of his subjects.

Pope Paul IV angrily released those Marranos who were citizens of Turkey, but condemned 25 others to the flames. Donna Gracia and Don Joseph, hoping to prevent other murders of this kind, resolved to organize a boycott of the port of Ancona. The citizens of Ancona soon began to complain to the Pope because of loss of business. Many Jews, however, opposed the boycott when the Pope threatened reprisals. Ultimately, Joseph's brave attempt to organize an economic boycott failed because of fear of further persecution.

The Sultan began to rely heavily on Don Joseph's political

advice. Joseph Nasi had an intimate knowledge of most of the countries of Europe. His agents throughout Europe would relay important information to him so that he could advise the Sultan properly. In recognition of his great services Sultan Selim made Joseph the Duke of Naxos and other important islands not far from Greece. This was the first time since the downfall of the Khazar kingdom that a Jew had ruled as a sovereign.

The Sultan's confidence in Don Joseph Nasi was so great that he would only touch food prepared in Joseph's household. There was always the fear that other food might be poisoned.

Thus, one of the Venetian representatives sent the following report to Venice:

"His Highness drinks much wine, and the said Don Joseph sends him many bottles of it from time to time, together with all manner of other delicacies. When His Serene Highness sees these flasks and delicacies, marked with his seal, he drinks the wine and eats the delicacies without any further thought, and shows thus that he trusts him, as being his most loving servant."

Joseph Nasi urged the Sultan to encourage Holland which sought freedom from Spanish tyranny. Turkey did lend Holland some diplomatic support. Holland finally succeeded in throwing off the Spanish yoke and became the first country in Europe to allow full religious freedom to its citizens.

Joseph Nasi also played an important part in the war between Turkey and Venice as a result of which the island of Cyprus was won by Turkey. There were rumors that the Sultan had promised to make Joseph the king of Cyprus, but this never materialized.

Throughout his life Don Joseph used his power and wealth to help the Jewish people. One of the many scholars whom he helped was Amatus Lusitanus, the famous doctor who was author of the Physician's Oath. When Lusitanus fled from Italy to Turkey so that he could practice Judaism openly, he received Joseph Nasi's help. Amatus Lusitanus, in appreciation, dedicated one of his books to Don Joseph.

"Not only are you learned," wrote the doctor, "but also a patron of learning. So great is your culture that you have no rival."

Synagogues and schools supported by Donna Gracia and Don Joseph flourished. It is no wonder that throughout Europe, Joseph Nasi was known as "The Great Jew" and "The Head of His Nation."

EXERCISES

I. Naples or Venice? (Review section 1, pages 61 to 62.)

1. Isaac Abravanel fled from Spain to _____.
2. Abravanel admired _____ because it was a great republic.
3. Abravanel helped the king escape from _____.
4. Abravanel tried to negotiate a treaty between Portugal and _____.
5. Abravanel died in _____ in 1508.

II. Choose the correct word or phrase. (Review section 2, pages 62 to 64.)

1. Abravanel's three sons were leaders of the Jews of _____. (Italy, Spain)
2. The rebirth of learning in Italy was called _____. (Inquisition, Renaissance)
3. A famous Marrano doctor was _____. (Amatus Lusitanus, Moses ben Maimon).
4. The first dated Hebrew book to be printed was the commentary by _____. (Abravanel, Rashi)
5. Jews managed to survive in Italy because _____. (Italy was divided into independent states, Italy was united under one central government).

III. Arrange these statements in the order in which the events occurred. (Review section 3, pages 65 to 66.)

1. Gracia Nasi married a Marrano banker.
2. Gracia Nasi was thrown into prison in Venice.
3. Gracia Nasi settled in Turkey where she supported schools and synagogues.
4. Gracia Nasi fled from Portugal to Antwerp.

5. Gracia Nasi settled in Ferrara, Italy where she openly declared her belief in Judaism.

IV. Why? (Review section 4, pages 66 to 69.)

1. Why did Don Joseph Nasi leave Portugal?
2. Why did Don Joseph Nasi ask Venice for an island for Jews?
3. Why did Don Joseph Nasi try to organize a boycott against Ancona, Italy?
4. Why did the Sultan rely on Don Joseph Nasi?
5. Why did Amatus Lusitanus dedicate a book to Don Joseph Nasi?

V. Questions for discussion:

1. Compare Italy and Turkey as lands of refuge for the Jewish refugees.
2. What events in Abravanel's life might have helped to convince him that a republic is better than an absolute monarchy?
3. How did Jews help the Renaissance in Italy?
4. Compare Donna Gracia Nasi and Queen Esther.
5. Why was Joseph Nasi called "The Great Jew"?

THINGS TO DO

1. *Picture Map*—Draw a picture map illustrating important events in the lives of Isaac Abravanel, Donna Gracia Nasi and Don Joseph Nasi.

2. *Memory Gem*—Memorize Shylock's famous speech beginning, "He hath disgraced me." The entire speech may be found in *The Merchant of Venice*, Act III, Scene 1.

CHAPTER VI

THE HOLY LAND

I. TIBERIAS

A LARGE Jewish community had remained in Palestine for hundreds of years after the destruction of the Second Temple in 70 C.E. The land declined under Rome, Byzantium and the Arabs. During the Crusades, Palestine became almost entirely desolate.

When Turkey gained control of the Holy Land in 1516 by defeating Egypt, Jews saw a new ray of hope. Refugees and pilgrims began to arrive in Palestine in increasing numbers.

For many years Joseph Nasi had helped his fellow-Jews escape from lands of persecution. If only Jews had a land of their own! Why could not the Jewish people rebuild the Holy Land? Perhaps Jews could once more make Palestine a land flowing with milk and honey.

In 1561, Don Joseph applied for permission to build Tiberias as a Jewish colony. The Sultan granted his request making him the prince of Tiberias and of seven villages in the vicinity. One of Joseph's enemies wrote that his ambition was to have himself proclaimed "King of the Jews."

Tiberias had been the chief city of Palestine after the destruction of the Second Temple. It had been the home of Judah the Prince who edited the Mishnah, and the site of the Sanhedrin. A small group of scholars, supported by Donna Gracia Nasi, already lived in Tiberias.

Don Joseph knew that there were many obstacles in the way. The first task was to build a wall around Tiberias so that the colonists would be protected from raiding Arabs. Unfortunately Joseph could not supervise the work personally, since the Sultan required his presence in Constantinople.

71

Joseph Nasi sent one of his loyal agents, Joseph ben Ardut, to take charge of the building of the wall. The agent was armed with an order from the Sultan saying, "All builders and porters in Damascus and in Safed shall go to build Tiberias; and he who does not shall bear his sin."

Construction of the wall progressed quickly until one of the Arab leaders began to incite the builders against the Jews.

"Do not permit this city to be built," said the Arab, "or it will be bitter for you in the end. For I have found it written in an ancient book that when Tiberias is built our faith will be lost."

Feelings ran high. There was a quarrel between the Jews and Arabs, and blood was shed. The governor of Damascus, however, fearing the anger of the Sultan, punished the Arab ringleaders, and the work was resumed.

The walls were completed on Chanukah in the year 1564. Donna Gracia made plans to move to Tiberias. A mansion was built for her, but we have no record as to whether she actually settled there or not. Her death in 1569 was a blow to the new colony.

Don Joseph knew that there must be a strong economic basis for the new colony. He tried to establish a textile industry with which Jews had long been associated. He imported wool from Spain for the manufacture of cloth. He planted mulberry trees for silk-worms, hoping to introduce silk-weaving. He encouraged agriculture and fishing.

Joseph Nasi then sent boats to the ports of Italy to help transport those who wished to settle in Tiberias.

The results of Don Joseph's hard work were soon noticeable. Mulberry, orange, pine and palm trees surrounded the strong walls of the city. Near Tiberias were vineyards and bee-farms kept by Jewish colonists.

A visitor wrote, "The habitations of the wilderness have been turned to a garden of Eden, and the parched soil like to the vineyard of the Lord."

Unfortunately, the war which broke out between Turkey

and Venice in 1569 interrupted the progress of the new colony. Arab marauders attacked the city, but Joseph Nasi was too much occupied with Turkey's foreign affairs to prevent bloodshed.

Don Joseph's death in 1579 was a blow from which the struggling colony never recovered. The Turkish grant was renewed and a Marrano named Alvaro Mendes was made governor. But without adequate support the colony began to dwindle away. After 50 years hardly a trace was left of Don Joseph's experiment.

No such noble venture, however, is fully lost. A century later, in 1740, another group of Jewish settlers came and rebuilt Tiberias on the ruins of Don Joseph's colony.

Joseph Nasi will long be remembered as one of the forerunners of the pioneers of modern Israel.

2. SAFED—CITY OF SAINTS

Many of those seeking refuge settled in the Holy City—Jerusalem. Others traveled to the beautiful city of Safed in the mountains of Upper Galilee. Never has there been a city like the Safed of the 16th century, for Safed was truly a city of scholars and saints.

The citizens of Safed were mostly weavers of wool, tailors, smiths, builders or merchants. Some were farmers and grew figs, grapes, olives or barley. All believed in the rule, "Love work." Even the greatest scholar depended on his own efforts rather than on servants.

A visitor describing the great men of Safed wrote, "None among them is ashamed to go to the well and draw water and carry home the pitcher on his shoulders, or to go to the market to buy bread, oil and vegetables. All the work in the house is done by themselves."

One of the most famous of Safed scholars was Rabbi Isaac Luria, also known as Ari (Lion). Rabbi Luria was a master of *Kabbalah*, secret mystical lore which had been handed down from generation to generation. Students of *Kabbalah* tried to hasten the coming of the Messiah by fasting and secret practices. Every act was designed to prepare them for the world to come. They tried to penetrate the mysteries of the spirit world and of the heavenly spheres.

Luria and the Kabbalists believed that Rabbi Simon Bar Yohai was the founder of the *Kabbalah*. Rabbi Simon and his son hid from the Roman soldiers in a cave for 13 years. It was at this time, believed the Kabbalists, that Simon devoted himself to the writing of the *Kabbalah*. Isaac Luria and his pupils would visit the grave of Rabbi Simon at Meron especially on *Lag B'Omer*, anniversary of Rabbi Simon's death. Huge fires were kindled in memory of the man whose teachings had illuminated their lives. The Kabbalists danced and sang in ecstasy through the entire night, and often saw strange visions concerning the redemption of Israel.

Luria's pupils strove for moral perfection. Love, charity and kindness were their guiding principles. They never spoke evil of their neighbors, refrained from anger, and guarded themselves from fraud and untruth.

Once a pupil named Samuel, dressed in his Sabbath finery, entered Luria's academy. The master called him to come forward and showed him great honor.

"The spirit of the blessed sages rests upon him today," said Isaac Luria.

All were eager to find out why Samuel had been honored by the master. Later they learned that the pupil, on his way to the academy, had passed a house whose inmates were weeping bitterly. Learning that their belongings had been stolen, Samuel gave them his own garments. He then clothed himself in his Sabbath garment, not possessing any other clothing, and proceeded to the academy.

Rabbi Luria's pupils would plead with him to rebuke them if he saw any defect or fault. Often a mere glance at the pupil's countenance was sufficient for the master to detect wrongdoing.

Once Rabbi Isaac said to Abraham, one of his most saintly

followers, "Thou shalt not defraud thy neighbor." The pupil examined all of his actions and could not remember any act of fraud or dishonesty. Fearing he had dealt unfairly with the weavers, Abraham called together all who had been in his employ.

"I am but human," he said. "If I have wronged you, I pray God to forgive me. I shall put this money before you. Take what you wish in satisfaction of any just claims."

The weavers all praised Abraham. One woman, however, took two silver coins. Abraham then realized he had not paid her in keeping with her skill.

When Rabbi Isaac Luria next saw Abraham, he said, "Your blemish is removed. Your sin is forgiven."

Although Luria and his pupils spent many days and nights in fasting, they also knew the meaning of joy and celebration. Festivals and holidays such as Purim and Passover were occasions for singing, dancing and rejoicing.

On Sabbath eve, in particular, they would dress in white and go out into the fields to greet the Sabbath with song and delight. It was then that the master would reveal the deep, hidden secrets of the *Kabbalah*. As the sun began to set and cast its last bright, red rays on the hills of Galilee the pupils sang a song of welcome, *L'cha Dodi*, a poem written by one of the Kabbalists of Safed. It was a song of praise which compared the Sabbath to a beautiful bride; it was also a prayer for the redemption of Jerusalem.

"Come, my beloved, to meet the bride,
And welcome the Sabbath at eventide.

In joy arise the Sabbath to greet,
The source of blessing and elation,
Ordained from God's celestial seat
As symbol of His divine creation.

O City of God, since ancient years,
Rebuild thy ruins and desolation;

Too long hast thou sat in the Vale of Tears,
For God will bring you consolation.

Come, my beloved, to meet the bride,
And welcome the Sabbath at eventide."

3. JOSEPH KARO

Safed's greatest scholar was Joseph Karo, author of the *Shulchan Aruk*, the standard code of Jewish law.

Joseph was born in Toledo, Spain in 1488. His family was descended from Judah the Prince, editor of the Mishnah. Joseph's father was a famous Rabbi and his first tutor.

When Joseph was 4 years old the evil decree of expulsion from Spain was pronounced by Ferdinand and Isabella. The family fled to Portugal, and after many hardships succeeded in finding refuge in Turkey.

Joseph Karo followed in his father's footsteps. He became a Rabbi and head of a Talmudical academy in Turkey. In 1529, Rabbi Karo met Solomon Molcho whose fiery visions of redemption stirred him greatly. He wrote letters of recommendation to help Molcho. Later, Solomon Molcho's death as a holy martyr at the stake made a profound impression upon him. Karo named one of his sons Solomon in honor of Solomon Molcho, and in his writings, often referred to the martyr as "Solomon, my beloved one."

Rabbi Karo yearned to settle in Palestine. He seemed to hear a voice within him saying, "Go up to the Holy Land. There you will teach Torah, and will train pupils who will become leaders in Israel."

Joseph Karo settled in Safed in 1536. Here he joined the scholars and saints who made Safed the greatest center of Torah in the world. After several years he became head of its largest academy, and was recognized as the leading Rabbi.

When Gracia Nasi and Joseph Nasi came to Turkey they began to support Karo's academy in Safed. Rabbi Karo was consulted by them concerning the boycott against Ancona, and gave his approval. They undoubtedly consulted him, too, about the establishment of a colony in Tiberias.

Joseph Karo was concerned about the lack of unity in religious practices among Jews. Each community seemed to have its own customs. There were many differences of opinion about Jewish law.

Some of the Rabbis proposed the formation of a new Sanhedrin in Israel of 71 Rabbis.

"The Sanhedrin will have final authority," they said. "The Sanhedrin can decide which practice to follow, and which law is correct."

Joseph Karo supported the plan for establishing a Sanhedrin. Perhaps Solomon Molcho's dream of Israel redeemed would come true. Then indeed a Sanhedrin would be necessary to proclaim the laws of Israel.

But there were many difficulties in the way. Where was the Sanhedrin to meet, in Safed or in Jerusalem? Who would select the judges of the Sanhedrin? Who would be the president of the Sanhedrin? What authority would the Sanhedrin have?

Because of all these problems no Sanhedrin was formed.

Joseph Karo now found another way of unifying the Jewish people. He spent many years studying each point of law. Where there were two opinions, he decided which point of view was supported by the majority. So great was his scholarship that all Jews accepted his decisions.

Rabbi Karo then arranged all laws in logical, well-organized fashion. He called the code *Shulchan Aruk* ("Prepared Table") since all matters were prepared in a neat and orderly manner. In each case he clearly indicated the basis for his decision by referring to the Mishnah and Talmud or to the codes of the Rambam and the other great authorities.

Karo succeeded in his purpose. The *Shulchan Aruk* was accepted by all Jewish communities. It became the standard code of Judaism which served to unify Jews the world over.

Joseph Karo passed away in Safed in 1575 at the ripe old

age of 87. A narrow, winding path leads to the street where Karo's academy once stood. On an old inscription honoring the author of the *Shulchan Aruk* are the words, "Happy is the mother who bore him."

EXERCISES

I. Complete each sentence. (Review section 1, pages 71 to 73.)

Damascus, Don Joseph Nasi, Joseph ben Ardut, Tiberias, Turkey

1. _____ gained control of Palestine by defeating Egypt in 1516.
2. _____ was given a grant to rebuild Tiberias and seven villages as a Jewish colony.
3. _____ was placed in charge of the building of the wall.
4. When the Arabs interfered with the building of the wall the Jews appealed to the governor of _____.
5. Don Joseph Nasi hoped to make silk-weaving the most important industry of the colony of _____.

II. Answer each question in a complete sentence. (Review section 2, pages 73 to 76.)

1. How did the inhabitants of Safed earn a living?
2. Who was Isaac Luria?
3. Why did the Kabbalists honor Simon bar Yohai?
4. What good deed did Luria's pupil, Samuel, perform?
5. How did Rabbi Luria and his pupils welcome the Sabbath?

III. True or false? (Review section 3, pages 76 to 78.)

1. Joseph Karo was born in Safed.
2. Joseph Karo admired Solomon Molcho.
3. Joseph Karo supported the plan for establishing a Sanhedrin.
4. Joseph Karo rejected the laws of the Mishnah and Talmud.
5. The *Shulchan Aruk* is a code of Jewish law.

IV. Questions for discussion:
1. Compare the problems confronting the builders of Tiberias and those confronting the builders of modern Israel.
2. Why is Safed called a "City of Saints"?
3. What has been the influence of the *Shulchan Aruk* on Jewish life?

THINGS TO DO

1. *Songs*—Learn some of the songs about the cities mentioned in this chapter.
Several popular Hebrew songs are:

> a—*Yerushalayim*
> b—*Al S'fat Yam Kinneret*
> c—*V'ulai*

2. *Class Newspaper*—Prepare a newspaper in which events concerning the building of Tiberias are reported. These are some of the topics that might be assigned to members of the staff:

(1) A report from Joseph ben Ardut to Joseph Nasi
(2) An editorial called, "We will continue to build"
(3) An eye-witness account describing the Arab attack
(4) A letter by one of the colonists to his family in Constantinople describing a visit to Safed
(5) Science column—Tiberias as a health resort
(6) An account of the trial before the governor of Damascus
(7) An interview with Donna Gracia Nasi reported by the Constantinople correspondent
(8) A statement by Joseph Nasi on the purpose of the colony
(9) Puzzles based on Jewish history
(10) Illustrations: Plan of wall around Tiberias; houses of Tiberias overlooking Lake Kinneret; fishing on the Kinneret; the Wailing Wall

CHAPTER VII

HOLLAND

HOLLAND will go down in world history as one of the first European countries to strike a blow for the cause of religious freedom. Finding the rule of intolerant Spain oppressive, brave little Holland fought courageously for liberty. After many years of struggle Holland succeeded in throwing off the yoke of cruel Spain in 1581.

As political adviser to the Sultan, Joseph Nasi had supported the cause of Dutch freedom. With the establishment of a Jewish community in Amsterdam, Joseph Nasi's co-religionists in Spain and Portugal were able to enjoy the benefits of this newly-won liberty.

The account of the origin of the Amsterdam Jewish community that has come down to us is indeed a romantic one. In 1593, a group of Marranos, led by Jacob Tirado, left Spain and Portugal in search of a haven of refuge. 100 years had passed since Judaism had been outlawed by Ferdinand and Isabella; yet still these families remained true to the faith of their fathers. Among those seeking freedom was the beautiful Maria Nunez.

The Marrano vessel which flew a Spanish flag was captured by an English ship, since Spain and England were then at war. The English captain, fascinated by the beauty of Maria Nunez, asked her to marry him. But Maria refused.

Hearing the romantic story, Queen Elizabeth asked to see the beautiful Marrano girl. Together the queen and the refugee drove in the royal carriage through the streets of London. It is very possible that William Shakespeare was among those who gathered in the streets to gaze at Maria as she drove by with the beloved queen.

Queen Elizabeth urged Maria to accept the ship-captain's proposal. Respecting the girl's wishes to settle in a country where she could live as a Jewess, Queen Elizabeth gave orders for the vessel to be set free.

The Marranos continued their journey northward. Near Emden, Germany a storm broke out almost wrecking the vessel. The Marranos landed on shore in order to repair the damage.

A small Jewish community lived in Emden. While strolling through the town Tirado and his friends wandered into the street where the Jews lived. Tirado noticed the *mezuzot* which decorated the doorposts. Recognizing the Hebrew letters, Tirado made inquiry and discovered that the inhabitants of these houses were Jews.

Tirado approached Rabbi Moses Halevy, leader of the small community. This was the first time in his life that he had met a person who openly professed Judaism.

"We are brothers," said Tirado his voice choked with emotion. "We too recite the *Shma Yisrael* daily even though we have been forced to practice Judaism secretly."

Rabbi Halevy welcomed the Marranos and offered his assistance to the newcomers.

"It is our earnest desire to return openly to Judaism," said Tirado. "If you help us we will reward you richly."

"I will gladly help you without reward," said Moses Halevy. "But it would be dangerous in Emden for men and women who were born Christians to convert to Judaism. In Amsterdam, however, the freedom-loving Dutch people will surely welcome victims of Spanish oppression. Let us meet in Amsterdam; there we can openly profess our belief in Judaism."

Everything went according to plan. But the troubles of the refugees were not yet over. On Yom Kippur the Dutch police, hearing the prayers of the Jewish worshipers, suspected a Spanish plot. They arrested all who had gathered to worship.

Jacob Tirado made an eloquent plea in Latin explaining that they were not Spanish spies but Jews fleeing from Spanish persecution.

Impressed by his eloquent words the police officer said, "I shall inform the authorities who will decide what is to be done. Meanwhile, you may continue your service. Pray for the peace of our city."

Later Tirado repeated his plea before the city officials who authorized the Jews to remain and to worship as they pleased.

Shortly after their arrival in Amsterdam, Maria Nunez married a fellow-refugee. Their wedding was celebrated by a festive dance in which all the newly-arrived members of the Jewish community participated.

A synagogue was established named *Beth Jacob* ("House of Jacob") in honor of Jacob Tirado. Moses Halevy served as the first religious leader.

Thus was founded the great Jewish community of Amsterdam.

2. RABBI MENASSEH BEN ISRAEL

The Marranos of Portugal and Spain rejoiced to hear the glad news that in Amsterdam Jews were free to worship as they pleased. Hundreds of families began to escape from the terrors of the Inquisition to this haven of refuge.

The Jewish community of Amsterdam soon became a large and flourishing one. Prosperous merchants engaged in trade with England, Germany, Italy, Turkey, India and the New World. Jews became respected citizens of Amsterdam. The famous painter Rembrandt, who lived in the Jewish section, loved to draw portraits of the picturesque Jewish types that he met. One of his paintings, for example, is called "The Jewish Doctor."

Among the Marranos who came from Portugal to Holland was Joseph ben Israel. He had been imprisoned and tortured by the Inquisition; his property had been confiscated. Broken in health but not in spirit Joseph ben Israel fled with his family

REMBRANDT AND MENASSEH BEN ISRAEL

to Amsterdam. Here they converted to Judaism and assumed Jewish names. Like Joseph of the Bible, Joseph ben Israel called his sons Ephraim and Menasseh.

The father was especially proud of Menasseh. The lad attended the excellent school maintained by the Jewish community. His progress in both his Hebrew and general studies was outstanding. The lad never tired of hearing his father tell of the secret practices of the Marranos.

In his book *Hope of Israel*, Menasseh later recorded one of the anecdotes told by his father:

"An hour-glass filled with the sand of Sambatyon ran all the week till the Sabbath. And I heard the same from my father. He told me that there was an Arabian at Lisbon who had such an hour-glass; and that every Friday at evening he would walk in the street called *The New Street* and show this glass to Jews who pretended to be Christians and say, 'Ye Jews, shut up your shops for now the Sabbath comes'."

When Menasseh was 18 years old he was asked, despite his youth, to serve as Rabbi of one of the Amsterdam congregations. Menasseh ben Israel used to say with a smile, "I went straight from the cradle to the pulpit."

Menasseh married a Marrano girl named Rachel Abravanel who was descended from Don Isaac Abravanel. Apparently the grandson of Don Isaac who had been seized in Portugal had lived all of his life as a Marrano and had passed on his belief in Judaism to his children.

Menasseh ben Israel and the other Rabbis were aware of the unusual nature of their community which consisted almost exclusively of men and women who had been brought up as Christians but who had secretly maintained a belief in Judaism. Menasseh devoted his efforts to explaining to these new Jews the meaning of the Bible and the laws of Judaism. His preaching was so effective that he was called "a swelling river of eloquence," and he was elected the official preacher of the Amsterdam community.

It was indeed a privilege to study under this inspiring

master. Many of his pupils became famous as scholars, authors and physicians. One of Menasseh ben Israel's pupils, Baruch Spinoza, is ranked among the world's great philosophers. Unfortunately, Spinoza's radical religious ideas later led to his excommunication while Menasseh ben Israel was away in England.

Eager to spread a knowledge of Judaism Menasseh set up his own printing press. Book after book rolled off the presses until Amsterdam began to rival Venice as a center of Hebrew publishing. Menasseh ben Israel's own books were read by Jews and Gentiles throughout Europe. Even in Spain and Portugal men secretly studied his writings about the Bible. In one case, unfortunately, a Portuguese diplomat was consigned to the flames by the Inquisition because of the interest he had shown in Menasseh ben Israel's writings.

In the eyes of the outside world Menasseh ben Israel was the spokesman for Judaism. They admired this Rabbi who had mastered ten languages and whose speeches and writings showed such learning and scholarship. When the queen of England visited the Amsterdam synagogue she was officially welcomed by Rabbi Menasseh ben Israel who delivered an eloquent oration. Gentile professors, inspired by Menasseh ben Israel, devoted themselves to the study of Hebrew. Christina, queen of Sweden, commissioned the Rabbi to assemble a Hebrew library for her palace.

Rembrandt, the great artist, was proud to claim Rabbi Menasseh ben Israel as a friend. He illustrated one of the Rabbi's books by drawing sketches of the visions of the prophets. Rembrandt's etching of Menasseh is a famous one. It shows the bearded Rabbi with a short cloak and a wide-brimmed Dutch steeple hat; his eyes seem to reflect deep wisdom and profound human understanding.

3. THE HOPE OF ISRAEL

One day a Marrano traveler arrived in Amsterdam with fantastic tales concerning the Lost Ten Tribes. He claimed that during his travels in South America he had met Indians who observed the Sabbath and the practices of Judaism. He believed that these were the Lost Ten Tribes.

Rabbi Menasseh ben Israel recorded the traveler's exploits and published a book about them. From all over Europe, especially England, came inquiries concerning the Lost Ten Tribes. In response to these letters Rabbi Menasseh ben Israel wrote his most famous book *The Hope of Israel*.

Menasseh ben Israel expressed in this book his belief that the prophecy of redemption would come true. The Lost Ten Tribes and Jews scattered throughout the world would soon be restored to the Holy Land. The secret Jews who had suffered so greatly at the hands of the cruel Inquisition would once again be free.

In every country the belief in the coming of the Messiah was intense. In the East, in Turkey, a false Messiah named Sabbatai Zevi raised the hopes of the Jews to fever pitch— hopes, alas, that were doomed to disappointment.

In his book *The Hope of Israel*, Menasseh ben Israel tried to prove that the Messiah could not be expected as long as the Jews were excluded from England. Did not the Bible say, "And the Lord shall scatter thee among all people, from one end of the earth even unto the other"? Before the redemption could come Jews must be found in England and in all other parts of the earth. If England admitted Jews the coming of the Messiah would be hastened.

Menasseh ben Israel's friends in England were greatly impressed by his stirring book. They urged him to apply to Cromwell for the readmission of Jews to England. Lord Oliver Cromwell, victor in England's civil war, was very sympathetic to the Jews. As a Puritan he looked upon them as the people of the Bible. He was also interested in the economic advantages that the Jewish merchants might bring to England.

Menasseh ben Israel wrote to Cromwell and was invited to come to England to negotiate concerning the matter. Menasseh set sail for England on September 2, 1655. This was the great adventure of his life.

4. MISSION TO ENGLAND

The Rabbi was cordially received by the handful of Marrano Jews already living in London. On Rosh Ha-Shanah services were held with Menasseh and his son officiating.

Soon thereafter Menasseh ben Israel met with Cromwell who was captivated by his engaging personality. Cromwell was especially stirred by the Rabbi's account of the suffering of the Marranos at the hands of the Inquisition. He favored the proposal that a formal proclamation be issued inviting Jews to settle in England.

Menasseh ben Israel then addressed a formal petition to the Council of State.

"With a gracious eye have regard unto us and our petition," he wrote. "Grant unto us free exercise of our religion that we may have our synagogues and keep our own public worship."

He added a pamphlet called "A Declaration to the Commonwealth of England" in which he showed how Jews were always loyal citizens of the countries in which they lived. He answered the slanders directed against Jews by citing Jewish law which makes it a sin to rob or defraud a stranger.

"The Jew is bound to show his charity to all men," wrote Menasseh ben Israel.

He then pointed out how Jews had enriched the ports of Holland, Germany and Italy. Once admitted to England they would enrich this country too.

Cromwell quickly appointed 28 men to serve on a committee to study Menasseh ben Israel's petition. He himself was strongly in favor of a formal proclamation encouraging Jews to settle in England.

It seems, however, as if Menasseh ben Israel had stirred up a hornet's nest. Prejudice again showed its vicious character. All the old lies, including the blood accusation, were revived. Merchants were afraid of competition. Ministers protested that Jews might try to convert others to Judaism.

For two years the debate dragged on. Menasseh ben Israel published a brilliant pamphlet, entitled *The Plea for the Jews*, denouncing one by one the slanders directed against the Jewish people.

Because of the strong opposition Cromwell decided to seek some other solution to the problem. The opportunity soon presented itself. When war broke out between England and Spain some of the Marranos living in London had to surrender their property because they were regarded as subjects of Spain.

A new petition carrying the signature of Menassah ben Israel and six Marranos was presented. In it they openly declared they were Jews, not Spaniards, and asked for permission to worship freely. Suit was brought by one of the Marranos for restoration of his property since he was a Jewish refugee and not a Spanish subject.

Cromwell and the Council of State ignored the petition but ruled that the property of the Marranos could not be confiscated since they were Jews and not Spaniards. In this manner Jews won the right, without a formal declaration, to live in England.

Rabbi Menasseh ben Israel was not satisfied with merely winning a test case. Was this sufficient to hasten the resettlement of the Jews in England and the coming of the Messiah? Meanwhile the Rabbi's son, who had accompanied his father to London, became ill and died. Embittered by his tragedy and convinced that his mission had ended in failure, Menasseh ben Israel returned to Holland. The English government felt responsible for Menasseh's support since he had come to England at their invitation. They voted him a pension, only a small portion of which was actually paid.

Rabbi Menasseh ben Israel arrived in Holland in October 1657 a sick and broken-hearted man. Almost immediately he was confined to his sick-bed. He died a month later at the age of 53.

Despite his feeling of disappointment, Menasseh ben Israel's mission was by no means a failure. Even though Cromwell had made no formal proclamation, Jews had won the right to settle in England. This victory was largely the result of Menasseh ben Israel's noble efforts.

The Jewish community of England began to grow and to thrive. Today it is one of the outstanding Jewish communities in the world. Rabbi Menasseh ben Israel may rightly be regarded as the founder of English Jewry.

On his tombstone the Rabbi's admirers inscribed these words:

"He is not dead; for in heaven he lives in supreme glory while on earth his pen has won him immortal remembrance."

EXERCISES

I. Name the country. (Review section 1, pages 80 to 82.)

1. _____ was one of the first European countries to grant its subjects religious freedom.

2. Tirado and his companions still practiced Judaism secretly even though _____ had expelled all Jews in 1492.

3. Maria Nunez drove in a royal carriage with Queen Elizabeth of _____.

4. Tirado found a small Jewish community in Emden, _____.

5. The refugees settled in _____ where they were allowed to worship as they pleased.

II. Why? (Review section 2, pages 82 to 85.)

1. Why did the Jews of Amsterdam become prosperous?

2. Why did Joseph ben Israel name his sons Ephraim and Menasseh?

3. Why did Menaseh ben Israel establish a printing press?

4. Why did the Rabbi think his congregation in Amsterdam was an unusual one?

5. Why did Jews and Gentiles admire Menasseh ben Israel?

III. Choose the correct word or phrase. (Review section 3, pages 85 to 87.)

1. The traveler claimed he found the Lost Ten Tribes in _____. (North America, South America)

2. _____ was a false Messiah. (Menasseh ben Israel, Sabbatai Zevi)

3. Menasseh ben Israel wrote _____. (*The Hope of Israel*, the *Shulchan Aruk*)

4. Friends of Menasseh ben Israel in _____ wrote suggesting he appeal for the readmission of Jews to their country. (England, France)

5. Menasseh ben Israel wrote about _____. (colonization in Palestine, the coming of the Messiah)

IV. Cromwell or Menasseh ben Israel? (Review section 4, pages 87 to 89.)

1. _____ wrote a petition asking for the admission of Jews to England.

2. _____ wrote "A Declaration to the Commonwealth of England."

3. _____ appointed a committee of 28 to consider the admission of Jews to England.

4. _____ and the Council of State ruled that Marranos in England were not Spaniards but refugee Jews.

5. _____ felt that a legal ruling permitting Jews to stay in England without a formal proclamation was not enough.

V. Questions for discussion:

1. Amsterdam has often been called "the Jerusalem of Holland." Why?

2. Compare Menasseh ben Israel and Joseph Karo.

3. Was Menasseh ben Israel's journey to England a failure? Give reasons for your answer.

THINGS TO DO

1. *Film*—Show the film "The Passover of Rembrandt Van Rijn." It may be obtained through the Jewish Theological Seminary of America, 3080 Broadway, New York City.

2. *Pictures*—There are many excellent pictures that can be brought to class. Volume I of *The Jewish Encyclopedia*, under "Amsterdam" contains pictures of the famous Dutch synagogues. Reprints of Rembrandt's Jewish portraits can be seen in Volume X. (Note especially the frontispiece to Volume X.) *The Jewish Encyclopedia* also has pictures of Menasseh ben Israel and Baruch Spinoza.

CHAPTER VIII

THE NEW WORLD

I. JEWS HELP IN THE DISCOVERY OF AMERICA

JEWS, especially Marrano Jews, played a prominent role in the discovery of America.

Many historians believe that Columbus himself was of Jewish extraction. In 1892, when the world celebrated the 400th anniversary of the discovery of America, the Spanish government invited a historian to study the records which might shed some light on the origin of Christopher Columbus. The historian came to the conclusion that Columbus was descended from a Jewish family that fled from Spain to Italy around 1391 to escape persecution. The explorer's son stated that Columbus was descended from King David.

Columbus' expedition would have been impossible without the aid of a Marrano named Luis de Santangel. Members of Santangel's family had been put to death by the Inquisition and he himself narrowly escaped punishment. Columbus, discouraged by the cool reception he had received in Spain, was ready to go to France to solicit the help of the French court. Santangel, however, was impressed by Columbus' scheme and intervened with Queen Isabella. It was Santangel who advanced the loan to finance the expedition. The popular story which relates how Queen Isabella pawned her jewels to purchase ships is merely a legend.

Don Isaac Abravanel was also a staunch friend of Columbus. He shares with Luis de Santangel and others the honor of having financed the Columbus expedition. An American historian, H. B. Adams writes: "Not jewels but Jews were the real financial basis of the first expedition of Columbus."

Columbus' ships were anchored at the port of Seville within

sight of the vessels on which the Jewish refugees fled from Spain in 1492. Columbus set sail one day after the exiles made their departure. The wailing of the Jews was almost the last sound he heard before setting sail.

Columbus began his account of his voyage with these words: "In the same month in which their Majesties issued the edict that all Jews should be driven out of the kingdom and its territories—in that same month they gave me the order to undertake with sufficient men my expedition of discovery to the Indies."

It is significant that Columbus should refer to the expulsion of the Jews. Was he perhaps thinking of his own family which fled Spain a century before because of persecution? Did he have some premonition that the land he would discover would prove to be a haven of refuge for the persecuted children of Israel?

Columbus mentions the names of two Jewish scientists on whose studies he depended. One was the poet, Bible commentator and astronomer, Abraham Ibn Ezra, who lived in the twelfth century. The other was Abraham Zacuto, astronomer to the king of Portugal, whose tables were used by Columbus. The copy used by the explorer with notes in his handwriting is still in existence.

Many of the members of the crew were Marranos. Rodrigo Sanchez joined the expedition at the personal request of Queen Isabella and was made Superintendent. Another Marrano named Marco was ship-surgeon. Mestre Bernal, who served as physician, had already suffered at the hands of the Inquisition because of his adherence to Judaism. The first man to sight land was a Marrano named Rodrigo de Triana. He later settled in Africa where he renounced Christianity and returned to his former faith.

The official interpreter for the expedition was Luis de Torres, a Marrano who was selected because of his knowledge of languages such as Latin, Arabic and Hebrew. Luis de Torres was the first European to touch American soil.

He and another seaman were chosen as ambassadors to the rulers of the new land. Little did Columbus know that despite the many languages Luis de Torres had mastered he would still have to communicate with the natives in sign language. The ambassadors were instructed to look for spices and other products. Beads were given to them to be used in exchange for food. They were told to return in six days.

Guided by two Indians whom they had met near the shore, Luis de Torres and his companion made their way inland to a large village. Here they were welcomed by the natives who invited them to partake of a strange-looking herb. They were the first but not the last Europeans to taste this herb—it was tobacco.

Luis de Torres brought back a detailed report to Columbus. He described the people, the animals, the plants and the strange sights he had seen. Later, Luis de Torres was rewarded by Ferdinand and Isabella with a royal pension for his faithful service. He settled in Cuba where he lived for the rest of his life.

Columbus wrote a letter describing his wonderful discoveries. This first letter was addressed to his friend Luis de Santangel, the Marrano Jew who had supported him so loyally.

The New World which they helped discover was destined to become a haven of refuge for the persecuted Jews.

2. BRAZIL

Portugal, like Spain, was greatly aided in its explorations by Jews and Marranos.

Abraham Zacuto, astronomer to the king of Portugal, provided the scientific information necessary for many of these voyages. We have already seen how Christopher Columbus relied on the tables prepared by Zacuto. King Manuel sent his pilots to Zacuto who would explain the use of the tables and the manner of determining the position of a vessel at sea by observing the sun or the North Star. He would discuss his theory of the origin of storms, and would supply the navigators with charts and with instruments. His *Perpetual Almanac* was used by many of the great explorers.

Vasco da Gama, before sailing on his voyage around the Cape of Good Hope, met Zacuto in a Lisbon monastery. The Jewish astronomer carefully briefed Vasco da Gama on his forthcoming expedition. Zacuto's tables were also used by Cabral who landed on the coast of Brazil in 1500 and claimed that country for Portugal, and by Americus Vespucius after whom America was named because of his many explorations in Central and South America. Despite his great contribution, Zacuto was forced to seek sanctuary in Turkey when King Manuel announced the decree of expulsion from Portugal.

The explorers were accompanied by Marrano navigators and seamen. Jews were quick to settle in the New World. They came seeking freedom from persecution and prejudice. They introduced the planting of the sugar-cane. They set up sugar-mills. They traded with the Indians and with the countries of Europe. They helped to conquer the wilderness.

The flame of Jewish faith burned brightly. Services were held regularly in the homes of colonists in Brazil, Mexico and Peru. In one community it was the custom to announce services by sending a Negro servant in party-colored clothes to play a tambour in the streets where Marranos lived. *Matzot* were distributed on Passover. The Sabbath was observed by the lighting of candles, and, at times, by abstention from work. On Yom Kipper, Marranos fasted and assembled for prayer.

But there was no escape from the terrors of the Inquisition. *Autos-da fé* were arranged in Mexico and in South America, and horrible punishments meted out to those who were suspected of observing Judaism.

Aided by the Marranos, the Dutch secured a foothold in Brazil by conquering the port of Pernambuco (also called Recife) in 1630. Almost immediately the Marranos openly announced their adherence to Judaism. They were joined by many immigrants from Amsterdam, among them Menasseh ben Israel's brother, Ephraim. Even Rabbi Menasseh ben Israel planned to leave Amsterdam for Brazil, but later changed his mind. Asser Levy and other Ashkenazic Jews from Germany or Poland also settled in the colony.

Congregations and religious schools were soon established. In 1633 a beautiful scroll of the Law with ivory rolls, a cloak of fine gold brocade and silver ornaments was imported from Amsterdam. Rabbi Isaac Aboab, a colleague of Menasseh ben Israel, was invited to become Rabbi of the new community. Thus, he has the honor of being the first American Rabbi. His life story is similar to that of Menasseh ben Israel's. He too had been born to a Marrano family in Portugal. At an early age he was brought to Amsterdam where his family openly professed Judaism. One of the Dutch poets called him, "The light of the Law and the example of virtue."

The community in Brazil flourished for several years. The colonists exported sugar and redwood, of which a dye was made, to their relatives in Amsterdam. They sent generous contributions to Jerusalem and to the synagogues of Amsterdam.

The danger of conquest by the Portuguese grew greater each year. There were many spies in Pernambuco who plotted to overthrow the Dutch colony. In 1645 a Jewish doctor and 4 other members of the congregation found documents in a boat which proved that Portugal was planning a revolt from within. With the help of this information the Dutch succeeded in capturing the conspirators.

Pleased with the loyalty of the Jewish settlers the government of Holland in 1645 sent a charter promising protection to them in case of peril.

The charter stated:

"As we have for some years now perceived the attachment which the Jewish Nation has to the improvement of the service of this State and particularly for the maintenance of the conquests in Brazil, just as this Nation recently has shown over there its loyalty and courage, so is it that we have taken the aforesaid Jewish Nation under our protection. The government now residing in Brazil shall favor and assist the Jewish Nation on all occasions as its loyalty and courage deserve; without permitting any difference between them and our other inhabitants in any way."

This is the first charter of equality granted to Jews in the New World.

The following year Portugal sent an army which laid siege to Pernambuco. For eight long years the Dutch put up a heroic resistance. Jews again distinguished themselves by their bravery. Rabbi Aboab delivered fiery sermons urging Jews to fight courageously.

Hopelessly outnumbered, exhausted by lack of food, the Dutch finally surrendered on January 27, 1654. True to their promises the Dutch included a provision in the terms of surrender allowing Jews to depart within 90 days, thus making it possible for them to escape the Inquisition.

Sixteen vessels carried the Jewish refugees and a few meager belongings away from Brazil. Most of the settlers, including Rabbi Isaac Aboab and the brother of Menasseh ben Israel, returned to Holland.

Thus ended the first Jewish settlement in the New World.

3. NEW AMSTERDAM

Not all of the refugees from Brazil returned to Holland. Some made their way to friendly settlements in the New World such as Dutch Guiana, Caracas, Jamaica and the Virgin Islands.

One hardy group of refugees, among them Asser Levy, sailed to New Amsterdam. They had landed first on the island of Jamaica in the West Indies but had decided to continue their journey northward. Their voyage is shrouded in mystery. Apparently they were captured on the high seas by pirates, but were ransomed by Master Jacques de la Motte, captain of a French boat named the *St. Charles.*

One-legged Peter Stuyvesant, governor of New Amsterdam, reluctantly allowed the refugees to land. Meanwhile,

Captain de la Motte harshly demanded immediate payment. He seized all goods belonging to the immigrants and sold them at public auction. Since there was still a balance due, three of the refugees, including Asser Levy, were thrown into debtors' prison. After several weeks, however, Captain de la Motte relented and agreed to wait until the relatives of his Jewish passengers sent the necessary funds from Amsterdam. Thus, Asser Levy and his two friends were released.

Governor Stuyvesant, unlike other Dutch officials, was intolerant and bigoted. He did not want to allow the Jews to remain in New Amsterdam. He felt that there was no room for new immigrants since the colony already boasted 200 families! Jews might become a public charge. Soon Jews would be followed by atheists.

Peter Stuyvesant wrote a strong letter to the directors of the Dutch West India Company requesting the expulsion of the Jews. He hurled vile insults at the Jewish people. He pleaded that Jews "be not allowed further to infect and trouble this new colony."

Governor Stuyvesant was aided by the minister of the colony who wrote to Holland, "It would create a still greater confusion if the obstinate and immovable Jews came to settle here."

The answer of the Dutch West India Company, dated February 15, 1655, was a complete victory for the Jewish colonists. There can be no doubt that Jewish leaders in Amsterdam, many of whom held shares in the Dutch West India Company, helped formulate the reply. The directors called attention to the charter of protection which had been granted to the Jews of Brazil in 1645. They mentioned the courage and loyalty shown by the Jewish colonists in Brazil, and the severe losses suffered by them after the fall of Pernambuco.

"You may therefore shut your eyes," wrote the directors. "At least not force people's consciences, but allow everyone to have his own belief, as long as he behaves quietly and legally."

ASSER LEVY AND PETER STUYVESANT

The directors agreed, however, that Jews must not be allowed to become public charges. Jews could remain "provided that the poor amongst them shall not become a burden to the community, but be supported by their own nation."

The Jews rejoiced at their good fortune. They organized a congregation called *Shearith Israel* ("Remnant of Israel") which is still in existence. They had indeed chosen an appropriate name, for their colony proved to be a haven of refuge for the persecuted remnant of Israel. The Jews of Amsterdam entrusted them with a scroll "of parchment with its green veil and cloak and band of India damask of dark purple."

4. ASSER LEVY AND THE STRUGGLE FOR EQUAL RIGHTS

The struggle for Jewish rights continued.

Peter Stuyvesant was not only wooden-legged, but, as far as the Jews were concerned, wooden-headed. They could remain but only as second-class citizens.

Prominent in the struggle for equal rights was Asser Levy. When the Indians threatened to attack, a watch was formed but Jews were not permitted to stand guard. Instead they were forced to pay a special tax.

Asser Levy and Jacob Barsimson insisted on their right to bear arms in defense of the colony.

Peter Stuyvesant denied their petition. He added, "As the petitioners are of opinion that the result of this will be injurious to them, consent is hereby given to them to depart whenever and whither it pleases them."

Asser Levy refused to leave New Amsterdam. Instead he appealed and won the right to stand guard and bear arms.

The next struggle for equality centered around the right to trade. The Jewish colonists had begun to trade along the Hudson and Delaware Rivers. They were harshly ordered by Stuyvesant to stop all trade.

The Jewish settlers wrote to Stuyvesant on November 29, 1655:

"The Honorable Lords Directors of the Chartered West-

India Company, masters and proprietors of this province, gave permission and consent to the petitioners, like the other inhabitants, to reside, navigate and trade here and enjoy the same liberties. They therefore request that your Honorable Worships will not prevent or hinder them herein, but will allow and consent that they may navigate and trade to and on the South River (Delaware River) of New Netherland, at Fort Orange (Albany) and other places situated within the jurisdiction of this Government of New Netherland."

Stuyvesant's reply was, "For weighty reasons the request is denied." He did not explain what the weighty reasons were. The governor, however, did make one concession. He allowed them to dispose of the goods they had already shipped to the Delaware River.

"Inasmuch as it has been reported that the suppliants have already shipped some goods, they are for the time being allowed to send one or two persons to the South River in order to dispose of the same, which being done they are to return hither."

Once again the colonists appealed to the directors of the Dutch West India Company in Amsterdam:

"It appears that Mr. Stuyvesant does not permit the Jewish Nation to enjoy in quietness the exercise of its religion. Nor does he permit them to buy and sell real estate, to trade and traffic in all places of the Company just like all other natives of this country, provided they support their own poor and pay their contributions together with all the other natives."

This appeal was endorsed by their relatives in Amsterdam who pleaded that Jews be given full religious freedom and be granted the "rights of housing, commerce, trade and liberty."

Again Governor Stuyvesant was rebuked and was ordered to grant Jews the right to trade.

The climax of the struggle for equal rights came in 1657. Asser Levy appeared in court and applied for a certificate as burgher, or citizen.

The court record reads as follows:

"Asser Levy, a Jew, appears in Court; requests to be admitted a burgher; claims that such ought not to be refused him as he keeps watch and ward like other burghers; showing a burgher certificate from the City of Amsterdam that the Jew is burgher there. Which being deliberated on, it is decreed, as before, that it cannot be allowed."

The entire Jewish community now joined with Asser Levy in an appeal to Peter Stuyvesant. The governor, it seems, had learned his lesson. He overruled the court and granted Asser Levy a burgher's certificate on April 21, 1657. This date is a milestone in the history of the Jewish people, for it marks the beginning of full citizenship in an American colony.

Asser Levy prospered as a citizen of New Amsterdam. His activities were varied indeed. He built a slaughterhouse; he owned a tavern. He bought and sold land. He was called upon as referee to settle business disputes. He was named executor of estates. He engaged in lawsuits against those who had broken contracts. He gave generously to Jewish and to Christian charities.

When the English fleet threatened to attack in 1664 Asser Levy advanced a large sum of money for the defense of the city. Four English men-of-war appeared in the harbor and demanded the surrender of Fort Amsterdam. Stuyvesant saw that resistance was hopeless. The burghers urged immediate surrender.

"Whether we turn us for assistance to the north or to the south, to the east or the west," argued the Dutch burghers, " 'tis all in vain."

The English allowed the Dutch soldiers to leave with military honors. New Amsterdam became New York.

The Jews continued to enjoy full civic and religious liberty. Little did Asser Levy and his friends realize that the settlement which they had founded would some day become the largest Jewish community in the world.

5. NEW ENGLAND

The Hebraic influence was strongly felt in New England even before the arrival of the Jews. The Pilgrims who came to Massachusetts regarded themselves as "The New Israel." They studied the Old Testament daily, many of them in the original Hebrew. They chose Biblical names such as Abraham, Samuel, David, Sarah and Deborah for their children. Their code of laws was entitled "Draft of the Model of Moses." Their colony was given a Hebrew name Salem ("peace"), a shortening of the name Jerusalem.

The holiday of Thanksgiving, modeled after the festival of *Sukkot*, is an interesting example of the Biblical influence. The Pilgrims felt that they were like the ancient children of Israel. They too had left their old homes in search of freedom. They too wanted to worship the one true God. They too had wandered in the wilderness and had been delivered from its dangers. Reading of the holiday of *Sukkot*, they said, "The children of Israel gave thanks unto God because He led them safely through the desert. We too will celebrate a holiday of thanksgiving unto God in gratitude for His many blessings."

When Harvard College was founded in 1636, all students were required to study Hebrew as one of the basic subjects. Not satisfied with the other translations of the Bible the Puritans studied the original Hebrew and composed their own translation. The first book published in America in 1640 was the *Bay Psalm Book*, a translation of the Hebrew Psalms. The printers used both Hebrew and English type for this famous book.

The Puritans, unfortunately, did not welcome any who differed from them in religious belief. Driven out by the Puritans, Roger Williams resolved to found a colony based on the doctrine of religious freedom. In his writings he argued that Jews would make good citizens. It is no wonder that Jews began to settle in Rhode Island.

In 1658 the second Jewish congregation in the colonies was

organized in Newport, Rhode Island. The community consisted of 15 families recently arrived from Holland.

The General Assembly of Rhode Island later assured the Jews of their rights under the law by stating:

"We declare that they may expect as good protection here, as any stranger, being not of our nation, residing amongst us in this his Majesty's colony ought to have, being obedient to his Majesty's laws."

Jews began to play a leading role in the life of Newport, then one of America's largest seaports. The community was enlarged from time to time by many new arrivals. As late as 1755, after the Lisbon earthquake, a group of daring Marrano merchants fled from Portugal to Newport. They had preserved their secret belief in Judaism for over 250 years.

The beautiful synagogue erected by the Newport congregation in 1768 still stands. It was built in an architectural style which made it blend with the rest of the colonial buildings in the city. In a sense this was a symbol of American Jewish life which seemed to blend so harmoniously with the life being created in the New World. The Newport synagogue, oldest existing synagogue building in America, was declared a national shrine by the United States Congress in 1947.

We have already seen how Dr. Samuel Nunez escaped from Portugal and became one of the early settlers of Georgia. The synagogue in Savannah, Georgia was built shortly after the founding of the colony. Other congregations were organized in Charleston, in Philadelphia and in Montreal.

The establishment of these congregations marks the beginning of a new and happy chapter in the history of the Jewish people. America was destined to become the haven of refuge for millions of Jews seeking liberty and religious freedom. Now at last they were able to walk with dignity, free and unafraid.

The beloved poet Longfellow caught the spirit of the Jews when he wrote, after having visited the cemetery of the Newport congregation:

"Pride and humiliation hand in hand
Walked with them through the world where'er they
went;
Trampled and beaten were they as the sand
And yet unshaken as the continent."

EXERCISES

I. Write a sentence about each of the following. (Review section 1, pages 91 to 93.)
  1. Luis Santangel
  2. Isaac Abravanel
  3. Abraham Zacuto
  4. Mestre Bernal
  5. Luis de Torres

II. Answer each question in a complete sentence. (Review section 2, pages 93 to 96.)
  1. How did Abraham Zacuto help the explorers of Spain and Portugal?
  2. Why did the Jews rejoice when the Dutch conquered Pernambuco?
  3. Who was Isaac Aboab?
  4. What did the Dutch government promise to the Jews in the charter of 1645?
  5. Why were the Jews forced to leave Brazil?

III. Complete each sentence. (Review section 3, pages 96 to 99.)

Asser Levy, Jacques de la Motte, Dutch West India Company, Peter Stuyvesant, *Shearith Israel*
  1. _____ was captain of the *St. Charles*, the boat which brought 23 Jews to New Amsterdam in 1654.
  2. _____ was among those placed in debtors' prison because the Jewish refugees did not have enough money to pay the ship captain.
  3. _____ tried to deny Jews the right to settle in New Amsterdam and to trade with other colonies.
  4. The refugees called their synagogue _____.

5. The _____ assured Jews of equal rights in New Amsterdam.

IV. Explain each of the following quotations. (Review section 4, pages 99 to 101.)

1. "Consent is hereby given to them to depart whenever and whither it pleases them."

2. "The Honorable Lords Directors of the chartered West India Company, masters and proprietors of this province, gave permission and consent to the petitioners, like the other inhabitants, to reside, navigate and trade here and enjoy the same liberties."

3. "They are for the time being allowed to send one or two persons to the South River in order to dispose of the same, which being done they are to return hither."

4. "It appears that Mr. Stuyvesant does not permit the Jewish Nation to enjoy in quietness the exercise of its religion."

5. "Asser Levy, a Jew, appears in Court; requests to be admitted a burgher."

V. Match. (Review section 5, pages 102 to 104.)

Column A	Column B
Thanksgiving	1. National American shrine
Harvard	2. Modeled after *Sukkot*
Bay Psalm Book	3. Believed in religious freedom
Roger Williams	4. First book published in America
Newport Synagogue	5. Required students to study Hebrew

VI. Questions for discussion:

1. What contribution did Jews make to the exploration and early development of the New World?

2. Amsterdam has been called "The Mother of New World Jewry." Why?

3. New York City named a public school after Asser Levy. In what way did Asser Levy contribute to Americanism?

4. What evidence is there of the Hebraic influence on the American colonies?

REVIEW QUESTIONS

for Units One and Two (pages 15 to 105)

1. Describe the main contributions of each of the following: Rabbi Meir of Rothenburg, Isaac Abravanel, Gracia and Joseph Nasi, Joseph Karo, Menasseh ben Israel, Asser Levy.

2. What were some of the causes of persecution of the Jews in Europe?

3. Identify each of the following: Cresques, Abraham Zacuto, Joseph of Rosheim, David Reubeni, Solomon Molcho, Amatus Lusitanus, Isaac Luria, Maria Nunez, Jacob Tirado, Luis Santangel, Luis de Torres, Isaac Aboab.

4. Discuss the attitude of each of the following toward the Jews: Richard the Lion-Hearted, Ferdinand and Isabella, Oliver Cromwell, Peter Stuyvesant, Roger Williams.

5. Tell about each of the following:

a—Burning of the Talmud (1242)
b—Imprisonment of Rabbi Meir of Rothenburg
c—Expulsion of Jews from England (1290)
d—Black Plague (1348)
e—Expulsion from Spain (1492)
f—The Inquisition
g—Marranos
h—Renaissance
i—Joseph Nasi's experiment in Tiberias
j—Jewish contribution to the discovery of America
k—The struggle for equal rights in New Amsterdam

6. Discuss the importance of each of the following communities in Jewish history: Rothenburg, Seville, Venice, Constantinople, Safed, Amsterdam, Pernambuco, Newport.

7. Tell why each of the following books is important: Abravanel's Commentary, Zacuto's *Perpetual Almanac*, Karo's *Shulchan Aruk*, Menasseh ben Israel's *Hope of Israel*, *Bay Psalm Book*.

8. Tell how Jews were treated in each of the following countries: Germany, England, France, Spain, Portugal, Italy, Turkey, Holland, Brazil, Colonial America.

TEST

on Units One and Two

I. Complete each sentence. (15 points)

1. _____ of Rothenburg helped Jewish courts of Germany by rendering legal decisions based on the Talmud.
2. _____ paved the way for the return of Jews to England; he was also author of *The Hope of Israel*.
3. _____ built a Jewish colony in the city of Tiberias. He was also Duke of Naxos.
4. _____, author of a famous Bible commentary, helped Jews maintain courage at the time of the expulsion from Spain.
5. The *Shulchan Aruk*, which became the standard code of Jewish law, was written by _____.

II. Choose the correct name or phrase. (15 points)

1. The author of the *Perpetual Almanac* was _____. (Cresques, Abraham Zacuto)
2. David Reubeni, who claimed to represent an independent Jewish tribe in the East, was helped by _____. (Joseph of Rosheim, Solomon Molcho)
3. The teacher of *Kabbalah* in Safed was _____. (Isaac Luria, Amatus Lusitanus)
4. One of the founders of the Amsterdam Jewish community was the Marrano _____. (Gracia Nasi, Maria Nunez)
5. The man who helped the Jews of New Amsterdam acquire equal rights was _____. (Isaac Aboab, Asser Levy)

III. Name the country in which each of the following events occurred. (24 points)

1. The Talmud was burned in 1242 after a public debate.
2. The leading Rabbi was imprisoned in 1286 but refused to be ransomed because of the unjust conditions proposed by the emperor.
3. Jews were expelled in 1290.
4. The first printed Hebrew book, Rashi's commentary,

was published here during the period of the Renaissance.

5. Marranos secretly practiced Judaism despite the establishment of the Inquisition by Ferdinand and Isabella.

6. Joseph Nasi became adviser on foreign policy to the ruler.

7. Rembrandt painted the portraits of Menasseh ben Israel and other Jews.

8. Jews established the first synagogue in the New World but were forced to leave in 1654.

IV. Match. (15 points)

Column A	Column B
Richard the Lion-Hearted	1. Appointed Isaac Abravanel to a position at the royal court
Ferdinand and Isabella	2. Founded a colony based on religious freedom
Oliver Cromwell	3. Reluctantly allowed the landing of 23 Jews
Peter Stuyvesant	4. Invited the Rambam to become his physician
Roger Williams	5. Negotiated concerning the return of Jews to his country

V. Why is each of the following cities important in Jewish history? (16 points)
   1. Constantinople
   2. Safed
   3. Amsterdam
   4. Newport

VI. Discuss any two countries showing how they extended or failed to extend religious freedom to the Jew. (15 points)

UNIT THREE

Eastern Europe

CHAPTER IX

POLAND

I. THE RISE OF POLISH JEWRY

WE HAVE already seen how the Jewish kingdom of the Khazars existed in southern Russia for about 300 years. Even after the fall of the Khazars, some Jews remained in Crimea and in settlements along the Black Sea.

Poland was another center of Jewish life in Eastern Europe. Poland had long been a commercial colony of Germany. Among the merchants who visited Poland were Jews, some of whom made their homes in this country. Other Jews came to Poland from southern Russia.

Information about the Jewish settlers of Poland in the early centuries has come down to us only in the form of legends. A popular legend, for example, tells how the Poles once assembled, after the death of their ruler, to choose a new king. The nobles, however, could not agree on a unanimous choice. Finally, to avoid further dispute, it was decided to choose as sovereign the first man to enter the city the next morning. It so happened that Abraham Prokhovnik, a Jewish merchant, was the first to arrive the following day. He was immediately proclaimed king, but he wisely declined the honor. Instead he nominated a well-known Pole who was subsequently elected by the nobles. A later legend tells of a Jewish girl named Esther who became queen of Poland.

As a result of the Crusades, when European Jewish communities were so savagely attacked, many Jews fled to Poland which had not yet been reached by the Crusaders. In 1096, for example, the Jews of Prague sought sanctuary in Poland. During the following century there was a steady flow of refugees from the Rhine and Danube provinces. They found shelter in Cracow, in Posen and in other cities along the borders of Austria and Germany.

It is natural that the Jews brought with them the language which they had spoken in Germany. This language, which came to be known as Yiddish, was really a form of German but included many Hebrew words. Later some Slavic words were added. Yiddish became the beloved mother tongue of Jews throughout Eastern Europe.

The development of Yiddish among the Ashkenazim of Eastern Europe is similar in many ways to the development of Ladino among the Sefardim. Yiddish is a combination of German and Hebrew; Ladino is a combination of Spanish and Hebrew. Yiddish, like Ladino, is written in Hebrew characters. Both Yiddish and Ladino were spoken for hundreds and hundreds of years after the Jews had left Germany and Spain, the countries in which these languages originated.

Jews in Poland prospered. For a while, Jews were placed in charge of the mint. That explains why many ancient Polish coins carry Hebrew inscriptions. One coin from the time of King Meshko, for example, bore the Hebrew inscription "Brachah Meshko" ("Blessings on Meshko"). Another Polish coin contained the Hebrew words, "Rejoice Abraham, Isaac and Jacob."

In 1264 King Boleslav the Pious granted the Jews a charter which assured them protection and fair treatment.

The charter begins with these words:

"The deeds of man, when unconfirmed by the voice of witnesses or by written documents, are bound to pass away swiftly and disappear from memory. Because of this, we, Boleslav, Prince of Great Poland, make it known to our contemporaries as well as to our descendants to whom this writing shall come down that the Jews, who have established themselves over the length and breadth of our country, have received from us the following statutes and privileges."

Procedure for court cases involving Jews and Christians is

prescribed. Jewish courts are given full authority in cases involving only Jews. Attacks on Jewish travelers are prohibited. Jews are not to be required to pay higher customs duties than their neighbors. Christian neighbors are warned to help Jewish victims in time of distress. Ritual murder charges are denounced.

Protected by this charter Jews enjoyed freedom. Some Jews became financial agents for the crown. Others were placed in charge of salt mines and forests, or supervised the collection of customs duties and wine taxes. Many exported farm products to Germany or imported articles of clothing. Others were engaged in trade or in handicrafts.

In 1492 there were about 50,000 Jews in Poland. Within a century and a half, by the time of Menasseh ben Israel, Poland boasted a Jewish community of 500,000. Polish Jewry had grown tenfold in numbers and in influence.

2. "THE COUNCIL OF THE FOUR LANDS"

Poland consisted, more or less, of three classes—nobles, peasants and Jews.

Some towns and villages were entirely Jewish; other cities had large Jewish sections. Jews were able to maintain their own culture, and to speak their own language. Jews were also granted the right of self-government.

Each organized community was known as a *kehillah*. The officers of the *kehillah* elected the Rabbi and the judges, supervised the schools and administered all public institutions. They were also responsible for the apportionment of taxes.

Since there were many problems confronting the communities the Rabbis and communal leaders would meet each year at the Lublin fair. In this way there grew up "The Council of the Four Lands" representing Great Poland, Little Poland, Galicia and Volhynia. For a while Lithuania was also part of the Council, but later formed its own assembly of leaders. "The Council of the Four Lands" was really a state within a state, for it had almost complete authority over Jewish life.

Let us imagine that we are attending the Lublin fair about the year 1600. It is springtime. We have just celebrated the joyous holiday of Purim and are preparing for the Passover season. Lublin is gay as people gather in the market-places to buy clothing, household goods and luxuries. Carts are piled high with sacks of grain. Peasants have flocked to the city to sell chickens and ducks, eggs and milk, fruits and vegetables.

"The Council of the Four Lands" is meeting in one of the synagogues. The president of the Council is a famous Rabbi. Near him are seated other Rabbis who are respected because of their piety and learning. Each city is represented by one delegate.

"This Council is almost like the Sanhedrin of old," whispers one of the listeners to his neighbors.

"Happy are we that we have lived to see the day when Jews are allowed to live in freedom and to govern themselves according to the laws of the Torah," replies his friend.

The Rabbi calls the Council to order. A message is read from the Polish king telling how much money must be paid in taxes by the Jews of Poland. A quota is assigned to each community.

At this point the delegate of Posen rises from his seat.

"The Jews of Posen have a serious problem," says the delegate. "We are forced to pay a special tax on salt to the duke of our province. This is a violation of our rights since only Jews are required to pay this tax."

After a lengthy discussion the delegates agree to send a *shtadlan*, or special agent, to Warsaw to plead with the king to revoke this unfair tax.

The delegates then discuss rules for electing the officers of the *kehillah*. This is especially important since disputes have arisen in one or two communities. They also agree on the qualifications needed by judges of the Jewish courts.

The Council then adjourns, as the sun is beginning to set and it is time for the evening service.

The following day the Council meets again. A large crowd

has gathered in the synagogue for the Rabbis have been asked to decide an important case. It seems that one of the richest merchants in Poland, after an argument with his children, has willed his estate to a friend. The children contest the will after the father's death.

The people eagerly await the decision. The oldest Rabbi then speaks:

"The Mishnah clearly tells us that one cannot disinherit his children. According to the law of Moses the children inherit, and one cannot deprive them of a right conferred upon them by the Torah. The property, therefore, belongs to the children."

There is much excitement when the Rabbi's words are heard. All seem to feel that it is a fair decision.

"Maybe the loser will not accept the decision of the Rabbis. Perhaps he will appeal to the Polish courts," whispers one of the members of the audience.

"He dare not do that," replies his neighbor. "That would create a scandal. Anybody who does not accept the decision of the Jewish court reads himself out of the community."

At that very moment the loser is seen approaching the platform. He announces that he knows the Rabbis have been impartial and he accepts their decision.

The crowd disperses but the session of "The Council of the Four Lands" is not yet completed. The Rabbis and delegates draw up a message for Polish Jewry.

They remind all Jews of the duty to educate children and to teach them a livelihood. They urge each community to set up a Yeshiva for advanced study. They warn Jews living in isolated villages not to imitate the drunkenness and vulgarity of the peasants. They thank the king for his generosity and kindness. The proclamation ends with the hope that the Messiah would redeem the people of Israel and that Zion would be speedily rebuilt.

The visitors now begin to return to their home towns. Some remain behind to complete their purchases. Others find this an excellent opportunity to arrange the betrothal of a son or daughter. What rejoicing there will be when the father informs his daughter that she is engaged to a young man of excellent family from another city! The bride may never have seen the groom before, but all are confident that the marriage will succeed if both families are known for their good character.

At last the Lublin fair is over and each one hurries home in order to be in time for the Sabbath. The delegates report to their communities about the problems that were discussed in Lublin, and each *kehillah* pledges its cooperation in carrying out the decisions of "The Council of the Four Lands."

3. EDUCATION

The school system was the glory of Polish Jewry.

Let us follow the educational career of a Polish Jewish boy. We will call him Solomon.

Solomon's father is a tailor in a small town near Lemberg. Solomon has two older brothers who have received an excellent Hebrew education. He has a sister who has not attended school since she is too busy with household chores, but who has been taught privately how to read and write.

Solomon is enrolled in the *heder*, or Hebrew school, when he is five years old. It is very difficult for his father to pay tuition to the *melamed* (teacher); but he refuses to ask for charity even though the *kehillah* provides for the education of all who cannot afford to pay.

"God is good," sighs the tailor. "He will help us provide for the education of our children."

Solomon visits the school for the first time on the holiday of *Shavuot*. Honey cakes have been baked for the child in the shape of the letters of the Hebrew alphabet. As the child learns each letter he is given the cake as a reward.

The teacher holds up an *aleph*.

"This is an *aleph*," says the teacher. "Tell me, Solomon, what is this letter?"

"*Aleph*," says Solomon with a smile.

"Here is your reward," says the teacher. "Eat the cake for the Torah is sweet, and its words and letters are sweet."

After the first brief lesson Solomon is taken to the synagogue which is beautifully decorated with leaves and branches in honor of *Shavuot*. Later Solomon is rewarded with fruits and nuts in celebration of this great day.

Solomon makes rapid progress. In a few months he has mastered the alphabet and is ready for the study of *Chumash* ("The Five Books of Moses").

He is fascinated by the story of the creation. "Let there be light," proclaims God and light illuminates the world. The child's world too is flooded with light, with the light of Torah and of Rabbinic wisdom.

Frequently the child is puzzled by a statement in the Bible. "Let us turn to Rashi," says the *melamed*.

And there in the words of Rashi, prince of commentators, Solomon always finds an appropriate answer.

The child is fascinated too by the stories of Adam and Eve, of Noah and the flood, of the patriarchs, of Joseph in Egypt and of Moses the lawgiver who received the commandments at Sinai.

"Why doesn't the Bible begin with the 10 commandments?" asks the lad.

"That is the very question which Rashi asks at the beginning of his commentary," replies the teacher.

Together pupil and teacher read Rashi's comment:

"The Bible begins with the story of creation to show that Israel has a just claim to the Land of Israel. Thus, if the nations of the world challenge Israel's right to the land, Israel can reply that the earth is the Lord's. He created it and He gave it to Abraham and his descendants who were righteous in His eyes, as told in the book of Genesis."

A deep love for the Land of Israel is implanted in the heart of the child who yearns to see the land with his own eyes.

Although the entire day is spent in study there is time too for play. On the Sabbath, especially, Solomon loves to walk with his father and older brothers in the fields or near the brook. On *Simchat Torah* there are gay parties as the children march with flags upraised behind the Torah. On Chanukah as the candles flicker the children spin the *dreidel,* or crowd around their elders seeking Chanukah *gelt* (money). On Purim, players go from house to house in mask and costume presenting the story of Mordecai and Esther. Sometimes they burn Haman in effigy.

But what better season than Passover! Now the pupils are free for several weeks to romp and play in the fields. And as the first springtime flowers begin to dot the countryside, Solomon thinks of the words of King Solomon which he has just been taught:

> "For lo the winter is past,
>   The rain is over and gone;
>   The flowers appear on the earth,
>   The time of singing is come."

Soon, all too soon, the Passover vacation is over and the second semester begins. But with the coming of summer Solomon is again free to play in the fields or to bathe in the river that flows past their village.

By the time Solomon is ten he has studied much of the Bible. He is proud of his beautiful Hebrew penmanship and can also perform simple operations in arithmetic. He knows little of the outside world except for what he has heard about the Land of Israel from travelers who sometimes pass through their village. Once a Jew from Safed stayed at their home for the Sabbath and told wonderful stories about the academies of learning in Safed, about the rebuilding of Tiberias by Don Joseph Nasi and about the Wailing Wall in Jerusalem. He also told about the secret Jews in Spain and Portugal who kept alive their religious beliefs despite cruel persecution.

Now Solomon begins the study of Mishnah. Soon he is

deep in the intricacies of the Gemara. When he arrives at the age of 13 he is called to the Torah in the synagogue and delivers a learned address.

Solomon's classmates have become apprenticed to carpenters, tailors, smiths and other artisans. But Solomon has decided to continue his studies. There is a small Yeshiva in his town where about 30 students study. This is indeed an achievement for a community with so few families. But Solomon is resolved to study in the finest Yeshiva of Poland.

Solomon travels to Posen to study in the Yeshiva of the great Rabbi known as the Maharal. He is given lodging by the Yeshiva. His food he receives through *essen teg* ("eating days"); that is, he eats at the homes of kind Jews eager to help a student of the Torah. In all, he is assigned to seven homes, a different home for each day of the week.

Solomon now devotes most of his time to study of Talmud. He drinks in the words of the Maharal who lectures daily at the Yeshiva on the Talmud. Sometimes he dips into the Rambam's *The Guide to the Perplexed*, or even into a Kabbalistic work by Rabbi Isaac Luria of Safed. He constantly refers to Karo's legal decisions in the *Shulchan Aruk*.

Now there is no time for play. Day and night Solomon pores over the sacred tomes until at last he wins the approbation of the Maharal.

"Well have you been named," says the great Rabbi. "You have been called Solomon and, indeed, like Solomon of old you have shown a love of wisdom."

Solomon is appointed an instructor at the Yeshiva to the great joy of his parents. Soon one of the leading merchants of Posen arranges the betrothal of his charming daughter to Solomon. All praise the brilliant young student who is destined some day to become a great Rabbi in Israel.

Indeed there were many Solomons in Poland, for Torah and learning were the most precious ideals of Polish Jewry.

EXERCISES

I. Answer each question in a complete sentence. (Review section 1, pages 111 to 113.)

    1. According to the legend, why was a Jew made king of Poland?

    2. Why did Jews migrate to Poland?

    3. Compare Yiddish and Ladino.

    4. How did Polish Jews earn a living?

    5. What were the provisions of Boleslav's charter?

II. Complete each sentence (Review section 2, pages 113 to 116.)

Council, *kehillah*, Lublin, *shtadlan*, Talmud

    1. Each organized Jewish community was called a _____.

    2. Polish Jewry was ruled by "The _____ of the Four Lands."

    3. A _____ was a special Jewish agent who tried to prevail upon the king to grant better conditions to Jews.

    4. In the Jewish courts all cases were decided according to the laws of the Bible and _____.

    5. Jewish parents often arranged the betrothal of their sons and daughters at the _____ fair.

III. Discuss the importance of each of the following in the education of a Polish Jewish lad. (Review section 3, pages 116 to 119.)

    1. The first lesson on *Shavuot*

    2. The *heder*

    3. *Chumash* and Rashi

    4. Jewish holidays

    5. Geography, penmanship, arithmetic

    6. The Yeshiva

IV. Questions for discussion:

    1. Discuss the economic conditions of the Jews of Poland.

    2. Why is "The Council of the Four Lands" called "a state within a state"?

Eastern Europe

3. Compare the education of a Polish Jewish boy and of a Jewish boy in your community.

THINGS TO DO

1. *The Council of the Four Lands*—Each member of the class is to pretend he is a delegate to "The Council of the Four Lands." The following items are on the agenda:

a—A *kehillah* refuses to accept its annual tax assessment claiming that it cannot pay because of a flood which ruined the crops.

b—A village in which three Jewish families reside asks for help in providing a Jewish education for the children.

c—A defendant who has lost a case refuses to abide by the decision of the Jewish court.

d—Two rival candidates appear, each one claiming to have been elected head of the *kehillah*.

e—A letter is received from the Rabbi of Safed in which he asks for money to help support the scholars in the Land of Israel.

2. *The Lublin Fair*—Dramatize one of the following scenes that might have taken place at the Lublin fair:

a—A merchant and a customer argue about the cost of a coat.

b—A tailor from Lemberg named Isaac tries to arrange for the betrothal of his son to the daughter of a wealthy merchant from Posen.

3. *Supplementary Reading*—The Maharal after having served in Posen became Rabbi of the Prague community. There are many legends about a *golem*, or mechanical man, which the Maharal was said to have created. According to these legends the *golem* saved the community from destruction by discovering the real culprit when Jews were brought up on trial on a ritual murder charge.

Read a biography of the Maharal or a book containing the legend of the *golem*.

CHAPTER X

"OUT OF THE DEPTHS
OF DESPAIR"

I. 1648—THE COSSACK REVOLT

THE YEAR 1648 and the decades following were eventful years in the history of the Jewish people. In Turkey, hopeful followers flocked to Sabbatai Zevi who claimed to be the Messiah. In Brazil, Jews heroically defended their city against invasion; when Pernambuco fell, 23 Jews sailed north and established a community in New Amsterdam. In Holland, Rabbi Menasseh ben Israel's writings about the Lost Ten Tribes led to the re-admission of Jews into England.

1648 was the turning-point in the history of Polish Jewry. The Jews of Poland, alas, like their brothers in the rest of Europe, were forced to drink deep of the cup of sorrows. They too were forced to cry out, "Out of the depths of despair, I call upon Thee, O Lord!"

In 1648 the peasant warriors of the Ukraine, who were called Cossacks, rose in revolt against their Polish rulers. They hated the Polish nobles and landlords who wrung from them the money which they had earned with the sweat of their brow. Since Jewish agents often served as tax-collectors for the nobles, the Cossacks directed their fury against Jews as well as Poles.

Led by the fierce and fanatical warrior, Chmelnitzki, the Cossacks spread ruin and destruction throughout the Ukraine. Swift riders sped north to bring news of the revolt to the Jewish communities.

"Flee for your lives!" gasped the messengers. "The Cossacks have rebelled!"

"What have we to fear?" asked the Jewish leaders. "We have never done them any harm."

"Already they have burned down synagogues and have wiped out all Jewish communities in their path. There is no time to lose!"

In panic Jews gathered their belongings and hastily began to move toward the fortified cities. Several thousand Jews, for example, entered Nemirov which was protected by strong walls on one side and by a deep river on the other side. The Jewish leaders took charge of the fort hoping to be able to defend it until help came from the Polish army. The Polish inhabitants joined in the defense.

The sentinels on the walls reported the advance of soldiers on horseback. The defenders took their posts ready to fight until their last breath.

"Don't you recognize the king's soldiers?" shouted one of the Polish inhabitants of the city. "These are not Cossacks. Open the gates!"

"How do we know they are not Cossacks?" asked the Jews.

"They carry the white Polish eagle on red flags. They are Polish soldiers who have come to save us."

Little did the Jews suspect that the Polish inhabitants of the city, hoping to save their own lives, had plotted with Chmelnitzki against the Jews.

The order was given to open the gates.

"We have been tricked! Cossacks!" cried some of the defenders as soon as the soldiers entered the city. But it was too late. The Cossacks showed no mercy.

"Convert or die!" shouted the Cossacks.

With the *Shma Yisrael* on their lips the Jews bravely met their death. Rather than betray their religion they preferred to die *al kiddush ha-shem* (as martyrs who sanctified the Name of God).

The chronicler who recorded these tragic events tells us that some of the peasants sought to marry captive Jewish maidens. One beautiful Jewish girl convinced her captor that she could cast a spell over bullets. Certain that the bullet would glide off without causing injury, the Cossack discharged his gun. The girl fell to the ground mortally wounded, but happy in the knowledge that she was saved from a fate worse than death.

Unhappy Poland, whose king had just died, could not organize effective resistance. In some cities Poles and Jews fought bravely side by side. In others Poles betrayed their Jewish neighbors, only to find that the Cossacks spared nobody. To make matters worse, Russia and Sweden joined in the invasion and added to the suffering of Poland.

When peace finally came after ten years, about half of Polish Jewry had been destroyed. Hundreds of cities had been partially or completely wiped out. Even the Crusades had not claimed as many Jewish victims. Communities spent large sums trying to ransom Jewish captives.

Slowly, Jews returned to their villages and cities striving to rebuild the ruins.

2. A FALSE MESSIAH

Is it any wonder that Polish Jews waited impatiently for the Messiah? Is it any wonder that they flocked enthusiastically to Sabbatai Zevi, who claimed to be the Messiah? Word had spread throughout world Jewry, "The Messiah has come! Sabbatai Zevi is the long-awaited Messiah!"

Sabbatai Zevi was born in a Turkish seaport named Smyrna on the 9th of Av in the year 1626. From his early childhood it could be seen that Sabbatai was not like other boys. He loved solitude and immersed himself completely in the mystic lore of the *Kabbalah*. He devoted his days to prayer and fasting, and scourged his flesh with lashes to do penance for his sins.

"The Messiah, who will redeem Israel, will be born on the 9th of Av." So was it written in the holy books.

"Was I not born on the 9th of Av?" thought Sabbatai. "Has not my life been one of holiness? Am I not different from other men?"

Thus was born within him this strange fantasy—that he

was the Messiah. Sabbatai's friends were entranced by their mysterious companion. When he sang the Psalms of David, his beautiful voice seemed to cast a spell over all who heard him. Children loved him for he was kind to them and would favor them with sweets and with gifts.

In 1648 Sabbatai decided to reveal himself to his small band of followers. He pronounced the secret Hebrew name of God, an act permitted only to the *Kohen Gadol* when he entered the Holy of Holies on the Day of Atonement.

"The Messiah has come!" shouted the followers in ecstasy. "The Messiah has come!"

Alarmed by Sabbatai Zevi's pretensions the Rabbis forced him to leave Smyrna. Sabbatai wandered from city to city, his followers increasing in number when they saw how righteous a life he led. Sabbatai Zevi would prostrate himself at the graves of pious men, his eyes filling with tears as he recited prayers in their memory.

Self-styled prophets arose who spread abroad the fame of Sabbatai Zevi.

"A parchment was found in a tomb stating that Sabbatai is the Messiah," said one.

"I have seen him converse with the Spirit of Elijah," declared another.

"He has performed miracles," announced a third.

"He will conquer the world and restore the children of Israel to the Holy Land in 1666," predicted a fourth.

1666 was the year to which all looked forward, for the mystics claimed to have found proof that this was the year in which the Messiah would usher in his heavenly kingdom.

After many wanderings Sabbatai Zevi settled in Jerusalem.

"Help us, O Messiah," was the anguished cry of the Jews of Jerusalem. "The Turkish governor has imposed a ruinous fine on our community. Who knows what calamity will befall us if we do not avert the evil decree?"

Living in poverty the Jews of the Holy City had lost one of their main sources of support when the riots broke out in

Poland in 1648. Kind-hearted Sabbatai promised to help. He quickly journeyed to Cairo where he obtained the necessary funds from Halabi, the Jewish treasurer of the Sultan, and a devoted follower of Sabbatai. The thankful Jews poured out their gratitude.

"Is not this indeed a miracle?" they asked.

Meanwhile, there appeared in Poland a beautiful woman named Sarah who called herself "The Messiah's Bride." Sarah had been found clad in a white sheet, wandering amidst the gravestones of a Jewish cemetery.

"Who are you?" people asked in terror.

"My parents were killed during the Chmelnitzki revolt," she replied. "I have just escaped from the nunnery where I have lived for many years. I was led forth by the spirit of my father who warned me that I must never forget my religion. He prophesied that I would become the bride of the Messiah."

Sarah wandered from country to country finally arriving in Italy. Messengers brought word of this strange woman to Sabbatai Zevi who believed that this was the hand of destiny. Sarah came to Cairo where she was wedded to Sabbatai amidst great festivity.

Was not this another good omen?

Among the Rabbis who believed in Sabbatai Zevi was Isaac Aboab of Amsterdam, the man who had formerly served as Rabbi in Brazil. As the year 1666 drew nigh hopes were raised to fever pitch. Many sold their homes and property, thinking that in a short while they would be miraculously transported to the Land of Israel.

Returning to his native Smyrna, Sabbatai Zevi publicly declared himself the Messiah on Rosh Ha-Shanah as the *shofar* was sounded. The congregation, delirious with joy, shouted, "Long live our King, our Messiah."

In January, 1666 the Turkish Messiah set sail for Constantinople, expecting a miracle that would place the Sultan's crown on his head. But tragic disappointment was to be his lot!

Sabbatai Zevi was seized as he landed, shackled with chains

and thrust into prison. Later, the Sultan gave him the choice of death or of accepting Mohammedanism. The false Messiah donned the turban as a sign of his acceptance of the religion of Mohammed.

Jews were shocked. The Sultan, pleased with Sabbatai Zevi's conversion, made him royal doorkeeper, showering favors upon him. Many of Sabbatai Zevi's followers claimed that their leader was only waiting until the proper moment would come when he would perform the long-awaited miracle. Sabbatai Zevi, himself, wrote to the Jews that his real purpose was to convert the Turks to Judaism.

At last the Sultan, tiring of Sabbatai's scheming, banished the false Messiah to a small village in Albania where he died in loneliness in 1676.

Was Sabbatai Zevi an impostor or did he suffer from a delusion? Some historians have judged him harshly; others feel he was the victim of his own fancies. Who can tell?

3. COURAGE IN THE FACE OF HARDSHIP

Weakened by the ravages of war and saddened by the downfall of Sabbatai Zevi, the Jews of Poland were plunged into despair. Their leaders helped them, however, to show courage in the face of hardship. An inner faith seemed to give them the strength to weather all storms.

In 1676, for example, "The Council of the Four Lands" issued the following message:

"Gravely have we sinned before the Lord. The unrest grows from day to day. It becomes more and more difficult to live. Our people has no honor among the nations. Indeed it is a miracle that in spite of all misfortunes we are still alive. The only thing left for us to do is to unite ourselves in one league, held together by the spirit of strict obedience to the commandments of God and to the precepts of our pious teachers and leaders."

Polish Jews continued to drink deep of the cup of sorrows. The causes of persecution were:

1—Political unrest
2—Religious prejudice
3—Economic rivalry
4—Oppression by the nobles

Ritual murder charges caused untold suffering. Church holidays, such as Easter and Christmas, became occasions for mobs to turn against their Jewish neighbors.

Poverty became the curse of communities that once were rich and prosperous. Merchants tried to restrict the privileges of the Jews. Guilds excluded Jewish artisans making it difficult for them to ply their trade.

Jews were forced to depend on the nobles who hired them to manage their estates or to collect taxes from the peasants. Many Jews served as innkeepers, paying dearly to the noble for the lease. Woe betide any Jew who failed to furnish the necessary funds on the prescribed day.

Here, for example, is the translation of a diary written by a Polish noble at a somewhat later time:

"The Jew Herschel failed to pay me the 91 *thalers* that he owes me. According to our agreement, if he fails to pay the amount due, I may put him and the members of his family in prison until he settles the debt. Yesterday, I gave orders to place him in chains and to throw him into the pigsty. His wife and children I did not touch, except for his youngest son, Eliezer, who was brought to my house to learn the prayers of the church. The boy is talented but refuses to repeat our prayers. After we gave him lashings he consented to eat pig-flesh."

Three weeks later the noble wrote:

"Jews came from Berditschev, and paid Herschel's debt, 91 *thalers* in all. They also brought me sugar and coffee as a gift. I freed Herschel, but tried to detain his son, Eliezer. The Jews protested so strongly, however, that I was forced to free him too. But I'm sure that the Jew will be unable to meet his next payment, and then I shall be able to snatch his son and convert him. I shall have to wait another two months."

The miracle of Jewish life was that Jews rose above their poverty. Industrious, honest, charitable, peaceful and loyal, they enriched the country in which they lived. Learning remained their great ideal. The light of the Torah helped to illumine their paths in the midst of great darkness.

EXERCISES

I. Complete each sentence. (Review section 1, pages 123 to 125.)

1. 23 Jews set sail for New Amsterdam when _____, a city in Brazil, was conquered by the Portuguese.
2. The peasant warriors of the Ukraine were called _____.
3. _____ led the revolt against Poland in 1648.
4. Many Jews took refuge in the city of _____, but were betrayed by the Poles.
5. Thousands bravely died *al kiddush* _____ (as martyrs).

II. Why? (Review section 2, pages 125 to 128.)

1. Why did Jews eagerly await the coming of the Messiah?
2. Why were Sabbatai's companions attracted to him?
3. Why were the Jews of Jerusalem grateful to Sabbatai Zevi?
4. Why did Sabbatai Zevi marry Sarah?
5. Why did many people sell their homes as the year 1666 drew near?
6. Why were Jews shocked by Sabbatai Zevi's final actions?

III. Choose the correct word or phrase. (Review section 3, pages 128 to 130.)

1. Jews were helped to show courage in the face of hardship by _____. (the followers of Sabbatai Zevi, "The Council of the Four Lands")
2. After 1648, religious prejudice in Poland _____. (decreased, increased)

3. Jews often depended for a livelihood on _____.
   (guilds, nobles)
4. The diary shows that nobles _____ tried to force
   Jews to convert. (never, sometimes)
5. When a Jew was in trouble with a noble, his Jewish
   neighbors _____. (tried to come to his aid, were
   afraid to help him)

IV. Questions for discussion:
   1. Why was 1648 an important year in Jewish history?
   2. Do you think that Sabbatai Zevi was an impostor or the
      victim of a delusion?
   3. How did Jews show that they could rise above their
      hardships?

THINGS TO DO

1. *Supplementary Reading*—The tragic story of the Cossack
revolt and its effect on the Jews is told in *Kiddush Ha-Shem: An
Epic of 1648* by Sholom Asch. Israel Zangwill's *Dreamers of the
Ghetto* contains an exciting chapter on Sabbatai Zevi called "The
Turkish Messiah." The autobiography of a Polish Jewish philosopher named Solomon Maimon gives us a vivid picture of conditions in Poland in the 18th century.

2. *Original Story*—Write an ending for the story of the noble
and the Jewish tenant, Herschel. (See page 129.)

CHAPTER XI

THE BAAL SHEM TOV—
FOUNDER OF *HASIDISM*

I. THE MASTER OF THE GOOD NAME

O F ISRAEL BEN ELIEZER, often called the Baal Shem Tov, it may be said that he gave Polish Jewry a new heart and a new spirit. He drove away the mood of despair, teaching men to worship God through joy and fervor.

Israel was born about the year 1700 in a village near the southern border of Poland named Okup. His parents, who had suffered greatly during the wars between Poland and Turkey, died when Israel was still a child.

When Israel's father felt death drawing near he called his son to him and said, "I know that some day, because of you, our people will see the light. My son, remember this throughout your life—God is with you. Therefore, you need fear nothing in all the world."

Israel treasured these words in his heart.

The kind people of the village took care of Israel. They sent him to the *heder* (school-room) where Israel learned Torah. But often Israel absented himself from the classroom. When his friends searched for him they would find him walking in the lonely woods or wandering joyously in green pastures. Later people said of him that he knew the language of birds and trees, of stones and rivers.

Although an excellent student, Israel devoted little time to Talmudic law. Instead he studied the secrets of the *Kabbalah*, hoping to master the mysteries of the universe.

When the boy grew up he became a teacher's aide. It was his duty to lead the young pupils to school. Sometimes a wolf would attack, but Israel bravely protected the children and drove the wolf away.

Israel married the sister of a learned Rabbi named Gershon Kitover. He was not welcomed by the Rabbi, however, since he seemed to possess so little learning. The Rabbi presented his brother-in-law with horses and a carriage, and Israel and his wife drove away to a little town in the Carpathian Mountains of Roumania where they lived in a small hut.

After each Sabbath, Israel would go to the nearby hills to quarry clay. For food he would put water and dough into a little pit, knead the dough and bake it in the sun. Twice a week his wife would drive the wagon to Israel's mountain shelter. She helped Israel load clay into the wagon and then took the lime to the city where she sold it for a small sum of money. Poor though he was, Israel was happy. His spirit seemed to soar above the lofty mountain-tops which surrounded him on all sides. He sang as he worked, and allowed the beauty of God's world to permeate his soul.

After seven years as a lime-digger, Israel turned to other occupations. At first he was a *shohet*.* Later he kept an inn, and for a time he was a *melamed* (teacher).

Israel cast a spell over all who met him. People came to him when they were ill for he had learned the magic of the healing herbs of the woods and the mountain-side. But not only could he heal, he could make whole; he seemed to make those who came to him whole in body and in mind. Many who were downcast and melancholy would regain the spirit of joy after being treated by Israel.

Far and wide Israel's reputation spread as a *Baal Shem* (a Master of the Name of God), a miracle-worker who had divine powers to heal and to cure. Out of love and affection people referred to him as Israel Baal Shem Tov (the Master of the Good Name). At first he traveled from town to town in Roumania, in the Ukraine or in Galicia, but later he settled

---

* A *shohet* is trained to slaughter poultry and cattle in accordance with the ritual laws designed to prevent undue pain to animals.

permanently in the village of Medzibuz. Here many disciples gathered to drink of his wisdom and to feel the influences of his blessed spirit.

The followers of the Baal Shem Tov came to be known as *Hasidim* (pious men). Their teachings were called *Hasidism*. So different was their mode of worship and their way of life that they formed a distinct sect. It was as if a fresh torrent of water had burst forth bringing swift changes into the religious life of the Jewish communities.

2. WORSHIP THROUGH JOY

Israel Baal Shem Tov taught that God is everywhere. "Sparks of God" are present in every creature, every tree, every stone, every object. In the words of the Bible:

> "Holy, holy, holy is the Lord of hosts;
> The whole earth is full of His glory."

To perceive these sparks of God which shine in all beings and in all things, one must learn to pray with all one's heart, with all one's soul and with all one's might. The best way to lift one's soul higher and higher, taught the Baal Shem Tov, is through *simcha*, or joy. Only through joyous fervor and ecstasy can one really commune with God.

The following legendary tale is an illustration of the Baal Shem Tov's teachings:

Once at the close of Yom Kippur, Israel tried through prayer to avert danger which threatened the Jewish community. He prepared to recite the blessing which must be said upon the appearance of the new moon. The heavens, however, were cloudy and did not permit the moon to shine through, thus making it impossible for the Baal Shem Tov to proceed with his prayer. In vain he sought, through concentration and absorption in holy thoughts, to dispel the clouds.

At that moment the *Hasidim* gathered in the outer room of Israel's house. Happy in the thought that they had satisfactorily completed the holy service of the Day of Atonement, they began to sing and to dance. It was a dance of pure joy, a dance of fervor and of enthusiasm. The merry dancers then entered the room where the Baal Shem Tov, absorbed in thought, tried to pierce the clouds so that the moon might shine through.

In their unbounded joy the *Hasidim* began to dance around their master. At the peak of ecstasy they begged Israel to join in the dance with them. At first the Baal Shem Tov merely looked on, refusing to enter the whirling circle. But so contagious was the mood of rejoicing that Israel was finally overcome by a spirit of elation, and he too joined in the dance.

At that moment one of the dancers pointed to the sky which could be seen through the open window and called out, "How beautiful the moon is! See how it has scattered the clouds of darkness!"

The *Hasidim* through their joyous dance had accomplished what the Baal Shem Tov could not earlier succeed in doing. Israel then recited the Blessing of the New Moon with such fervor that his prayers flew straight to the throne of God, and his prayers were answered.

3. THE TEACHINGS OF THE BAAL SHEM TOV

When catastrophe threatened, the Baal Shem Tov helped not only through prayer but through good deeds. On several occasions Jews were falsely accused of ritual murder. Israel immediately hastened to the aid of the victims and their families. He and his followers gave generously to help those in trouble. Innkeepers who could not meet their debts were often saved from imprisonment because of the Baal Shem Tov's assistance.

Israel also saved the people from spiritual disaster. A false Messiah, named Jacob Frank, appeared claiming to be the reincarnation of Sabbatai Zevi. Shocked by the rapid spread of Frank's influence, the Baal Shem Tov did all in his power to combat this new movement.

Although a student of the *Kabbalah*, Israel opposed those

who taught that one can please God by torturing the body through constant fasting.

Once he was asked, "How can we best serve God? Is it not true that formerly pious men would often fast from one Sabbath to the next? Yet you have taught that it is sinful to mortify the flesh and torment the body."

"It is not necessary to torment one's body through fasting," replied the Baal Shem Tov. "I have come into this world to point another way, namely that man should try to attain to three loves: the love of God, the love of Israel and the love of Torah."

The Baal Shem Tov believed that since every man has a spark of God no sinner is beyond redemption. "No man has sunk so low," he taught, "that he cannot raise himself to God."

Often, according to the Baal Shem Tov, one finds a purity of soul in a simple man or in a child not to be found even in the heart of a righteous scholar. This is well illustrated by the tale of the village whistler.

A Jewish peasant who prayed each Yom Kippur in the synagogue of the Baal Shem Tov was ashamed of his dull-witted son who had never mastered the letters of the prayer-book. When the lad attained the age of thirteen, even though he could not recite the Hebrew prayers, he accompanied his father to the synagogue. In his pocket the boy carried a small whistle which he always blew when he sat in the fields near the calves and the sheep.

Hour after hour the boy sat silent in the House of Prayer. At last he said, "Father, I have my whistle with me. I want to blow on it."

"Do not disturb the prayers of those around you," warned the father. "Put the whistle away."

Moved by the solemn services, his heart overflowing with a desire to pray to God, the child could restrain himself no longer. He quickly placed the whistle in his mouth and blew a loud note.

"How dare you interrupt the service?" angrily declared the worshipers.

The Baal Shem Tov quieted the congregation, and then continued with the service.

Later he said, "It is only because of the peasant lad that our prayers have reached God. The synagogue was heavily laden with impure prayers which could not ascend to heaven. This boy's prayer, expressed in the form of a whistle, proceeded from a pure and simple heart and rose straightway to the throne of God."

The doctrine of the Baal Shem Tov appealed especially to the common man—the peasant, the laborer, the water-carrier. They too now had a place of honor in the House of Prayer, a place formerly reserved for students and scholars. Did not the Master teach that all men could attain unto pure communion with God?

4. THE LEGEND OF THE BAAL SHEM TOV

After the death of Israel Baal Shem Tov in 1760 his disciples continued to teach his doctrines throughout the many towns and villages of southern Poland. Legends began to cluster around the name of the saintly teacher. These legends helped to spread his teachings and his influence.

Here, for example, is a wondrous tale of how the Baal Shem Tov saved the soul of a Jew who once renounced Judaism.

On the day of his death Rabbi Israel called unto one of his disciples named Jacob and said, "After I die, you must wander from one place to another and must tell of my deeds and repeat my words."

Jacob obeyed his master's wishes. Once he heard that there was a Baron in Rome who gave rich rewards to any who could repeat the sayings of the Baal Shem Tov. Jacob journeyed to Rome to the home of the Baron who rejoiced at his coming.

After the Sabbath prayer, when all were gathered around the table, the Baron turned to Jacob and said, "Now tell us a tale concerning your master."

Suddenly Jacob's mind went blank. For the life of him he

could not remember a single story about the Baal Shem Tov. For three days the Baron kept urging Jacob to relate an incident from the life of his teacher but to no avail. Finally Jacob prepared to leave.

Just as he was entering the carriage he remembered part of a story which he related to the Baron.

"Once the Baal Shem Tov and I traveled to a distant country," he said. "There we found the Jews panic-stricken, for on this day the wicked ruler had threatened to seize a Jew and to cast him into the flames. All was in readiness in the public square, but the Jews in fear had tightly closed the shutters of their windows. When the ruler and his retinue drew up to the public square my master ordered me to go to the ruler and say,

" 'Rabbi Israel commands you to come to him at once.'

"Trembling I did as my master bade me. The ruler replied he would come in two hours.

" 'Go back and tell him to come this instant!' said Rabbi Israel.

" 'I am coming immediately,' said the ruler when I repeated my master's words.

"The ruler quickly left the public square after calling a halt to the entire proceedings. He came to the house where we were staying and followed the Baal Shem Tov into an inner room. After about three hours of conversation my master returned to me and said, 'All is well. Let us go home'."

Jacob ended his story abruptly.

"Go on," said the Baron. "Tell me the end of the tale."

"That is all I know," replied Jacob.

To his surprise the Baron embraced Jacob and said, "You have saved my soul from torment! I was the wicked ruler whom you commanded to appear before the Baal Shem Tov."

Jacob looked at him in amazement. The Baron added:

"Know that I am descended from a long line of Rabbis, but my desire for power and wealth made me abandon the faith of our fathers. I grew in riches and in cruelty. But one night

I dreamed that I saw my ancestors seated around a table. At the head of the table was Rabbi Israel. Before them my soul was brought for judgment. They condemned me to eternal torture until Rabbi Israel proclaimed, 'Let him repent, for the gates of Heaven are always open to receive the penitent sinner.'

"On the day of the execution," continued the Baron, "when you commanded me to appear before Rabbi Israel I knew I dare not disobey. Your master advised me to divide my fortune into 3 parts. With one part I would buy my freedom, the second part I would give to charity, and with the third part I would retire to a distant country, do good deeds as a Jew and pray for forgiveness.

"Rabbi Israel's final words were, 'When my disciple comes to you and tells you your own story, that will be a sign that your sins have been forgiven by the Almighty.'"

The Baron then added, "When you came to my home I recognized you immediately as the Baal Shem Tov's messenger. I was dismayed when you could not remember anything, for I was afraid that I would never be pardoned. But now, thank God, I know that Rabbi Israel has interceded for me in Heaven, and I am saved!"

Thus, according to the legend, even after death the Baal Shem Tov succeeded in communicating with the living.

Hasidism spread rapidly throughout Poland and Eastern Europe. In the spirit of the Baal Shem Tov, the *Hasidim* began to worship with soul-stirring ardor and fervor; with unbounded joy and enthusiasm they strove to commune with God through song and dance and ecstatic prayer.

In the words of a modern author, "The number of Israel's followers grew, for his teaching had that beauteous simplicity that goes directly to the hearts of the common folk."

EXERCISES

I. Arrange in the order in which these events occurred. (Review section 1, pages 132 to 134.)

   1. Israel became a lime-digger in the Carpathian Mountains in Roumania.

   2. The last words of Israel's father were: "My son, remember this throughout your life—God is with you."

   3. The Baal Shem Tov settled in Medzibuz where many *Hasidim* gathered around him.

   4. Israel earned a living as a *shohet*, then as an innkeeper, then as a teacher.

   5. Israel married the sister of Rabbi Gershon Kitover.

   6. Israel often absented himself from *heder* in order to wander through the fields or the forest.

II. Answer each question in a complete sentence. (Review section 2, pages 134 to 135.)

   1. According to the Baal Shem Tov, where can one perceive sparks of God?

   2. What is the importance of *simcha* (joy)?

   3. What prayer did Israel recite after the Day of Atonement?

   4. How did the heavens change after the joyous dance of the *Hasidim?*

   5. What is the meaning of the legend?

III. True or false? (Review section 3, pages 135 to 137.)

   1. The Baal Shem Tov refused to help innkeepers because they were ignorant.

   2. Jacob Frank was a false Messiah.

   3. The Baal Shem Tov believed that God wants us to torment our bodies through constant fasting.

   4. The Baal Shem Tov said that his mission in life was to teach three loves: the love of God, the love of Israel and the love of Torah.

   5. Israel rebuked the lad who whistled because he disturbed the service.

IV. Choose the correct name. (Review section 4, pages 137 to
     139.)

Baal Shem Tov, Baron, Jacob

1. The _____ died in 1760.

2. _____ wandered from town to town telling of his
   master's good deeds.

3. The _____ lived in a rich palace in Rome.

4. The _____ told his disciple to command the wicked
   ruler to come to him immediately.

5. The _____ decided to repent and to return to Judaism.

6. _____ could not remember the entire story.

7. When the _____ heard the story he knew that God
   had pardoned his sin.

V. Questions for discussion:

1. Why did the teachings of Israel Baal Shem Tov spread
   so quickly?

2. Discuss the teachings of the *Hasidim* concerning the following:
   a—Worship through joy
   b—Love of Israel
   c—Repentance
   d—"Sparks of God"

3. Discuss the meaning of each of the following anecdotes
   and legends:
   a—The dance of the *Hasidim* after the Day of Atonement
   b—The village whistler
   c—Jacob and the Baron

THINGS TO DO

1. *Music and Art*—Listen to recordings of *Hasidic* songs. A
famous composition inspired by the founder of *Hasidism* is the
Baal Shem by Ernest Bloch.

Among the many artists who have drawn pictures of the
Hasidim is Marc Chagall. Many reprints of his paintings have
been published and can be shown.

2. *Supplementary Reading*—Stories about *Hasidim*, such as I. L. Peretz' "If Not Higher," can be found in numerous anthologies. *The Golden Mountain* by Meyer Levin, from which the concluding quotation in this chapter is taken, contains some excellent *Hasidic* legends. *The Hasidic Anthology* by Louis I. Newman is a collection of *Hasidic* lore which includes parables, fables, sayings and anecdotes on subjects such as repentance, prayer, truth, Torah, love, kindness, humility and charity.

The BAAL SHEM TOV

A HASIDIC DANCE OF JOY

CHAPTER XII

THE VILNA GAON

1. ELIJAH OF VILNA

THE BRIGHTEST STAR in the firmament of European Jewry was Rabbi Elijah of Vilna. His brilliant scholarship and his saintly character have won him an immortal place in the hearts of the Jewish people.

Elijah was born in Vilna in 1720. Vilna was the largest city of Lithuania which then belonged to Poland. Already by the age of 6, Elijah gained fame as a child prodigy when he delivered a learned address in the Grand Synagogue of Vilna. He not only mastered all branches of Hebrew learning, but studied also arts and sciences. He believed that without a knowledge of subjects such as mathematics and astronomy one could not fully understand the Talmud and Jewish law.

At the age of 20, Elijah traveled from city to city in Poland and Germany thus becoming acquainted with the great Rabbis and scholars of his day. There were many hardships he had to endure. Once, for example, when he alighted from his carriage to recite the afternoon prayer, his coachman ran away with his belongings and his money. But hardships and poverty were accepted cheerfully by the student. He knew that this was his lot in life, in keeping with the Talmudic saying: "This is the way to study the Torah; eat bread and salt, drink water by measure, sleep on the earth, and live a life of care."

When Elijah returned to Vilna his fame as a scholar spread throughout the world. Recognizing his genius, Jews gave him the title of Gaon ("Excellency"). Of course, the title was unofficial, for Elijah refused to accept any position offered to him lest it interfere with his studies.

Elijah was gifted by nature with such a wonderful memory that he could remember entire books, almost word for word, after one reading. But Elijah refused to depend on memory alone. Study, he believed, required hard labor. He would repeat passages in the Bible or Talmud hundreds of times so that he would never forget them. He refused to leave any book until every word was crystal clear in meaning.

"Unless learning is acquired through hard labor," he would say, "it is of no real value. If an angel were to appear to me and offer to explain all the mysteries of the Torah, I would spurn his offer. One cannot really discover the truth without searching for the truth.

A story told by his favorite disciple, Hayim of Volozhin, illustrates Elijah's method of study. One Friday morning a messenger came to Hayim with this message:

"Rabbi Elijah is ill and wishes to see you at once."

At the master's home Hayim was met by Elijah's wife.

"What is wrong?" asked the pupil.

"For three days and nights Elijah has hardly slept," she replied. "He refuses to take food, so occupied is he with an obscure passage whose meaning is not clear to him. I am afraid he will become very ill."

Hayim repaired to Elijah's room where he found the scholar, weak and fatigued, studying the Jerusalem Talmud. Elijah was happy to see his pupil.

"Two heads are better than one," said Elijah. "Perhaps the two of us can unravel the meaning of this passage."

Master and pupil worked together until at last they solved the difficulty. Elijah's countenance flushed with delight. He called for food for the first time in three days, and joyfully prepared to usher in the Sabbath.

2. THE INFLUENCE OF THE VILNA GAON

Although Elijah did not establish any official school, many disciples flocked to him for guidance and inspiration. Like Akiva in ancient Israel, Elijah would lecture to his admirers about the intricacies of Jewish law.

One of his pupils was Hayim of Volozhin, a prosperous cloth manufacturer, who left his business to devote himself to study and to Torah. Another pupil, Benjamin of Sklov, was a physician who gave up a lucrative practice to study under the Vilna Gaon. Another follower of Elijah was a mathematician who, at the suggestion of the Gaon, translated Euclid's geometry into Hebrew so that students of the Talmud could also master this important branch of mathematics. Other disciples of the Vilna Gaon continued their pursuit of business or of trade, but devoted their leisure hours to scholarship. It is no wonder that Vilna came to be known as the Jerusalem of Lithuania.

Under the influence of the Vilna Gaon these pupils rediscovered the beauty of the Bible, often neglected by students of the Talmud. Elijah's insistence on understanding the true meaning of a passage bore fruit. Grammar became a useful tool for arriving at the real meaning of the text. Thus, many current fantastic explanations were rejected by Elijah and his pupils. The Vilna Gaon's commentaries on both Bible and Talmud are of great value in helping us understand these sources of Judaism.

In addition, Elijah emphasized the importance of many great works which had long been ignored. The Jerusalem Talmud which was produced in the Land of Israel, for example, did not enjoy as much authority as the Talmud of Babylon. This was because the Holy Land had been laid waste under Roman rule, and only a few scholars remained. Nonetheless, the Jerusalem Talmud contains great spiritual treasurers. The Vilna Gaon helped to restore the study of the Jerusalem Talmud and of other important Rabbinic works.

Elijah did not approve of the *Hasidic* movement which had gained so many adherents in Poland. He believed that the emphasis of the *Hasidim* on faith rather than study was dangerous, since learning was the great ideal of Judaism throughout its history. Their method of worship lacked dignity and decorum. But above all, he opposed their superstitious belief

in the miraculous powers of their leaders whom they called
Zaddikim (saints).

When the *Hasidim* began to establish synagogues in Lithuania, their opponents decided to issue a *herem* or ban prohibiting the spread of the movement. Elijah, believing that
Hasidism would have a harmful effect on Judaism, agreed to
sign the ban. A mass-meeting was held in the Grand Synagogue of Vilna; a thousand candles were lighted, the *shofar*
was sounded and the decree of excommunication was read
from the pulpit. The *herem* was read again at the fairs where
hundreds of merchants gathered yearly. As a result, *Hasidism*
made little headway in Lithuania. Many years passed before
peace was restored between the *Hasidim* and their opponents.
Today we realize how much beauty there is in the teachings
of the Baal Shem Tov, although many of the criticisms of the
Vilna Gaon were undoubtedly true.

In one respect there was perfect agreement between Elijah
and the *Hasidim*—in their love of *Eretz Yisrael*. No Jew can
hope to attain spiritual perfection outside of the Land of Israel,
believed the Vilna Gaon. He prayed for the day when the
children of Israel would return to Zion and restore the Land
of Israel. One of his books is a geography of the Holy Land.
He himself set out on a journey to Jerusalem, but turned back
before he had completed his journey.

"As with Moses, one cannot enter the Holy Land unless
Heaven decrees it," he said. Apparently he felt that further
preparations were necessary before a new community could
be established.

When one of his pupils, Benjamin Riveles, earned a fortune
through the sale of forest-land, Eljiah urged him to organize
an expedition to Palestine. A committee called "Vision of
Zion" was enthusiastically formed. At first only a few individuals migrated to Palestine, but in 1809, eleven years after
the death of Elijah, an entire community of his pupils settled
in the Holy Land. They built a Yeshiva in Safed which they
named after the Vilna Gaon. Together with the many

Hasidim who had also come to the Land of Israel, Elijah's pupils served as the nucleus of the new Ashkenazic community which was to play a historic role in the rebuilding of Zion.

The Vilna Gaon died in 1798 at the ripe old age of 78. World Jewry deeply mourned his passing, for Elijah embodied the Jewish ideals of wisdom, learning and righteousness. Other nations accorded their greatest honors to a ruler or to a general; Jewry's highest tribute was paid to the man of learning. As one author wrote, "Go and see how rich we always were in excellent men. In every town and every village you would find scholars, saints and philanthropists. Their merits could sustain worlds, and each of them was an ornament of Israel."

Five years after the death of Elijah, his disciple, Hayim, established a Yeshiva in Volozhin so that students could study in accordance with the methods of the Vilna Gaon. The Yeshiva of Volozhin attracted hundreds of pupils, and became one of the world's greatest Talmudical colleges.

Elijah's epitaph describes him as "The light of the world, and the source of wisdom and knowledge."

3. JEWS IN RUSSIA

An iron wall separated Russia from the rest of the world. Jews were forbidden to enter Russia, although merchants occasionally were permitted to trade at Russian fairs. Prisoners-of-war taken captive during the wars between Russia and Poland were treated with great cruelty.

In 1708 when the Russian army occupied several Polish cities, Jewish communities were in great danger from the rioting troops. A brief Hebrew entry in a local *kehillah* journal describes how Peter the Great prevented serious bloodshed:

"In the year 5468 (1708) there came the Caesar, who is called the Czar of Muscovy, by the name of Peter, with his whole suite, an immense, numberless host. Robbers and murderers from among his people fell upon us, without his knowledge, and it almost came to bloodshed. And if the Lord Almighty had not put it into the heart of the Czar to enter our synagogue in his own person, blood would certainly have been shed. It was only with the help of God that the Czar saved us, and took revenge for us, by giving orders that thirteen men from among the rioters be immediately hanged, and the land became quiet."

Unhappy Poland grew weaker and weaker. Russia, Austria and Prussia combined against the dying kingdom and divided the soil of Poland among them. The first partition of Poland took place in 1772. A second partition took place in 1793.

Under the leadership of brave Kosciusko, who once served alongside of George Washington, Jews and Poles fought courageously in the streets of Warsaw against Russian invaders. Kosciusko appointed a Jew named Berek to head a Jewish Legion which showed dauntless bravery. But all to no avail! The third and final partition took place in 1795. Poland was now completely dismembered.

The Jews of southern Poland, including those in the province of Galicia, had now fallen under the rule of Austria. The Jews of Danzig and Posen in northwestern Poland became subjects of Prussia. The bulk of Polish Jewry, over a million Jews, were now subject to the Russian Czar.

A series of restrictions were adopted by the Russian government which brought Jewish communities to the brink of ruin:

1—Jews were forced from villages into towns. Jewish innkeepers were deprived of the right to maintain inns, under the false charge that they were responsible for the drunkenness of the peasants.

2—Jewish merchants were required to pay a double tax. Those who would not pay the tax were forced to leave Russia after paying a large fine.

3—The *kehillah* was deprived of most of its authority except in religious matters. Jews forced to appear in government courts were treated harshly and unjustly.

4—A Pale of Settlement was established beyond which boundary Jews were not allowed to go. A sort of iron curtain divided East from West Russia. Within these limits, Jews were compelled to maintain a shadowy existence.

The Vilna Gaon died three years after Lithuania had become a Russian province. Thus, his death came shortly after the end of an important era. Economically and politically, the future of the Jews in Eastern Europe seemed bleak indeed. Spiritually, however, the Jews could not be crushed. The torch of learning and faith which the Vilna Gaon and his disciples held high still burned brightly, illumining the path of the Jewish people.

EXERCISES

I. Choose the correct word or phrase. (Review section 1, pages 144 to 145.)

1. Elijah was born in _____. (Vienna, Vilna)
2. Elijah studied both Hebrew and _____. (agriculture, science)
3. As a student, Elijah lived a life of _____. (luxury, poverty)
4. Elijah was called Gaon because of _____. (his genius, the office to which he was elected)
5. Hayim of Volozhin was the Vilna Gaon's _____. (pupil, teacher)

II. Write a sentence about each of the following topics. (Review section 2, pages 145 to 148.)

1. The pupils of Elijah
2. The Jerusalem Talmud
3. The Vilna Gaon's opposition to *Hasidism*
4. Elijah's love of the Holy Land
5. The Yeshiva of Volozhin

III. Match. (Review section 3, pages 148 to 150.)

Column A	Column B
Peter	1. Restricted area
1772	2. Final partition of Poland
Kosciusko	3. Czar of Russia
1795	4. Fought for American and Polish freedom
Berek	5. Head of Polish-Jewish Legion
Pale of Settlement	6. First partition of Poland

IV. Questions for discussion:

1. Compare the Baal Shem Tov and the Vilna Gaon.
2. In what way was the Vilna Gaon a genius?
3. How were the Jews affected by the partitions of Poland?

THINGS TO DO

1. *Map*—Draw an outline map of Eastern Europe. Locate the following places:

a—The Four Lands—Great Poland, Little Poland, Galicia, Volhynia

b—Sections and Countries—Crimea, Ukraine, Roumania, Lithuania

c—Cities and Villages—Vilna, Volozhin, Danzig, Posen, Warsaw, Moscow, Prague, Vienna, Lublin, Berditschev, Nemirov, Okup, Medzibuz.

2. *Council of Rabbis*—Set up a Council to discuss the question whether *Hasidic* synagogues should be banned in Lithuania. Allow a representative of the *Hasidim* to present his case.

3. *Letter from a Legionnaire*—Berek succeeded in escaping from Warsaw to Paris. Write a letter in which Berek describes his experiences as commander of the Jewish Legion in Poland.

UNIT FOUR

The Dawn of Emancipation

CHAPTER XIII

MOSES MENDELSSOHN—FATHER OF JEWISH EMANCIPATION

1. THE GHETTO

A T THE TIME of the American Revolution there were only about three million Jews in the world. Half of these lived in Poland and Russia under wretched conditions. A large number lived in Turkey, or in countries under Turkish control such as Roumania. There were also important Jewish communities in Central Europe, in Holland, in Italy and along the Mediterranean as well as a scattering of Jews in Asia and Africa, in France and England and in the American colonies.

Central Europe was divided into hundreds of little states and principalities under the rule of an emperor whose domain was known as the Holy Roman Empire. In reality the emperor had little power, each state exercising full control over its own affairs. Among the more important states were Austria, Bavaria and Prussia.

There were Jewish communities in many of the German-speaking cities such as Vienna, Frankfort and Berlin. Jews were restricted to a special section known as the ghetto. The ghetto was usually located in the least desirable section of the city, often near the river-front or along swamps. Streets were narrow and poorly maintained. Fires were frequent; since gates were often closed it was sometimes impossible for the victims of the fire to escape.

A wall separated the ghetto from the rest of the city. In the wall was a gate through which Jews would enter or leave. The gate was closed at night, and was guarded by non-Jews so that none could leave the ghetto after dark. Often Jews were required to wear a yellow badge or a distinctive hat to set them off from the rest of the population.

Most occupations were closed to Jews. They could not own farms or engage in manufacturing. Peddling and pawnbroking were the occupations usually forced on Jews. In some cases, where the ruling prince was more tolerant, Jews were allowed to serve as artisans. There were Jewish tailors, shoemakers, carpenters, goldsmiths, stone-cutters and metal-workers. Sometimes a Jewish family would gain wealth and would receive protection from the prince as court-Jews.

Special taxes, often of the most humiliating kind, were imposed on Jews. They were taxed for buying and selling, for coming and going, for being Jews, for getting married. In some cities only one member of a Jewish family was allowed to marry—others who wished to marry were forced to migrate. In the city of Dresden, Jews were forced to pay the same entrance fee as was paid for oxen.

The wall separating Jews from the rest of the population was more than a physical wall. Strong barriers divided Jews from others, making second-class subjects of them. Jews led their own lives behind the ghetto walls, and organized their own schools, courts and institutions.

Despite all restrictions, however, Jews maintained their faith and morale. "A merry spirit smiled on Jewish life," writes one author. Joyousness remained a vital part of daily Jewish life. Darkness and gloom were dispelled by the light of the Torah as Jews prayed for the coming of a better day.

2. MOSES MENDELSSOHN

The man who did the most to break down the ghetto walls was Moses Mendelssohn.

Moses, son of Mendel, was born in Dessau, Germany in the year 1729. His father was a Torah scribe who earned a living by copying scrolls of the law on parchment. It was from him that Moses inherited both his love of learning and his beautiful handwriting. Moses' mother was said to be a lovable woman with sterling traits of character.

Moses was so young when enrolled in *heder* that often on cold winter days his father would carry him there wrapped up in a cloak. His teacher, Rabbi David Frankel, inspired the lad to study not only Bible and Talmud, but also *The Guide to the Perplexed* by Moses ben Maimon. Thus, the young student was encouraged to judge everything in the light of reason. Moses had been born with a curvature of the spine. Illness and excessive stooping over his books created an unsightly hunch.

"I owe it to Moses ben Maimon," the student used to say, "that I have such a misshapen body; but I love him nevertheless for he has sweetened many a bitter hour of my life, and has thus compensated me tenfold for what damage he has done to my body."

Shortly after Moses celebrated his *Bar Mitzvah*, Rabbi Frankel was elected Rabbi of the Berlin congregation. Moses decided to follow his teacher. He traveled the 80 miles from Dessau to Berlin on foot. Weary and footsore, he arrived at the Rosenthal Gate, the only one by which Jews were allowed to enter Berlin. Here he was stopped at the gate by a Jewish official whose duty it was to prevent undesirables from entering the city.

According to tradition the official demanded of the sickly youth:

"Why have you come to Berlin?"

"To study," was the lad's reply.

"Where?"

"With Rabbi Frankel."

The name of the learned Rabbi was sufficient to gain admittance for his humble pupil. Rabbi Frankel welcomed the youth, and provided for him. Apparently, Moses earned a meager livelihood copying the Rabbi's manuscripts. Often his supper consisted of little more than dry bread, and at times he went to bed hungry. After seven years of hard study Moses mastered science, philosophy, Latin, German, French and English; of course, he continued with his study of Bible and

Talmud. In 1750, a rich Berlin silk manufacturer, Isaac Bern-hard, offered Mendelssohn the post of tutor to his children. Later he became a bookkeeper in the Bernhard factory, a position which he kept to the end of his life.

The turning-point in Mendelssohn's life came in 1754 when he met a young Gentile author named Gotthold Lessing. The friendship of Mendelssohn and Lessing has become proverbial. Like David and Jonathan these two friends remained loyal to each other throughout life, their friendship proving to be a blessing for both German literature and Jewish history. Even before meeting Mendelssohn, Lessing had written a play called "The Jew" in which he depicted a Jew as a gallant hero.

Mendelssohn's broad culture gained him membership in a coffee-house where the outstanding scholars, authors and scientists of the day would often meet. Here Moses excelled as a chess-player, and, despite a slight stammer, as a conversationalist. Once it was proposed that each member describe his own defects in verse. Mendelssohn, a stammerer and a hunch-back, wrote:

> "Great you call Demosthenes,
> Stuttering orator of Greece;
> Hunchbacked Aesop you deem wise;
> In your circle, I surmise,
> I am doubly wise and great.
> What in each was separate
> You in me united find—
> Hump and heavy tongue combined."

Mendelssohn's marriage to Fromet Gugenheim of Hamburg was romantic indeed. The story goes that the girl hesitated at first because of Mendelssohn's deformity.

"Do you believe that matches are made in heaven?" asked Fromet.

"Certainly," replied Moses. "In fact, a strange thing hap-pened in my case. You know that it is even said that at the birth of a child an announcement is made, 'So-and-so shall marry so-and-so.' When I was born it was announced that my future wife would be hunchbacked. 'Dear God,' I said. 'A girl ought to be beautiful. Give me the deformity, and let the girl be pretty and graceful.' "

Fromet decided to marry Moses, and theirs was a very happy marriage.

Moses Mendelssohn and his friend Lessing collaborated by writing books on philosophy as well as criticism of poetry. Mendelssohn's writings attracted attention because of the author's learning, his good common sense, his fairness and his fearlessness. He did not hesitate to criticize even the poetry of Frederick II, King of Prussia. The article by Mendelssohn was confiscated and the author ordered to appear before the Attorney-General. Mendelssohn was in danger of being expelled from Berlin.

"Look here!" said the Attorney-General angrily. "How can you venture to write against Christians?"

"When I play at nine pins," replied the Jewish philosopher, "I knock down the pins whether my companions be Christian or Jew."

The Attorney-General smiled, realizing that Mendelssohn meant that any author, whether king or subject, had to be willing to be the target of criticism. The ban on the article was removed and Mendelssohn was released. King Frederick II himself read the article by Mendelssohn and praised it.

Moses Mendelssohn saw how important it was for him to acquire legal status. He applied to Frederick the Great for the privilege of residence.

"Since the days of my boyhood," he wrote, "I have lived in Your Majesty's dominions and I desire to settle therein permanently. I take the liberty of petitioning humbly that Your Majesty may graciously condescend to grant me and my children Your Majesty's most gracious protection."

Frederick ignored the petition. At last, his favorite court-philosopher presented a second petition in behalf of Mendelssohn. The king accorded the privilege of residence to Mendelssohn, but refused to extend it to his children. When Moses Mendelssohn was nominated as a member of the Berlin Academy of Science, Frederick crossed his name off the list.

Nonetheless, Mendelssohn's fame as a philosopher spread far and wide. His books were read in every country of Europe, and were translated into many languages.

The hunchbacked philosopher became known as "The Jewish Socrates."

3. THE FIGHT FOR EQUAL RIGHTS

Mendelssohn's great ambition was to obtain equal rights for the persecuted.

He complained that Prussia, which boasted of its tolerance, was hemmed in on all sides by intolerance.

"Sometimes in the evening I go for a stroll with my wife and my children," he wrote in a letter to a friend. " 'Father,' asks a child in his innocence, 'what is that boy calling after us? What have we done to them?' 'Yes, father,' says another, 'they always run after us in the street and call us: Jews! Jews! Is it such a disgrace among these people to be a Jew?' Alas! I cast down my eyes and I sigh within myself: oh men, how could you let it come to this?"

In 1774 the governor of Baden, Switzerland ruled that the number of Jews in his area was to be kept within certain limits. As a result, Jews who had recently married were to be expelled. The community appealed to Mendelssohn to intercede in their behalf. So great was Mendelssohn's influence that his letter had the desired effect. The decree was rescinded and the Jews allowed to remain.

The Prince of Dresden signed a decree that Jews who failed to pay the personal tax on the appointed day were to be expelled immediately. As the result of unavoidable misfortunes hundreds of poor Jews were unable to pay their taxes promptly. They too appealed to Mendelssohn to prevent expulsion.

The philosopher wrote to one of the Prince's advisers:

"The last post has just brought the news that hundreds of my coreligionists are to be driven out of Dresden. Among these are a number I know personally, of whose honesty I am certain. They have lost their money and are perhaps unable to bear the burdens imposed upon them. I am sure they have come to this not by their own fault, but by misfortune. Kind and benevolent father, where are they to find shelter and protection? Expulsion is the hardest punishment for a Jew, almost equivalent to extermination from God's earth where prejudice turns them back from every frontier by force of arms. And human beings are to suffer this punishment though they are not guilty of any crime, merely because they hold different convictions and have been impoverished by misfortune. The innocent poor, no matter what their customs and religion, cannot be refused fire, water and shelter."

Again Mendelssohn's plea was heeded and the decree of expulsion revoked.

In 1777, the government inspector at Konigsberg complained that the Jewish prayer *Alenu* contained an attack on Christianity. The inspector had been appointed to supervise synagogue worship to make sure that nothing disrespectful of Christianity was recited by Jewish worshipers. The Jewish community appealed to Mendelssohn to defend them. Mendelssohn proved so convincingly that the prayer was free of any bias against Christianity that the charge was dismissed completely. Frederick the Great went even further and abolished the position of synagogue inspector altogether.

In 1783 the Jews of Alsace, which was ruled by France, requested Mendelssohn to help them in their fight for equal rights. Mendelssohn asked his friend Wilhelm Dohm, a Gentile author who wrote on political topics, to assist. Dohm then wrote a remarkable work called *On the Civil Emancipation of the Jews*. Dohm argued that Jews would make excellent citizens because of their industriousness, their good character, their wisdom and their steadfast loyalty. He demanded that they be granted full religious equality and the right to engage in industry, to own farms and to hold public office.

Dohm's book created a sensation. Mendelssohn was delighted. When opponents attacked Dohm's views, Mendelssohn arranged for the translation of Menasseh ben Israel's famous book, *The Plea for the Jews*, into German. Mendelssohn wrote a preface to the translation in which he pleaded for equality.

"It is curious to see," he said, "what different forms prejudice assumes throughout the centuries to oppress us and to place difficulties in the way of our reception as citizens. . . . Christians continue to keep us away from arts, sciences and useful industries; all the roads to useful improvement are blocked. . . . They tie our hands and then blame us for not using them."

Mendelssohn and Dohm won many supporters who upheld the doctrine of equality for all. Mendelssohn rejoiced that "an all-kind Providence had let him live long enough to see the day when people were beginning to take the rights of humanity to heart."

4. NATHAN THE WISE

Lessing, loyal friend of Moses Mendelssohn, struck a blow for freedom by writing a play called *Nathan the Wise*. The hero is a wise and noble Jewish merchant who lived in Jerusalem during the time of the Crusades.

When asked by Saladin, ruler of Egypt, which of the three major religions is the true religion, Nathan the Wise replied by telling the following parable:

Once there was a man who possessed a precious ring. Whoever wore the ring was beloved of all. Before his death the father gave it to one of his sons who thus became leader of the family. And so it continued from generation to generation until the ring passed into the hands of a man who had three sons, all equally precious in his eyes. The father went to an expert jeweler who forged two rings which looked exactly like the original ring. The father secretly gave one of the rings to each of his sons before his death.

After the father's death a violent quarrel sprang up among the brothers, each one claiming to possess the true ring. When the matter was brought before a judge he said, "It is impossible to tell who has the true ring and who has the false ring. However, this ring possessed a magic quality—the man who wore it was loved by all because of his noble qualities. Let each man act nobly so that he will be beloved of all, and thus prove that he indeed is the wearer of the true ring."

The meaning of the parable was clear. Each man believes that his is the true religion, yet nobody can really say which is true and which is false. Let, therefore, each man act nobly thus proving that his beliefs are fruitful and a source of blessing.

Lessing's play reminded everybody of Moses Mendelssohn. They knew that Lessing was inspired by Mendelssohn's character when he described a wise and noble man who pleaded that all religions be respected, and that men be judged by their deeds.

When Lessing died shortly after the publication of *Nathan the Wise*, Mendelssohn mourned for the man who had been his friend throughout life. Recognizing that many years would pass before the world would accept Lessing's great teachings, Mendelssohn wrote, "He was indeed more than a century ahead of his time."

Meanwhile, Moses Mendelssohn continued the plea for tolerance in a brilliant book named *Jerusalem*. In this book the philosopher considers the relation between church and state. Thought is free, argues Mendelssohn. No state has the right to interfere with men's religious beliefs. It should not reward one church nor punish another. Religious acts must begin in the heart, and cannot be bought with rewards nor enforced with punishment. Any church which relies on the state to force people to accept its doctrines is a failure, for religion must use instruction and not compulsion. Let the state enforce law and order, but leave religion to the conscience of each individual.

Germany's greatest philosopher, Immanuel Kant, wrote to Mendelssohn, "I consider this book to be the announcement of a great reform moving forward no matter how slowly, a reform which will affect not only your nation but also others. You have known how to combine with your religion a degree of liberty of conscience we should never have thought possible and which no other religion can boast of. You have clearly and thoroughly demonstrated the necessity of unrestricted liberty of conscience."

5. *Haskalah* OR ENLIGHTENMENT

Mendelssohn knew that there was a mental as well as physical ghetto whose walls had to be broken down. He devoted his efforts to guiding the Jews of Europe along the lines of self-improvement. Enlightenment, or as it was called in Hebrew *Haskalah*, became the slogan of the day.

The chief aims of the *Haskalah* were:

1. Political and social emancipation
2. Economic and vocational reconstruction
3. Westernization of schools and customs
4. Spread of science among the Jewish people
5. Revival of Hebrew poetry and literature
6. Emphasis on Biblical study
7. Scientific study of Jewish history and culture.

One result of Mendelssohn's ideas on education was the establishment of the *Jewish Free-School* in Berlin. The curriculum included Bible, Talmud, mathematics, bookkeeping, geography, French and German. Similar schools were soon set up in Breslau, Dessau, Frankfort and other cities.

Under the leadership of Mendelssohn and a gifted Hebrew author Naphtali Wessely, a Hebrew magazine called *Ha-Meassef* ("The Gatherer") was published. This magazine served to revive Hebrew as a literary language, and soon became a leader in the struggle for emancipation and enlightenment.

Here is an original fable which Mendelssohn wrote for this magazine:

"The sun lit up the face of the earth and shone on plant and on grass of the field. A young lad jumped and capered in the green fields, joyful and with merry heart, when suddenly he beheld his image in his shadow. And the lad was delighted with the shadow, for with each step he took the shadow jumped along in front of him. Eager to capture the shadow, the boy began to chase after it; but the shadow ran as fast as he did. He skipped, and the shadow skipped before him, and he saw that he could not succeed in overtaking the shadow. Deciding to ignore the shadow, the lad turned toward the sun and went on his way.

"But as he walked quietly and confidently, he looked behind—and behold the shadow was following him! How true indeed are the words of our sages: Honor flees from him who pursues honor."

This was a fitting parable to describe the life of the gentle philosopher. For he, shunning honor and glory, had gone through life modestly and humbly, only to be pursued by the honor he so richly deserved.

Perhaps Mendelssohn's crowning achievement was his translation of the Five Books of Moses into German. This was accompanied by a splendid commentary prepared by Mendelssohn, Wessely and other members of their circle. The translation served as a two-way bridge, helping the older generation learn German and the younger generation learn Hebrew and Bible.

The plea for tolerance which Mendelssohn had made to the Gentile world he directed also to his fellow-Jews. Let not Judaism use force in trying to compel Jews to abide by the Torah. He emphasized this thought in his preface to *The Plea for the Jews*.

"True divine religion," he wrote, "knows of no other force than that of winning by argument, or convincing and rendering blessed by conviction. True divine religion needs neither arms nor fingers for its use; it is all spirit and heart."

Was Mendelssohn thinking of the excommunication of a man like Baruch Spinoza? The power of excommunication, he wrote, is indeed a dangerous one.

"All the nations of the earth, hitherto, appear to have been infatuated by the error that religion can be maintained by iron force. . . . Thank the God of your forefathers, thank the God who is all love and mercy, that that error appears to be gradually vanishing. The nations are now tolerating and bearing with one another, while to you also they are showing kindness and forbearance, which with the help of Him who disposes the hearts of men, may grow to true brotherly love. . . . Love and ye will be beloved."

Mendelssohn pleads with the younger generation, however, not to abandon the laws of Judaism. In his book *Jerusalem*, he warns all Jews to hold fast to the religion of their fathers. If equality means surrender of Judaism, he will have none of it. His own observance of the customs of Judaism set an inspiring example.

To Jew and Gentile alike, Mendelssohn proudly affirmed: "I declare before God that I shall adhere to my principles."

Moses Mendelssohn's death in 1786 was mourned by all. Of him it was said as was once said of Moses ben Maimon, "From Moses to Moses there was none like Moses."

EXERCISES

I. True or false? (Review section 1, pages 155 to 156.)

1. There were 3 million Jews in the colonies at the time of the American Revolution.
2. Jews lived in a special walled section of each city known as the ghetto.
3. Jews usually were not allowed to engage in agriculture or in manufacturing.
4. Jews paid the same taxes as their neighbors.
5. Despite hardships there was much merriment and joy among the Jews.

II. Who am I? (Review section 2, pages 156 to 160.)

1. I was a Torah scribe in the city of Dessau. My son became a great philosopher.
2. I was a Rabbi in Dessau, and then was called to a post in Berlin. I inspired one of my pupils to devote himself to a life of study.
3. I was a hunchbacked philosopher whom people called "The Jewish Socrates."
4. I was a German author who wrote a play in which the hero was a Jew.
5. I was king of Prussia. I granted Mendelssohn the right to remain in Berlin, but refused to admit him to the Academy of Science.

III. Why? (Review section 3, pages 160 to 162.)

1. Why did Mendelssohn complain about conditions in Prussia?
2. Why did the Jews of Baden, Switzerland fear expulsion?
3. Why did the Jews of Dresden fail to pay the tax on the appointed day?
4. Why did the inspector condemn the prayer *Alenu?*
5. Why did the Jews receive Dohm's book with enthusiasm?

IV. Complete each sentence. (Review section 4, pages 162 to 164.)

Jerusalem, Lessing, Mendelssohn, Nathan, Saladin

1. _____ wrote a play about a wise and noble Jew.
2. _____, ruler of Egypt, asked which is the true religion.
3. _____ told the story of the three rings.
4. _____ wrote that the state should not interfere in religious matters.
5. Kant praised the book _____ because it demanded religious liberty for all.

V. Explain each quotation. (Review section 5, pages 164 to 166.)

1. "Honor flees from him who pursues honor."
2. "True divine religion needs neither arms nor fingers for its use."

3. "Love and ye will be beloved."
4. "I declare before God that I shall adhere to my principles."
5. "From Moses to Moses there was none like Moses."

VI. Questions for discussion:

1. What were the disadvantages of ghetto life?
2. How did Mendelssohn help the cause of emancipation?
3. What were the aims of the *Haskalah* (Enlightenment)?
4. Discuss the importance of each of the following publications:

> a—William Dohm's *On the Civil Emancipation of the Jews*
> b—Mendelssohn's preface to *The Plea for the Jews*
> c—Lessing's *Nathan the Wise*
> d—Mendelssohn's *Jerusalem*
> e—Mendelssohn's transelation of the Five Books of Moses
> f—*Ha-Meassef*

THINGS TO DO

1. *Original Story*—Write a story about a Jew in Baden whose marriage is prevented by the threat of expulsion. Let the story end happily.

2. *Dramatization*—Dramatize the following scenes in the life of Mendelssohn: a) Mendelssohn at the gate of Berlin b) Mendelssohn and Fromet Gugenheim c) Mendelssohn before the Attorney-General.

CHAPTER XIV

THE FRENCH REVOLUTION
AND JEWISH EMANCIPATION

THREE YEARS after Mendelssohn's death came the French Revolution. Events moved quickly, and Mendelssohn's dream of equal rights was closer to realization than he had dared hope.

Although Jews had been expelled from France in 1394, there were almost 60,000 Jews in France at the time of the French Revolution. In the district of Avignon, where the popes had formerly ruled, Jews were allowed to live without interference; many Marrano Jews had settled in Bordeaux where they openly returned to Judaism; Alsace-Lorraine which was ceded to France in 1648, after the Thirty Years' War, contained many German-speaking Jews.

Mendelssohn's plea for equality had found its way to the heart of liberty-loving Frenchmen. Montesquieu, famous author of *The Spirit of the Laws*, wrote:

"You Christians complain that the Emperor of China roasts all Christians in his dominions over a slow fire; you behave much worse toward Jews, because they do not believe as you do."

Count Mirabeau, statesman and orator, was an eloquent champion of Jewish rights. A warm friend of Mendelssohn's, he paid tribute to the Jewish philosopher. In the course of his remarks he added:

"If you wish the Jews to become better men and useful citizens, then banish every humiliating distinction, open to

them every avenue of gaining a livelihood; instead of for-
bidding them agriculture handicrafts and the mechanical arts,
encourage them to devote themselves to these occupations."

The fall of the Bastille on July 14, 1789 was a turning-point
not only in French history but in Jewish history. At first the
riots which followed the fall of the Bastille claimed many
Jewish victims. Alsatian Jews were forced to flee for refuge
to Switzerland. On August 23, 1789, however, inspired by the
American proclamation that all men are created equal, the
French patriots adopted the Declaration of the Rights of Man.

"Men are born and remain equal in rights," declared this
famous document.

One clause of the Rights of Man read, "No one shall be
molested on account of his religious opinions."

Count Mirabeau, the great orator who had defied the king,
pleaded with the National Assembly to carry out this clause
by passing laws in behalf of the oppressed Jewish community.
All to no avail! It seemed at first as if the three catchwords of
the Revolution, "Liberty, Equality and Fraternity" were intended for all but Jews.

The Sefardic Jews of Bordeaux selfishly pleaded their own
case saying they had nothing to do with the Jews of Alsace.
The few but rich Jews of Bordeaux were granted citizenship
in 1790. A year later the French Constitution was drawn up
without any reference to Jewish equality.

When the final draft of the Constitution was presented on
September 27, 1791 a deputy rose to protest against the exclusion of Jews.

"I believe that freedom of thought does not permit any
distinction in political rights on account of a man's creed,"
he said. "The recognition of this equality is always being
postponed."

The deputy then made a motion that a decree be passed
stating "that the Jews in France enjoy the privileges of active
citizenship." The motion was accepted with enthusiasm, and
the next day all laws discriminating against Jews were abol-

ished. King Louis XVI, who had not yet been deposed, signed the decree.

Cerf Berr, one of the Alsatian Jewish leaders, wrote to his fellow-Jews throughout France:

"We have at last again obtained the rights of which we have been deprived for eighteen centuries. How deeply at this moment should we recognize the wonderful grace of the God of our forefathers! God chose the noble French nation to reinstate us in our due privileges, and to bring us to a new birth."

2. NAPOLEON

The struggle for equal rights was forgotten during the Reign of Terror when innocent and guilty alike were sent to the guillotine. Among the Jewish patriots was Abraham Furtado of Bordeaux who barely escaped with his life. His property was confiscated by the government. Rabbi David Sinzheim of Strasbourg wandered from city to city in order to escape imprisonment during the anti-religious campaign.

The Reign of Terror was succeeded by a Directory government until Napoleon Bonaparte assumed power in 1799. Napoleon showed a friendly interest in Jewish problems from the very beginning of his career. During the Palestine campaign of 1799 when Napoleon fought against the Turks, he issued a proclamation that if Jews rallied to his banner he would restore Palestine to the Jewish people. Although successful in several battles in Palestine, Napoleon suddenly abandoned the campaign when France was attacked by a coalition of European countries.

Napoleon's armies spread the doctrine of equality throughout Europe. The Jews of Rome removed the yellow badge which they had worn for centuries. The ghetto walls of Venice fell, and Jews were given full equality. Holland, which was the first European country to give Jews religious liberty, now extended equal political rights as well; prominent Jews were soon elected to public office.

Napoleon carved out a new kingdom in West Germany where he enthroned his brother, Jerome. The tolerant new king immediately granted full equality to all Jews. With one stroke of the pen, the Jewish poll tax and other discriminatory taxes were wiped out. In 1811, with the guns of Napoleon thundering away outside of the city, the Duke of Frankfort gave Jews full citizenship after extracting a large sum of money from the Jewish community. In 1812, Prussia accorded Jews equal rights, except that they could not hold public office. The hated Inquisition was abolished in Spain and Portugal, and the few Marrano families remaining, after 300 years of persecution, were able to breathe more freely.

Is it any wonder that Jews joined with other Frenchmen in declaring, "We owe toward Napoleon, our emperor, love, respect, obedience, fidelity, military service, and the taxes laid for the defense and preservation of the empire"?

3. THE ASSEMBLY OF NOTABLES AND THE GRAND SANHEDRIN

The truth of the matter was that Napoleon was not at all free of prejudice. When complaints were brought by Alsatians against Jews to whom they owed money, Napoleon called a special meeting of his advisers to consider the Jewish question. He spoke harshly saying that Jews were a state within a state, and that like the aristocrats they oppressed the peasants.

Several of his advisers, however, courageously defended the Jewish community. They pointed out how loyally Jews had fought for France, how many were awarded prizes for bravery. They stated that Jews were forced into moneylending, but that the rate of interest charged was in keeping with the law. They also praised Jewish industriousness, showing what splendid progress Jews had made in various vocations since equality was accorded to them.

Napoleon decided to assure the loyalty of the Jewish community by calling Jewish representatives together to consult with him. He issued a call to all the Jewish communities of

France to select representatives to take part in an Assembly of Notables. Several German and Italian Jewish communities were also invited to send representatives.

On July 26, 1806, about a hundred distinguished Rabbis and leaders met in a beautiful Parisian palace. Spirits ran high, for this was the first time in centuries that a Jewish parliament had met to promote the welfare of the Jewish people.

Abraham Furtado who had been an outstanding patriot during the days of the French Revolution was elected president. Furtado came of a Marrano family which had secretly remained loyal to Judaism for over 250 years. When Lisbon, capital of Portugal, was overturned by an earthquake his mother miraculously escaped. She left Portugal, and openly returned to Judaism. Her son Abraham was raised as a proud and staunch Jew.

Napoleon proposed a series of questions to the Assembly of Notables. Did Jews consider themselves loyal Frenchmen? Would they abide by the laws of France? Could they engage in manual labor? Did Judaism permit a man to have more than one wife? Would Judaism recognize French divorce law? Did Judaism permit usury? Does Judaism permit intermarriage?

The answers to these questions were prepared by a group of delegates headed by the brilliant Rabbi David Sinzheim of Strasbourg. The representatives answered "Yes" as one man when questioned as to whether they were loyal to France and to its laws. Some delegates called out, "Even unto death." Manual labor was honored among Jews, many great Rabbis having earned a livelihood by the work of their hands. Western Jews were not permitted to have more than one wife since the tenth century. No Jewish marriage would be celebrated if a civil impediment existed.

Usury, or excessive interest, was denounced by the delegates. Rabbi Sinzheim prepared a reply to Napoleon's question in which he pointed out that in ancient Israel, Jews were commanded to share with one another, and therefore loans should be extended without any interest. Later, where money

was loaned for business reasons, a small amount of interest was permitted. Under no circumstances could the creditor oppress either Jew or Gentile by charging excessive interest. Jews as a whole were not to be blamed because of the sins of a small group of moneylenders.

The question concerning intermarriage was the most difficult to answer. The delegates were strongly opposed to intermarriage since they feared that it would lead to conversion and assimilation. They realized, however, that Napoleon would not be saitsfied with such an answer. In their reply they stated that a Jew who marries out of the faith is still accepted as a Jew; the Rabbis, however, could not perform a religious ceremony where one of the parties did not believe in the ceremony.

Napoleon was delighted with the work of the Assembly. Were their decisions binding on all Jews? To make certain that their answers would be accepted as law, Napoleon decided to revive the Sanhedrin. It was the Sanhedrin of 71 members in ancient Jerusalem which made the laws for the Jewish nation.

The call for elections to the Grand Sanhedrin was published in Hebrew, French, Italian and German. The proclamation declared: "This great event, which will be remembered forever, will serve the remnant of the people of Abraham as the beginning of a new era of redemption and salvation."

The Grand Sanhedrin met on February 9, 1807 with great festivity. The delegates assembled in one of the synagogues of Paris where Rabbi David Sinzheim greeted them in Hebrew. Tears appeared in the eyes of those assembled when Rabbi Sinzheim lifted the Torah and recited a prayer of thanksgiving to God.

Rabbi Sinzheim was elected president of the Grand Sanhedrin. Abraham Furtado reported on the decisions of the Assembly of Notables. The 71 members, seated in a semi-circle like the Sanhedrin of old, endorsed the work of the Assembly of Notables. They cast the decisions in the form of laws binding on all Jews of France. In this dramatic manner, they called to the attention of Europe that Jews could be both loyal citizens and true to their religious heritage.

Meanwhile, Napoleon was in Central Europe waging war against Prussia and Russia. Word spread among the leaders of the Grand Sanhedrin, that in the absence of Napoleon enemies of the Jews were preparing a series of anti-Jewish laws. Abraham Furtado headed a mission to Napoleon at the battlefield where he pleaded in behalf of the Jews. Napoleon promised to continue to treat Jews as equals.

Despite his promise—not the first promise that Napoleon broke—laws discriminating against Alsatian Jews were passed in 1808. Debts owing to them were suspended for ten years; also they were forbidden to move during that time to other sections of France. These laws, called "The Infamous Decrees," were never fully enforced.

Even though Napoleon was not entirely free of prejudice he must be credited with having destroyed many of the ghettos of Western and Central Europe. By spreading the doctrine of "Liberty, Equality and Fraternity" he ushered in a new era for the Jew.

4. REACTION

Many of the rights extended to the Jew during the reign of Napoleon were really only paper rights. Prejudice was so strong that Jews often were unable to take advantage of their legal rights.

An example of this prejudice may be found in the writings of Fichte, one of Germany's leading philosophers. He wrote concerning Jewish emancipation:

"The only way I see by which civil rights can be conceded to them is to cut off all their heads in one night and to set new ones on their shoulders, which should contain not a single Jewish idea."

Finding all avenues of advancement closed to them many German Jews sought escape through conversion. Among the converts were Mendelssohn's own children. His grandchild, Felix Mendelssohn, the great composer, was born a Jew, but brought by his father to the church while still a child. These converts often found, however, that they had sold their birthright for a mess of pottage. They were rejected by both Christian and Jew. (A century after his death Felix Mendelssohn's memory was desecrated in Germany because he was of Jewish origin.)

Napoleon's defeat was the signal for many countries to withdraw the rights they had granted the Jews. "The cup of freedom was dashed from their lips," writes one author, "just when they were beginning to sip."

It is true that at the Congress of Vienna the allies who defeated Napoleon agreed to retain the rights which had been granted to the Jews. But few rulers took this clause seriously. Frankfort which had taken a large sum of money from the Jews in return for a promise of equal rights, kept the money but not the promise. In Austria, Jews were forced back into the ghetto. Prussia canceled many concessions that had been made to the Jews. In Bremen an attempt was made to exclude all Jews. In Italy, Jews were thrust out of their new homes. Only France and Holland remained true to the ideal of equality.

The dreams of freedom seemed to turn to ashes. Yet once having tasted of freedom, Jews would not rest content until their rights were restored. They joined forces with others who worked and fought for an extension of human rights. A generation was to pass before there was a new birth of freedom.

EXERCISES

I. Fill in the correct date. (Review section 1, pages 169 to 172.)

   1. Jews had been expelled from France in _____.
   2. The Bastille fell on July 14, _____.
   3. The Rights of Man were proclaimed on August 23, _____.

4. The Jews of Bordeaux were granted citizenship in
   _____.

5. Jews of France were made citizens by the Constitution
   of _____.

II. Match. (Review section 2, pages 172 to 173.)

Column A	Column B
Furtado	1. Granted Jews rights in return for money
Turks	2. Served as delegate to Grand Sanhedrin
Napoleon	3. Spread idea of equality throughout Europe
Jerome	4. Fought French in Palestine
Duke of Frankfort	5. Granted Jews of West Germany equal rights

III. Choose the correct word or phrase. (Review sections 3 and 4,
     pages 173 to 176.)

1. Charges were brought against Jews by _____. (Alsatians, Parisians)

2. Napoleon's advisers said that Jews were _____. (loyal, disloyal)

3. The Assembly of Notables said Jews were in favor of _____. (intermarriage, obedience to the laws of France)

4. The Assembly of Notables objected to _____. (manual labor, usury)

5. The leading Rabbi of the Grand Sanhedrin was _____. (Furtado, Sinzheim)

6. Felix Mendelssohn, the composer, was Moses Mendelssohn's _____. (son, grandson)

7. After Napoleon's defeat, Jews _____. (received many new privileges, were deprived of many privileges)

IV. Questions for discussion:

1. How did the French Revolution advance the cause of Jewish emancipation?

2. Was Napoleon a friend of the Jews?

3. What did the Assembly of Notables and the Grand Sanhedrin accomplish?

4. Which events that took place within the generation after his death would have pleased Moses Mendelssohn? Which events would have displeased him?

THINGS TO DO

1. *Panel Discussion*—a) Arrange a discussion on the question, "Should the Sanhedrin be revived today?"

b) Invite the Rabbi of your synagogue to lead a discussion on the subject, "The attitude of Judaism toward intermarriage."

2. *Class Newspaper*—Prepare a newspaper dated February 10, 1807, the day after the opening meeting of the Grand Sanhedrin. These are some of the topics that might be assigned to members of the staff:

a. An editorial about the importance of the Grand Sanhedrin for French Jewry

b. An interview with Napoleon about equal rights for Jews

c. A human interest story about the life of Abraham Furtado

d. A late bulletin about rumors of war between France and Russia

e. A letter from a delegate to his family in Strasbourg

f. A report of the service on February 9, 1807 in the synagogue of Paris

g. An article on France's greatest Jew—Rashi

h. A report about preparations in France for Purim and Passover

i. An interview with Rabbi Sinzheim about the questions which Napoleon put to the Assembly of Notables and the Grand Sanhedrin

j. A letter from a reader about usury, manual labor, obedience to French law or one of the other questions to be discussed by the Sanhedrin

k. An article on "Hillel—President of the Ancient Sanhedrin"

l. Drawings: a Parisian synagogue; the Grand Sanhedrin in session; Jewish delegates before Napoleon; a French Rabbi studying Rashi's commentary

CHAPTER XV

MOSES MONTEFIORE–
DEFENDER OF JEWISH RIGHTS

I. THE JEWS OF ENGLAND

MOSES MONTEFIORE, staunch defender of Jewish rights, was the outstanding English Jew of the 19th century. His life is a mirror of Jewish strivings and problems over a period of a hundred years. Like Moses Mendelssohn he became the symbol of an era in Jewish history.

English Jewry had prospered since Menasseh ben Israel had helped found the first synagogue of the new community in London in 1655. Marranos, especially, came to London where they could practice Judaism openly. They set up a thriving trade with their fellow-Marranos in Amsterdam, Bordeaux, Venice, Leghorn, West Indies and other great ports. English woolens, Italian hats, Turkish goods, corals and precious stones were among the products bought and sold by these prosperous traders. A number of Marranos found their way to London after the Lisbon earthquake in 1755. As late as 1795, many members of the London congregation said they had come to England to escape the Inquisition; one wrote that his mother had been burnt alive by the Inquisition. Many Jews from Poland and Germany also crowded into England.

Moses Montefiore's family came from Leghorn, Italy. He was born in that city when his parents returned from England for a visit in 1784. Thus, he was but a child when Mendelssohn died and when the French Revolution broke out. He was tutored in Hebrew by his uncle, a man of great learning. During the Napoleonic Wars he served as a captain in the

English militia. Six-feet-three and broad of frame, he impressed all with his great height, and military bearing.

Moses became a broker on the London Stock Exchange for his wealthy brother-in-law, Nathan Rothschild. The English government owed a great debt to Rothschild who helped finance its wars against Napoleon. Thanks to his financial genius and widespread connections, England was able to forward to Europe the money with which to pay the Duke of Wellington's soldiers. Rothschild and Montefiore were among the first to learn of Napoleon's escape from Elba. It was Rothschild, through his special couriers, who brought the news of Waterloo to an anxious Prime Minister.

Rothschild and Montefiore had helped to prevent a collapse of the stock market by keeping up prices through extensive buying of stocks. Another notable service to the government was the issue by Nathan Rothschild and Moses Montefiore in 1835 of a loan to carry into effect the abolition of slavery in England.

In 1836, Moses Montefiore was made sheriff of London, the second Jew to be elected to that high office. He would not attend the inauguration dinner, however, because it fell on Rosh Ha-Shanah. As a tribute to Montefiore, the dinner was postponed. The next year Queen Victoria was crowned queen, and Moses Montefiore led a delegation which brought a gift from the Jewish community. Later, Moses Montefiore was knighted by Queen Victoria. His coat of arms was built around a banner which contained the word "Jerusalem" in Hebrew.

Jews in England still suffered from many disabilities. They could not engage in retail trade in London. They could not practice law before the bar. They could not obtain college degrees. They could not serve on juries. With the exception of sheriff, they could not hold public office. Theoretically, they could not even vote since they might be required to take an oath on "the true faith of a Christian." In reality, the oath was seldom required.

As president of the Board of Deputies of British Jews, Moses Montefiore played a leading role in removing these disabilities. One by one, laws were passed giving Jews equal rights. In 1845, for example, he headed a delegation to the Prime Minister requesting that obstacles to the holding of municipal office by Jews be removed. A law was passed stating that any member of the Jewish faith could take an oath for municipal office in a form acceptable to his conscience. Shortly thereafter a Jew named David Salomons was elected alderman, and in 1855 Lord Mayor of London.

The last major obstacle to full equality was the inability of a Jew to serve in Parliament, since each member had to take an oath on "the true faith of a Christian." Moses Montefiore, David Salomons and the Rothschilds bent all their energies to bring about a change in this procedure.

In 1847, Baron Lionel de Rothschild, nephew of Montefiore, was elected to Parliament by the City of London. Since he would not take the oath, he could not serve. A bill was introduced to change the oath. The Prime Minister argued in favor of the change saying that every Englishman, regardless of creed, is entitled to all the honors and advantages of the British Constitution. The bill was passed by the House of Commons, but defeated by the House of Lords who claimed that Jews are "voluntary strangers."

Rothschild was elected four more times during the next ten years, but each time was rejected by Parliament when he failed to take the oath. After many years of wrangling the opponents of Jewish equality finally decided to yield. A bill allowing Jews to take an oath in keeping with their religious beliefs was passed in 1858, and Baron Rothschild took his seat in the House of Commons. It was Lionel de Rothschild who made possible English control of the Suez Canal by advancing the necessary funds to Prime Minister Benjamin Disraeli in 1875.

With the seating of Baron Rothschild in Parliament, English Jews had at last won full political equality.

2. THE DAMASCUS AFFAIR

But Montefiore fought for Jewish equality not only in England—he became the defender of Jewish rights wherever they were threatened. Together with his beloved wife, Judith, he would travel to remote corners of the world in order to defend the good name of the Jew.

Perhaps the most famous of the affairs in which Montefiore served as the champion of Jewish rights was the Damascus Blood Accusation of 1840. Jews of Damascus, Syria were falsely accused of having taken the life of Father Thomas, a monk and physician, for ritual purposes. Jews and Christians alike were shocked by the revival of this horrible slander. The governor of Damascus arrested an innocent Jewish barber, and forced a confession by means of cruel torture. Following this false confession, eight of the leading Jews of Damascus were arrested and forced to undergo excruciating torture. Two of the Jews died under torture. The other six, in spite of the tortures, refused to confess to any guilt.

The governor then arrested 60 Jewish children, and confined them without food, thus hoping to force a confession of guilt from their parents. An investigation led to the discovery of some bones near the home of a Jew. This heightened suspicion until it was found that the bones were not those of a man but of a sheep. Unfortunately, the governor of Damascus was aided in his schemes by Ratti Menton, the cruel and corrupt French Consul, who announced that the guilt of the Jews had been proved.

Moses Montefiore and his friends decided to come to the aid of the innocent. A group of Jewish leaders met at the home of Montefiore to consider what steps might be taken. Among those who attended the meeting was Adolphe Crémieux, a statesman and leader of French Jewry. A delegation pleaded with the British Prime Minister for assistance. The English government gave instructions to British representatives in the East to aid the accused in every way possible. It also ordered its own inquiry to see what the truth of the matter was.

Since no protests seemed to help, it was decided to send a delegation headed by Montefiore to the East. Queen Victoria granted an audience to Montefiore before he left, and assured him of all possible assistance.

Moses and Judith Montefiore, Crémieux and other members of the delegation journeyed to Egypt to intercede with Pasha Mehemet Ali, who then controlled Syria. They asked for the right to proceed to Damascus to examine the evidence and to cross-examine the witnesses. When the request was refused, Montefiore, supported by the British Consul and representatives of other European governments, demanded the immediate liberation of the accused. Mehemet Ali, fearing the wrath of Europe, bowed to this request and granted a pardon to the prisoners. Since this seemed to imply guilt, Montefiore asked that "pardon" be changed to "honorable liberation." This request was granted, and the prisoners were soon released.

The political turn of events was such that, at that very time, Egypt lost control of Syria to Turkey. Montefiore and his party proceeded to Constantinople to obtain a confirmation of Jewish rights from the Sultan of Turkey. They were received with great honor. The Sultan then issued a declaration protecting Jewish rights.

"For the love we bear to our subjects," wrote the Sultan, "we cannot permit the Jewish nation to be vexed and tormented upon accusations which have not the least foundations in truth. The Jewish nation shall be protected and defended."

The world rejoiced with Montefiore that justice had prevailed. Upon his return to England he was granted a special honor by Queen Victoria "in commemoration of these his unceasing exertions in behalf of his injured and persecuted brethren in the East and of the Jewish nation at large."

3. SPOKESMAN FOR WORLD JEWRY

The condition of Jews in Russia at this time was deplorable. A few years after the Damascus Affair, the Czar of Russia announced that all Jews near the borders of Germany and

Austria would be forced to move. This meant utter ruin for almost 100,000 Jews. Russian Jews appealed to Sir Moses Montefiore for help.

Moses Montefiore and his wife, accompanied by a large party, set out for Russia on March 1, 1846. The journey by coach over bad roads and over the thawing ice of rivers was a dangerous one. After a month of arduous travel, Montefiore reached St. Petersburg on April 1, 1846. Several days later he was received in the friendliest manner by Czar Nicholas I.

Montefiore has left an interesting impression of this interview in his diary. The Czar mentioned that the laws of Russia did not even permit a Jew to sleep in St. Petersburg.

"I trust your Majesty will see fit to alter them," said Montefiore.

"I hope so," replied the Czar.

Montefiore then made a strong plea for relaxing the many unfair laws directed against Jews. The Czar promised that he would do everything possible to improve their conditions. He boasted that he had even placed Jewish soldiers in his guards. Montefiore inquired whether these soldiers had any chance of promotion and was assured that they did.

Montefiore adds in his diary, "I repeatedly said that the Jews were faithful, loyal subjects, industrious and honorable citizens."

The Czar replied, "If they are like you."

In honor of Montefiore's visit, the palace guard for the day was made up of Jewish soldiers. On the Sabbath an officer of the Minister of War escorted Montefiore to the synagogue.

The general effect of Montefiore's visit to Russia was of great value, and the decree of expulsion from the border communities was revoked.

As a reward for his great achievement Queen Victoria made Montefiore a Baronet. The Prime Minister wrote:

"I have the satisfaction of acquainting you that the Queen has been graciously pleased to confer on you the dignity of a Baronet. This mark of royal favor is bestowed upon you in consideration of your high character . . . and in the hope that it may aid your truly benevolent efforts to improve the social condition of the Jews in other countries by temperate appeals to the justice and humanity of their rulers."

The succeeding years were marked by unceasing labors in behalf of the Jews of Palestine, Persia, Morocco and Turkey. One of the outstanding events of Montefiore's long career was his visit in 1867 to Roumania. For hundreds of years Roumania was part of the Turkish Empire. Jews were treated with tolerance and prospered. The Baal Shem Tov, for example, had lived for a while in Roumania, and found many supporters there. Serious persecution of the Jewish inhabitants began when Roumania was granted autonomy in 1856.

Urgent appeals for help reached the Board of Deputies of British Jews when riots broke out in 1866. Large numbers of Jews were declared vagrants and forced to leave the country. At the Turkish border, 10 Jews were thrust across the frontier. Since they had no passports they were turned back; the Roumanian guards thereupon drove them into the waters of the Danube where they were drowned.

Sir Moses Montefiore decided to visit Roumania in 1867 as the representative of the Board of Deputies of British Jews. He was received most courteously in Bucharest by Prince Charles, ruler of Roumania. The mobs, however, stirred up by anti-Jewish newspapers, threatened to grow violent. Montefiore and his party were openly threatened with death. An angry crowd gathered in front of Montefiore's hotel, and hurled vile insults at the Jews.

Undaunted, Sir Moses appeared in front of an open window and cried, "Fire away, if you like! I came here in the name of justice and humanity to plead the cause of innocent sufferers."

Although warned not to appear in public, Montefiore drove through the streets in an open carriage.

"Everyone shall see me," he said. "It is a holy cause, that of justice and humanity."

Prince Charles wrote to Montefiore: "I am glad that you

have come to Roumania to convince yourself that the religious persecution . . . does not exist. If it has happened that the Israelites have been disturbed, these are isolated incidents for which my Government cannot assume the responsibility. I shall always consider it a point of honor to respect religious liberty."

Montefiore's mission was successful in that he received promises of help from the ruler of Roumania. Unfortunately, however, these promises were not sincere and were never fully kept.

4. THE HOLY LAND

Each Sabbath day, Montefiore would wear a ring on which was engraved the word "Jerusalem." This was a symbol of the strong love he felt for the Holy Land.

Moses Montefiore made his first trip to the Holy Land in 1827. Thereafter he paid six more visits to Palestine. On each trip he was accompanied by his wife, until her death in 1862. No danger would deter Judith Montefiore from accompanying her husband. Once the cholera plague broke out in Palestine when they were en route, and Moses tried to dissuade his wife from making the perilous trip. She replied in the words of Ruth, "Entreat me not to leave thee."

The impression that the Holy Land made on Moses Montefiore may be gathered from the following description written by him as his boat approached the shores of Palestine:

"Myriads of celestial luminaries were now emitting their silvery rays of light in the spangled canopy over us. Sure and steady our ship steered towards the coast of the land so dearly beloved, summoning all to sleep, but few of the passengers retired that night. It was silent all around us—silent, so that the palpitation of the heart might almost be heard. It was as if everyone had the words on his lips, 'Ah, when will our eyes be gladdened by the first glance of the Holy Land?' The words of Judah Halevi, which he uttered when entering the gates of Jerusalem, now came into my mind: 'The kingdoms of idolatry will all change and disappear; thy glory alone, O Zion, will last forever.' "

Since there were no hotel accommodations the Montefiores would set up tents in the fields. Sometimes, they traveled on camels. At night because of brigands they would post an armed guard to protect them from attack. Sometimes on moonlit nights they rode at night to avoid the heat of the day.

Here is Montefiore's account of one such trip:

"I was longing to see Jerusalem, and decided to start on Saturday night. We waited for the rising of the moon, and twenty minutes past eleven o'clock started for Jerusalem. Those were exciting moments which presented themselves to my mind, now and then as we ascended and descended the hills and dales on the road; the moon throwing her long and dark shadow. They recalled to memory how much exposed the traveler was in former years to the attacks of a Bedouin, or some feudal lord. . . . Just as I concluded these meditations, two Bedouins in full speed dashed along from behind some hidden rock, and directed their course right up to our carriage.

" 'Good Heaven,' I thought. 'What in the world will they do with us?'

"But Dr. Loewe, who was with me in the carriage, suddenly called out as loud as he could, '*Shalom Aleichem*, Rabbi B.——. *Shalom Aleichem*, Rabbi L.——.'

"Turning around to me, he said, 'These are not Bedouins, though they are dressed exactly like them, and gallop along the hills like the sons of the desert, but they are simply our own brethren from Jerusalem.'

"And so it was. A minute afterwards they pulled up the reins of their fiery chargers, and stood before us.

" 'A happy and blessed week to you, Dr. Loewe,' they shouted. 'Where is Sir Moses? How is he? When will he enter Jerusalem?'

"As I bent my head forward, they saluted me, and stated to me the object of their coming. . . . They again saluted, galloped off, and soon disappeared."

Sir Moses distributed charity in the Holy Land with a lavish hand. He helped build hospitals, schools and synagogues. In time of famine he arranged for the shipment of food; in time of plague, for the shipment of medical supplies.

His chief goal, however, was not charity. He hoped to rebuild the economy of Palestine. He helped organize agricultural settlements. He built a windmill in Jerusalem, stipulating that the poor should be allowed to grind their flour without charge. He arranged for training in weaving and other skills. He tried to create an adequate water supply in Jerusalem. He suggested the building of a railroad by the government. He founded the Palestine Society to encourage and to finance colonization. He urged young people to find employment in the cultivation of the vine, the olive and the mulberry. He bought a plantation and experimented with the growing of oranges, lemons, citrons, apples, peaches, almonds, dates, apricots, pears, figs and bananas.

His greatest contribution, perhaps, was the building of model houses outside of the wall of old Jerusalem, thus laying the foundation for the new city. This is what he wrote:

"If you put the question to me thus: What scheme do you propose? I would reply, 'Begin with the building of houses in Jerusalem. Select land outside the city; raise, in the form of a large square or crescent, a number of suitable houses. Let each house have in front a plot of ground large enough to cultivate olive trees, the vine, and necessary vegetables, so as to give the occupiers a taste for agriculture.

"The houses ought to pay a moderate rental, by the amount of which there should be established a loan society, on safe principles, for the benefit of the poor working-class, the trader, agriculturist or any poor deserving man.

"If the amount of your funds be sufficient, build houses in Safed, Tiberias and Hebron on the same plan.

"And if you now address me saying, 'Which would be the proper time to commence work?' my reply would be, 'Commence at once: begin the work this day, if you can.'"

Montefiore's plan succeeded. The model houses built outside of the walls of the old city were named in his honor, and became the nucleus for the new city. Montefiore may be called the founder of New Jerusalem!

5. A CENTURY OF PROGRESS

At the end of his long life, Montefiore could look back on a century of progress for the Jewish people. Except for Eastern Europe, the battle of emancipation had been won. In 1867, Austria extended equal rights to its Jewish subjects. The unification of Italy in 1870 and of Germany in 1871 brought emancipation to the Jews of these lands. That same year the Universities of Oxford and Cambridge removed their restrictions so that Jews could qualify for degrees. Switzerland granted full equality in 1873.

Jewish population had tripled since the year of Montefiore's birth. There were now almost 10 million Jews in the world. This increase was due to many reasons:

1. The Industrial Revolution brought about the growth of large cities. Here Jews found greater economic opportunities and freedom from oppression.

2. Emancipation encouraged Jewish growth. In Frankfort, for example, the Jewish community was formerly permitted to arrange only 12 weddings a year. Now, all restrictions were lifted. Expulsions of Jews became a thing of the past. With the fall of the ghetto, Jews could breathe more easily.

3. Scientific advances helped to improve health conditions. Plagues were less widespread. The death rate fell, and the life span was extended.

Despite some conversions, Jewish morale had not been broken. Jews proudly adhered to the religion of their fathers. The Jews of one country willingly extended aid, in time of need, to their brothers in distress. In France, for example, Adolphe Crémieux had founded the Alliance Israélite Universelle whose motto was, "All Israelites are brothers." The Alliance built schools in Algiers, Morocco, Syria, Palestine,

Egypt and other countries where French influence was strong. Crémieux worked hand in hand with Montefiore to uphold the honor of the Jew.

Moses Montefiore served as president of the Board of Deputies of British Jews for over 30 years. Younger men finally succeeded him in the leadership of this group, but age did not diminish Montefiore's willingness to aid his brothers. When at the age of 93 he learned that many Jews were suffering as a result of the Russo-Turkish war he organized a relief fund. He offered to travel to Turkey to help. His telegram read:

"Should my presence in Constantinople or Adrianople be deemed in any way beneficial to the sufferers, I shall be ready to proceed there without delay."

This was certainly an extraordinary offer for a man of 93.

Montefiore's 100th birthday was celebrated by Jews throughout the world. A procession, miles in length, composed of civic officials and delegates from far and near, paraded past Montefiore's home. The harbor was illuminated and large bonfires were lighted to mark this unique event. One of the most interesting features of the procession was the traveling carriage in which Montefiore rode through the countries of Europe when on his historic missions. Like Moses the Lawgiver "his eyes were not dim, nor his natural force abated."

Montefiore breathed his last on July 28, 1885 at the age of 101. He had become almost a legend. As one author wrote, "His had become a name with a magic touch, uplifting the whole race in its own self-respect and self-confidence."

EXERCISES

I. Moses Montefiore or Lionel de Rothschild? (Review section 1, pages 180 to 182.)

1. _____ was born in Leghorn, Italy in 1784.

2. _____ was elected sheriff of London.

3. _____ was elected by the City of London to serve in the House of Commons.
4. _____ led a Jewish delegation to congratulate Victoria when she became queen.
5. _____ was the first Jew to serve in the House of Commons.

II. Complete each sentence. (Review section 2, pages 183 to 184.)

Crémieux, Mehemet Ali, Montefiore, Sultan, Victoria

1. _____, as head of the Board of Deputies of British Jews, helped free the imprisoned Jews of Damascus.
2. _____, a leader of French Jewry, was part of the delegation which secured Justice for the Jews of Damascus.
3. _____ knighted Montefiore in honor of his achievements in behalf of the Jews.
4. _____ of Egypt ordered the governor of Damascus to free the prisoners.
5. "The Jewish nation shall be protected and defended," wrote the _____.

III. True or false? (Review section 3, pages 184 to 187.)

1. The Czar threatened to expel all Jews from Russia.
2. There were many Jews in the army of the Czar.
3. The decree was revoked because of Montefiore's appeal to the Czar in behalf of the Russian Jews.
4. Roumania granted all Jews equality when it won autonomy from Turkey.
5. Although Montefiore's life was threatened in Bucharest, he continued with his mission in behalf of the Jews of Roumania.

IV. Explain each quotation. (Review section 4, pages 187 to 191.)

1. "Entreat me not to leave thee."
2. "The kingdoms of idolatry will all change and disappear; thy glory alone, O Zion, will last forever."
3. "They recalled to memory how much exposed the

traveler was in former years to the attacks of a Bedouin."

4. "Begin with the building of houses in Jerusalem."

5. "Commence at once: begin the work this day, if you can."

V. Answer each question in a complete sentence. (Review section 5, pages 190 to 191.)

   1. When did Jews gain equal rights in Austria? In Italy? In Germany?

   2. What were the reasons for the growth of Jewish population?

   3. Where did the Alliance Israélite Universelle build schools?

   4. Why did Montefiore offer to travel to Turkey?

   5. How was Montefiore's 100th birthday celebrated?

VI. Questions for discussion:

   1. How did Montefiore and Rothschild help the Jews of England gain equality?

   2. What were some of the changes that took place in Jewish life during Montefiore's life-time?

   3. What was Montefiore's greatest achievement?

   4. Discuss the meaning of this quotation: "His had become a name with a magic touch, uplifting the whole race in its own self-respect and self-confidence."

THINGS TO DO

1. *The Jew in English Literature*—Form committees to bring in reports about the Jew in English literature. Among the books that might be discussed are Shakespeare's *Merchant of Venice*, Scott's *Ivanhoe*, Byron's *Hebrew Melodies*, George Eliot's *Daniel Deronda* and the novels by Disraeli, England's Prime Minister.

2. *Chart of Famous Jews*—Make a chart listing the names and accomplishments of famous Jewish leaders from the 13th through the 19th centuries. Include the following: Rabbi Meir of Rothenburg, Don Isaac Abravanel, Solomon Molcho, Donna Gracia Nasi, Don Joseph Nasi, Rabbi Isaac Luria, Rabbi Joseph Karo, Menasseh ben Israel, Asser Levy, the Baal Shem Tov, the Vilna Gaon, Moses Mendelssohn, Rabbi David Sinzheim, Sir Moses Montefiore.

CHAPTER XVI

RUSSIAN JEWRY

I. UNDER THE RULE OF THE CZARS

THE JEWS of Russia remained loyal during the Napoleonic wars. The Russian Czar, out of gratitude, adopted a more lenient policy for a few years. Soon the evil days returned. When Russia was stricken by famine in 1821 the blame was placed on the Jews. The old law compelling Jews to move from the villages to the towns was revived. The Jewish Pale of Settlement was a giant ghetto shutting in millions of helpless souls.

Czar Alexander I instructed his ministers to lessen the misery of those expelled by finding employment for them in their new homes. But no makeshift jobs could make the lot of these refugees happier.

Here is the description by one historian of what happened:

"Hordes of hapless refugees, with their wives and children, began to flock into the overcrowded towns and townlets. There they could be seen, stripped almost to their shirts, wandering aimlessly in the streets. They lived in frightful congestion, as many as ten of them being squeezed into a single room. They were huddled together in the synagogues, while many of them, unable to find shelter, remained on the streets with their families facing the winter cold. Sickness and mortality began to spread among them."

This was only a preview of the suffering Russian Jews were to undergo under the new Czar, Nicholas I who ascended the throne in 1825. Czar Nicholas set up a rule under which young men were drafted into the army for a period of 25 years. Jewish youths were required to undergo a special period of training for 6 additional years in cantons or army camps. Scenes of horror took place as children of 9 or 10 were snatched from their homes and impressed into service, perhaps never to see their parents again.

The Czar's frank purpose was to destroy Judaism by making these youths convert. Horrible tortures were used at the camps to force the young "cantonists" to betray their religion. Even the brutal guards were often moved by the loyalty and courage shown by the young soldiers who bravely clung to the faith of their fathers.

The experience of the "cantonists" is vividly portrayed in many a novel or short story. In the story "Tov" by I. L. Peretz we read of a youth, named Judah, who wandered with his teacher into the forest. There, surrounded by the trees and birds, the teacher mysteriously informed him:

"You are going on a long journey. Your name is Judah. Remember your name. Remain a Jew."

The next day the lad was kidnapped and impressed into service. Many years of torture and hardship followed. The soldier was falsely accused of a crime, but told he would be acquitted if he converted. To escape further torture Judah almost yielded, but suddenly his teacher appeared to him in a vision and he remained steadfast. One night while on guard he heard a passing civilian say that it was the first night of Passover.

Passover—the word brought back memories; Passover—the holiday of freedom. An irresistible desire came over him to recite the *Haggadah*—but he could not remember a single word. If only he could remember the first word; once he knew the entire *Haggadah* by heart. And then it came to him. "Slaves were we unto Pharaoh in Egypt." . . . One word after another came pouring forth—the words flowed like a river. And Judah was overjoyed.

And suddenly there appeared before him a vision of the teacher. The teacher smiled and whispered one word to him. He listened intently. The word was "Tov" ("Good!")

It was as if the teacher had said, "Good! Well done, Judah! You have remembered your name, and you have remained true to your name and to your faith."

What the author Peretz has described in story form was indeed the soul-searing experience of thousands of youths who despite 31 years of hardship in the army of Czar Nicholas remembered they were Jews, and remained true to their precious heritage.

2. THE RUSSIAN NIGHTMARE

Czar Nicholas earned among Jews the title of Haman II. It is no wonder that they refused to send their children to Crown schools which the government set up for them. They feared, and rightly, that this was only a step toward conversion. Nicholas also tried forcibly to make Jews change their mode of dress.

Montefiore's visit in 1846 helped avert a decree of expulsion from the border cities. His plea for equality, however, fell on deaf ears.

Toward the end of his career Nicholas was involved in the Crimean War against France and England. To increase the number of Jewish soldiers, Nicholas raised the quota of those to be conscripted. There were new scenes of horror as heads of families were snatched by their captors to serve as cannon-fodder in the corrupt Russian army.

The clouds of darkness lifted for a while when Alexander II ascended the throne. Eager to introduce reforms, he freed 40 million serfs who had worked the soil as servants of their feudal lords. Jews too benefited. The cantons or army schools for Jewish youth were abolished, and Jews were conscripted in the same manner as non-Jews. Some Jews were given the right to settle in the interior of Russia, and soon there were flourishing communities in Moscow, in St. Petersburg and in other cities. As railroads were built and industry expanded, Jews found new means of employment. Some Jews gained prominence as physicians.

Although Alexander freed the serfs, he refused to grant political freedom. His refusal to free the Russian people from political slavery cost him his life.

He met his death on March 1, 1881 in one of the streets of St. Petersburg when dynamite bombs were hurled at him by a group of terrorists. Newspapers and government officials, in search of a scapegoat, began to insinuate that Jews were responsible for the assassination. Although there was no truth in the charge, it was enough to spark bloody pogroms (riots). Rumors began to spread that the new Czar, Alexander III, had given orders to exterminate the Jews. The scenes that took place were similar to the massacres during the Crusades. Where Jews organized self-defense units as in Odessa, they were arrested for carrying arms.

The United States, Great Britain and other countries joined in the cry of protest. The riots were succeeded by a series of legislative pogroms. Official policy was frankly proclaimed by the head of the Russian Church who said that the way to deal with the Jews was to let one third die, force one third to emigrate, and compel the remaining third to convert.

In May, 1882 the government adopted the infamous May Laws. Claiming that the Jews were responsible for the riots, since they "exploited" the people, the government set up new restrictions. Jews were expelled from many towns and villages. There were also wholesale expulsions from Moscow, St. Petersburg, Kiev, Kharkov and other forbidden cities. Leases and mortgages held by Jews were canceled. There were further restrictions on occupations. Everywhere Jews were at the mercy of police officials who demanded immense bribes if Jews were not to suffer severe penalties. Again an iron curtain separated the Jewish Pale of Settlement from the rest of Russia.

Russian Jews now knew that their only hope lay in escape. Societies were formed to help those who wished to migrate to America or England. Many Jews believed that the time had come to establish a homeland in Palestine.

One of the prophets of the new era was Dr. Leo Pinsker. A physician who had been honored because of his heroic efforts in behalf of the sick in time of plague, he had long believed in emancipation. But now he saw that this was an empty dream. He published a pamphlet called *Auto-Emancipation* (that is, self-emancipation). Jews could not wait for others to grant them emancipation; the time had come for Jews to free themselves. They must declare themselves a nation and ask for political recognition and a homeland. The natural place for such a homeland is Palestine. Only by breaking their own chains of servitude, could Jews win freedom.

Pinsker inspired a large number of Jews with his eloquent words: "Let 'Now or Never!' be our watchword. Woe to our descendants, woe to the memory of our Jewish contemporaries, if we let this moment pass by!"

3. HEBREW LITERATURE

The *Haskalah* or Enlightenment movement spread from Germany to Eastern Europe. Hebrew was revived as a literary language. Great authors and poets in Russia added a glorious chapter to the story of Hebrew literature.

Among the most famous of these authors is Abraham Mapu who, in 1854, wrote the first modern Hebrew novel, *The Love of Zion*. Living in the valley of tears which was Jewish life during the days of Nicholas I, Mapu dreamed of a better day when the free Hebrew nation lived on its own soil in the ancient Land of Israel.

The hero of this novel is a shepherd lad named Amnon who tends his sheep near the city of Bethlehem. In the springtime the beautiful Tamar, daughter of a Jerusalem prince, visits Bethlehem where she is attracted by the songs and dances of the shepherds. She plucks some flowers for the shepherd lad when suddenly a lion jumps out of the thicket. Amnon's arrow pierces the lion, and the grateful Tamar invites him to her home in Jerusalem.

In Jerusalem, Amnon hears the prophet Isaiah prophesy that some day peace will prevail.

> "And they shall beat their swords into plowshares,
> And their spears into pruning-hooks;
> Nation shall not lift up sword against nation,
> Neither shall they learn war any more."

That day of peace has not yet come, and Amnon himself is taken prisoner by the enemy. But the Assyrian army which came down like a wolf on the fold, suddenly falls prey to the plague. The Assyrians lift their tents and flee, thus freeing Jerusalem. Amnon and Tamar are reunited in the joyful city.

Thousands of copies of this romantic novel were sold among the Russian Jews who read of the glories of ancient Israel. Yeshiva students would hide copies of *The Love of Zion* between the pages of their heavy Talmuds, and secretly read of the adventures of Amnon and Tamar. And in their hearts was reawakened the love of Zion and the dream of returning to their ancient homeland.

4. YIDDISH LITERATURE

In order to appeal to the masses some of the authors began to write in Yiddish, which was the language of daily speech among Russian Jews. Writers like Sholom Aleichem, the humorist, and I. L. Peretz have created immortal works.

I. L. Peretz became famous as the master of the short story. Especially popular are his *Hasidic* tales. Peretz realized that the attitude of the *Hasidim* toward their leaders was superstitious; nonetheless, he caught the inner beauty of *Hasidism*. He depicted the *Zaddik*, or *Hasidic* Rabbi, as one who was close to the people and who understood the needs of the people.

His heroes are plain, simple people who have tasted the cup of suffering. This is true, for example, of the story "Bontshe Schweig." Bontshe was called by this name because he was always silent, because he could not give expression to the misery which filled his life. Bontshe suffered and suffered in silence. He made no impression on life itself—even when he walked there was no impression of his footstep on the earth beneath him. When he died, just a thin board was stuck into the earth to mark the spot where he lay buried. A day later, a strong wind uprooted the board and carried it some distance away. Bontshe was completely forgotten in this world.

But in the next world it was different. There Bontshe was received with heavenly acclaim and loud praises. And when Bontshe was called before the court of last judgment, the defending attorney stood up and recited his many virtues and told of how he had endured all suffering in silence.

When the prosecuting attorney was called upon, he stood up and said, "I have nothing to say against Bontshe. He suffered in silence, and I too will be silent."

The presiding judge thereupon turned to Bontshe and said, "Bontshe, seldom are we privileged to receive a soul of such extraordinary virtue. Your reward shall be great. Tell me, what is your wish; and no matter what it may be, it will be granted."

At first, Bontshe was bewildered, but when he realized that the court meant him, he turned to the court and said, "Please— each morning I should like to have a hot roll and butter."

To Bontshe, a hot roll and butter represented the height of luxury. For Peretz knew that there were millions in the Pale of Settlement who were deprived not only of bread and butter, but of many of the necessities of life. He depicted their suffering and became their champion. But he also showed how they rose above their poverty because of their courage and morale, and because of an inner strength and an inner faith which enriched their lives.

EXERCISES

I. Choose the correct word or phrase. (Review section 1, pages 194 to 196.)

   1. The Russians blamed the famine of 1821 on the _____. (French, Jews)

   2. In 1821 Jews were expelled from the _____. (cities, villages)

   3. Jewish youths were forced to serve as "cantonists" by _____. (Alexander I, Nicholas I)

   4. "Cantonists" served _____. (21 years, 31 years)

5. In the story "Tov," Judah's teacher appears to him in a vision during the holiday of _____. (Passover, Purim)

II. Discuss each topic. (Review section 2, pages 196 to 198.)

1. Crown schools
2. Montefiore's visit to Czar Nicholas
3. The attitude of Alexander II to the Jews
4. The May Laws
5. Pinsker's *Auto-Emancipation*

III. Who am I? (Review section 3 and 4, pages 198 to 200.)

1. I was the author of the first modern Hebrew novel, *The Love of Zion*.
2. I was the shepherd lad in *The Love of Zion* who saved Tamar from a lion.
3. I was the prophet who predicted that "nation shall not lift up sword against nation."
4. I was the author of short stories in Yiddish. I saw the inner beauty of *Hasidism*.
5. I was the suffering but silent hero of a short story. I was praised in heaven because of my many virtues.

IV. Questions for discussion:

1. How did the Czars differ in their attitudes toward the Jews?
2. Compare Russian Jewry and English Jewry.
3. What were the virtues of the heroes of the stories mentioned in this chapter?

REVIEW QUESTIONS

for Units Three and Four (pages 109 to 201)

1. Explain the importance of each of the following Jewish leaders: the Baal Shem Tov, the Vilna Gaon, Moses Mendelssohn, Moses Montefiore, Abraham Mapu, I. L. Peretz.
2. Discuss the attitude of each of the following rulers to the Jewish people: Napoleon Bonaparte, Queen Victoria, Nicholas I, Alexander II, Alexander III.
3. Identify: Chmelnitzki, Sabbatai Zevi, Rabbi David Frankel, Count Mirabeau, Gotthold Lessing, Abraham Fur-

tado, Rabbi David Sinzheim, Baron Lionel de Rothschild, Adolphe Crémieux, Dr. Leo Pinsker.

4. Explain the influence of each of the following publications: *Jerusalem, Nathan the Wise,* Mendelssohn's
translation of the Bible, *Ha-Meassef, The Love of Zion,
Auto-Emancipation.*

5. Discuss one problem of the Jews in each of the follow-
countries: 17th century Turkey, 17th and 18th century Poland, 18th and 19th century Germany, 18th
and 19th century France, 19th century England, 19th
century Syria, 19th century Palestine, 19th century
Russia.

6. Tell why each of the following is important in Jewish
history: Boleslav's charter of 1264, the Cossack rebellion of 1648, the French Revolution of 1789, the partitions of Poland in 1772, 1793, 1795, the Grand Sanhedrin of 1807, the defeat of Napoleon at Waterloo in
1815, the Damascus blood accusation of 1840, the
May Laws of 1882.

7. Discuss the goals and achievements of each of the following movements in Jewish life: *Hasidism,* emancipation, *Haskalah* (Enlightenment).

8. Explain each of the following terms: Ladino, *kehillah,
heder, melamed, Yeshiva, Zaddik,* ghetto, "cantonists."

9. Mention one event of importance in Jewish life con-
nected with each of the following places: Lublin,
Nemirov, Constantinople, Medzibuz, Warsaw, Vilna,
Volozhin, Berlin, Paris, London, Damascus, Jerusalem.

10. Discuss each of the following topics: "The Council of
the Four Lands"; education in Poland; conditions in
the ghetto; the Jewish Pale of Settlement; the rise of
Jewish population in the 19th century.

TEST

on Units Three and Four

I. Name the country in which each of the following took
place. (20 points)

1. The Cossack rebellion in 1648 under Chmelnitzki brought
about the ruin of many Jewish communities.

2. Sabbatai Zevi, the false Messiah, was born in this country, and gained many followers here.
3. Jewish youths were forced to serve as "cantonists" and in the army for 31 years.
4. Jews were given full political equality in 1858 when those elected to office were allowed to take an oath in keeping with their religious convictions.
5. Montefiore urged the Jews of this country to buy land, cultivate the soil and build new houses.

II. Who am I? (24 points)

1. I believed that God must be worshiped through joyful prayer. I told many parables to help people of simple faith. I was the founder of *Hasidism*.
2. I was the author of great commentaries that help explain the real meaning of the Bible, the Babylonian Talmud and the Jerusalem Talmud. I opposed *Hasidism* because of the superstitious belief of the people in *Zaddikim*.
3. I fought for emancipation of the Jews in Germany and in Europe. I translated the Bible into German, wrote for *Ha-Meassef*, and inspired the *Haskalah* (Enlightenment) movement.
4. I was president of the Grand Sanhedrin called by Napoleon in 1808. I helped the emancipation of French Jews by making clear the Jewish attitude toward civil law, usury, intermarriage etc.
5. I was champion of Jewish rights in Europe. I interviewed the rulers of Egypt and Turkey in 1840, the ruler of Russia in 1846, the ruler of Roumania in 1867. In each case I helped better the condition of the Jews.
6. I wrote stories in Yiddish about *Hasidism*. One of my stories is about a Jewish "cantonist" who remains true to Judaism. Another story "Bontshe Schweig" tells about a man who suffered in silence.

III. Which book deals with each of the following? (16 points)

1. Mendelssohn argues in this book that the state should not interfere with religious beliefs.
2. In this play by Lessing a Jew tells Saladin a parable about 3 rings.

3. This is the first modern Hebrew novel. A shepherd named Amnon falls in love with the beautiful daughter of a Jerusalem prince.

4. Dr. Leo Pinsker argues that Jews must free themselves and not wait for others to emancipate them.

IV. Select the correct city. (20 points)

Berlin, Constantinople, Damascus, London, Lublin, Medzibuz, Paris, Vilna, Volozhin, Warsaw

1. A representative of each *kehillah* met here at the time of the great fair. The representatives served as delegates to "The Council of the Four Lands."

2. Sabbatai Zevi expected to declare himself Messiah in this city. Instead he was thrown into prison.

3. Jews gathered here to gain inspiration from the Baal Shem Tov.

4. This city was known as the Jerusalem of Lithuania. The Rabbis of this city were opposed to *Hasidism*.

5. The pupils of the Gaon of Vilna formed a Yeshiva here which became one of the great centers of learning in Russia.

6. Jews were admitted to this city through a special gate. Mendelssohn came here to study under Rabbi David Frankel.

7. Jews of this city fought bravely under Kosciusko to defend Polish freedom.

8. The Rights of Man and the Constitution of 1791 proclaimed here gave Jews full equality.

9. This city admitted Jews in 1654 after a plea by Rabbi Menasseh ben Israel. It is capital of a country whose queen honored Jewish leaders who fought for equal rights for the Jewish people.

10. Montefiore and Crémieux helped free the Jews of this city who had been falsely accused of murder.

V. Discuss two of these topics. (20 points)

1. Education in Poland

2. Steps toward emancipation in Europe

3. The rise of Jewish population

4. Problems of Jews in *one* of these countries: Germany, England, Russia

UNIT FIVE

Jews in America

CHAPTER XVII

CITIZENS OF A NEW COUNTRY

I. THE REVOLUTIONARY WAR

THE 2500 Jews who lived in the 13 colonies at the time of the Revolution played an important part in the economic life of the New World. Some, especially in Newport, Rhode Island were merchant princes whose ships sailed the seven seas. In the South there were a few plantation owners. Some were fur-traders; others were craftsmen working in wood and metal, or tailors, bakers and candlemakers.

The Biblical ideal of liberty burned brightly in the hearts of the colonists. On the Liberty Bell which pealed the glad tidings of independence were inscribed the words of the Bible, "Proclaim liberty throughout all the land unto all the inhabitants thereof." The story of Moses who had freed his people from slavery in Egypt, inspired these liberty-loving patriots. Later, Franklin and Jefferson proposed that the seal of the United States be inscribed with a picture of the children of Israel escaping from Pharaoh by crossing the Red Sea. At the bottom were the words, "Rebellion to tyrants is obedience to God." Although the seal was never officially adopted, it shows us how the Israelite struggle for freedom served as an inspiration to the founding fathers.

Outstanding among the many brave Jewish soldiers who fought for American independence was Francis Salvador of South Carolina. He has been called, "The Southern Paul Revere." Salvador was a plantation owner who ardently embraced the cause of American liberty. He was one of the leading members of the First Provincial Congress and the Second Congress of South Carolina. He was on many important committees, and his advice carried weight.

The Cherokee Indians in South Carolina were encouraged by the British to attack the colonists. On July 1, 1776 the Indians overran the frontier, forcing many of the refugees to take shelter in the home of Francis Salvador. As soon as he learned the news, Salvador mounted his horse and galloped 28 miles to the residence of Major Andrew Williamson who was in command of the American forces. Gathering a small force, Williamson advanced to attack on July 3.

The Indians ambushed the American soldiers, pouring down heavy fire from their guns. Williamson's horse was shot from under him, but he was unhurt. Francis Salvador received three wounds and fell to the ground unable to move. After defeating the Indians, Williamson returned to take care of the wounded. He found Salvador in the bushes, scalped and mortally wounded.

This is how Williamson described the scene in his letter to the president of South Carolina.

"When I came up to him, after dislodging the enemy, and speaking to him, he asked whether I had beat the enemy. I told him yes. He said he was glad of it, and shook me by the hand—and bade me farewell."

Thus died Salvador, the day before the Declaration of Independence was signed, on the altar of American liberty.

Although there were some Jewish Tories, the large majority followed the lead of the eloquent patriot, Rabbi Gershom M. Seixas. He was a native American, born in New York in 1745, son of a Marrano Jew who came to America from Lisbon, Portugal. Gershom Seixas devoted himself to Jewish studies and was elected Rabbi of the *Shearith Israel* Congregation at the age of 21. He has the honor of being the first American-born Rabbi. Rabbi Seixas was in the pulpit when messengers brought word that the British were approaching. The sermon he preached on that occasion in behalf of liberty was so eloquent that all who were present wept.

Rabbi Seixas and the members of the congregation decided to flee from the British, and to remove the ceremonial objects of the synagogue. The departing patriots took with them the scrolls of the law, the candlesticks and the prayer-books. Rabbi Seixas brought these precious objects to his father's home in Connecticut where he stayed until 1780. He then moved to Philadelphia where he served as Rabbi of the *Mikveh Israel* Synagogue. The Rabbi was not the only ardent patriot in the family. One brother was an officer of the New York Militia. Another brother, who was a colonel in the Georgia Brigade of the Continental Army, took part in many dangerous missions.

Rabbi Seixas returned to New York in March, 1784. The historic ceremonial objects which he had guarded so zealously were restored; they are now on display in the present synagogue of the *Shearith Israel* Congregation. Gershom Seixas helped administer the oath at Washington's inauguration. He was also one of the original incorporators of Columbia College, serving as a trustee for almost 30 years. When the American nation was sharply divided later by partisan politics, Rabbi Seixas frequently raised his voice in behalf of unity. Until his death at the age of 81, he remained one of the outstanding religious leaders of the new country.

2. HAYM SALOMON

Haym Salomon rendered valuable service to his country as patriot and as financial agent.

He was born in Poland in 1740, and came to New York shortly after the French and Indian War. When the Revolution started, Haym Salomon was busily engaged in providing supplies for the American troops. For a time he was in the Lake George region of New York, helping the soldiers under the command of General Schuyler. Haym Salomon returned to New York City which was captured by the British on September 15, 1776. Salomon was accused by the British of being a spy and was thrown into the Provost, an old prison notorious for its dreadful conditions.

Haym Salomon might have rotted away in the old prison

like many another prisoner if it were not for his knowledge of languages. Finding it difficult to communicate with their Hessian mercenary soldiers, the British were greatly in need of interpreters. Salomon, who had traveled widely in Europe, knew French, German, Polish, Russian, Italian and Hebrew. He was freed and employed as an interpreter and supply agent by the Hessian officers.

Salomon proved to be of great service to the American prisoners. He helped them with money and arranged for their escape. He also spoke to the Hessian officers in their own language urging them to resign, since they were fighting for money against men who were struggling for freedom.

After he was released from prison Haym Salomon married Rachel Franks, daughter of a prominent member of the *Shearith Israel* Congregation. Meanwhile, the British officers learned of Salomon's activities in behalf of the Americans. Fortunately, Salomon was able to escape before they could imprison him a second time. He fled to Philadelphia in 1778, leaving behind, as he himself writes "his distressed wife and a child of a month old." Later the family was reunited.

In Philadelphia, Haym Salomon became a merchant and prospered. As financial agent and broker, he helped the French Consul and served as paymaster of the French army. His great skill came to the attention of Robert Morris who called on Haym Salomon to aid the American government by arranging for the sale of government securities. Salomon sold about a quarter of a million dollars worth of securities, a vast sum for those days. He also negotiated the war subsidies from France and Holland. He thus rendered a valuable service, and helped to finance the Revolution.

The generous Haym Salomon was always ready to assist delegates to the Continental Congress, like Thomas Jefferson and James Madison, who were in need of funds. He refused to accept any reward for this service.

Thus, James Madison, referring to Haym Salomon wrote: "The kindness of our little friend in Front Street near the coffee-house, is a fund that will preserve me from extremities."

Madison added that Salomon "obstinately rejects all recompense."

Haym Salomon was one of the active leaders of the Jewish community. He was an officer of the *Mikveh Israel* Congregation, and helped Rabbi Seixas raise funds for the new synagogue building erected in 1782. He frequently sent money to his relatives in Poland, and was overjoyed to receive news of his parents in 1783.

In a letter to his family he adds: "Should any of my brother's children have a good head to learn Hebrew I would contribute towards his being instructed."

The problem of separation of church and state had not yet been solved in America. Pennsylvania, for example, gave full political rights to all religious groups except that each official had to take an oath, "I do acknowledge the Scriptures of the Old and New Testament to be given by divine inspiration."

Rabbi Seixas, Haym Salomon and three other members of the community drew up a petition that this oath be changed. In their petition they called attention to the valuable patriotic services rendered by Jews. They wrote:

"The conduct and behavior of the Jews in this and the neighboring states has always tallied with the great design of the revolution. . . . The Jews of Charleston, New York, Newport and other posts occupied by the British troops, have suffered for their attachment to the revolution."

Although the petition was not immediately granted, it gained many supporters. In 1790 the Pennsylvania Constitution provided equal political rights for all religious groups.

Unfortunately, Salomon did not live to see that day for he passed away in 1785.

Salomon's brother-in-law Colonel Isaac Franks was also an outstanding patriot. He joined General Washington's forces at the age of 17. He took part in the Battle of Long Island and in the retreat to New York. He was captured by the British and held prisoner for three months, but escaped to the

Jersey shore in a small leaky rowboat with one paddle. He served in the army with distinction until after the defeat of the British.

Later, in 1793 Colonel Franks' home served for a while as the nation's Capitol when it was leased by President Washington while a yellow fever epidemic was raging. The bill for occupancy was rather amusing. In addition to the rent which was $66 for 2 months, Washington paid for a missing flatiron, one fork and four plates.

Francis Salvador, Rabbi Gershom Seixas, Haym Salomon and Colonel Isaac Franks are typical of the patriotic Jews who made a great contribution to the cause of American liberty.

3. LAND OF THE FREE

The spirit of the new nation was aptly expressed by Thomas Jefferson in the Declaration of Independence, "We hold these truths to be self-evident, that all men are created equal, that they are endowed by their Creator with certain inalienable rights, that among these are life, liberty and the pursuit of happiness."

The delegates to the Constitutional Convention were aware of the crimes committed by many European states which forced all citizens to accept one religion. Jonas Phillips, a former president of the Philadelphia congregation and a Revolutionary War veteran, sent an eloquent letter to the Convention pleading for religious freedom in this country. He pointed to the sacrifices made by Jews during the Revolutionary War, saying: "They have supported the cause, have bravely fought and bled for liberty."

The Constitution included a ruling that no religious test shall be required of those elected to federal office. The First Amendment, adopted in 1791, provided: "Congress shall make no law respecting an establishment of religion or prohibiting the free exercise thereof."

It might be added that the framers of the Constitution were inspired by the Biblical ideals of brotherhood and justice.

They regarded the rules drawn up by Moses as an example of a just constitution. The president of Harvard College called the government of the children of Israel under Moses "a perfect republic." They remembered how Samuel the Prophet had warned against the tyranny of kings, and in his spirit they tried to set up a government free from oppression. One historian wrote, "Hebraic mortar cemented the foundations of American democracy."

The Constitution said nothing about election of state officials. New York State was the first to extend equality to all religious groups in 1777. In Virginia an attempt was made to adopt Christianity as the state religion. Jefferson and Madison, however, fought for religious freedom for all. In 1786 they succeeded in securing the passage of a law which removed religious discrimination. Thomas Jefferson regarded this as one of his three greatest achievements. He requested that the following epitaph be placed above his grave:

"Here was buried Thomas Jefferson, author of the Declaration of Independence, of the Statute of Virginia for Religious Freedom, and Father of the University of Virginia."

Within a few years Georgia, Pennsylvania, South Carolina and Delaware followed the example of New York and Virginia. Other states moved more slowly. The fight in Maryland for equal rights for all religious groups was particularly bitter. It was led by a man named Thomas Kennedy. Year after year Kennedy would introduce a bill in the Maryland House of Delegates granting full political rights to all citizens regardless of creed.

"Religious liberty does not exist in Maryland," he wrote in his report, "for religious liberty cannot be said to exist under any government where men are not permitted to worship God in the manner most agreeable to the dictates of their own consciences. . . . It becomes our interest, as well as our duty, to let the world know that in Maryland, as well as in the other states, civil and religious liberty is enjoyed in its fullest extent."

Kennedy showed how absurd it was for Maryland to exclude Jews from state office when several Jews living in Maryland were already serving in federal posts. He pointed out that a Jew born in Maryland was qualified according to the Constitution, to serve as president of the United States, yet he was barred by Maryland from holding state office.

Thomas Kennedy's opponents made a burning issue of what they called "The Jew Bill." Kennedy was defeated when he ran for reelection. The cause of civil liberty was so vital, however, that Kennedy would not admit defeat. He ran for office again in 1824, and reintroduced the bill which was passed by one vote on the last day of the session. The bill which finally became law in 1826 made provision for a special oath for officials professing the Jewish religion.

A full half century was yet to pass before every state in the Union followed suit. It was not until 1876 that the State of New Hampshire abolished all discriminatory clauses. Thus Jews throughout the United States had now become equal before the law.

4. GEORGE WASHINGTON AND THE JEWISH CONGREGATIONS

As first president of the United States, George Washington set an example of good will for all to follow.

After his election to the presidency the Hebrew Congregation of Savannah sent Washington a letter of congratulations. They praised his heroism in time of war and his wise guidance in time of peace. They also expressed gratitude that his fine example had helped to dispel the "cloud of bigotry and superstition." They ended by wishing him happiness, good health and long life. Washington replied by thanking them for their good wishes. He rejoiced that enlightened nations were beginning to show liberality toward all religious groups. May God who delivered the Hebrews from bondage in Egypt, he wrote, "continue to water them with the dews of Heaven."

The congregations of Charleston, New York, Philadelphia and Richmond later sent a similar letter. They stated that

Washington's sword had opened the way to freedom, which his wise leadership was now making secure. They ended with these words, "To the eternal God who is thy refuge, we commit in our prayer the care of thy precious life." Washington's reply was most cordial. He not only asked God's blessings on the Hebrew congregations, but expressed satisfaction that the spirit of good will shown toward each other by various groups in America "stands unrivalled in the history of nations."

Perhaps the most eloquent of the precious Washington letters was the one sent to the Jews of Newport. When Washington visited Newport, Rhode Island in the summer of 1790, the Hebrew Congregation sent him a letter of welcome. They gave thanks unto God that they were free citizens of a country which did not encourage bigotry and persecution. They prayed that "the angel who conducted our forefathers through the wilderness into the promised land, may graciously conduct you through all the dangers and difficulties of this mortal life." The letter was signed by the leader of the congregation, Moses Seixas, older brother of Rabbi Seixas.

Washington was grateful for the cordial welcome he received in Newport, since many people in Rhode Island were strongly opposed to the newly-adopted Constitution. In his reply to the Hebrew Congregation he stated that tolerance was not enough. All groups had inherent natural rights, and the government "which gives to bigotry no sanction" only requires that people conduct themselves as good citizens.

The full text of the letter follows:

"Gentlemen,

"While I receive with much satisfaction your address replete with expressions of affection and esteem; I rejoice in the opportunity of assuring you that I shall always retain a grateful remembrance of the cordial welcome I experienced in my visit to Newport from all classes of citizens.

"The reflection on the days of difficulty and danger which are past is rendered the more sweet from a consciousness that they are succeeded by days of uncommon prosperity and security. If we have wisdom to make the best use of the advantages with which we are now favored, we cannot fail, under the just administration of a good government to become a great and a happy people.

"The citizens of the United States have a right to applaud themselves for having given to mankind examples of an enlarged and liberal policy, a policy worthy of imitation.

"All possess alike liberty of conscience and immunities of citizenship. It is now no more that toleration is spoken of, as if it was by the indulgence of one class of people, that another enjoyed the exercise of their inherent natural rights. For happily the government of the United States, which gives to bigotry no sanction, to persecution no assistance, requires only that they who live under its protection should demean themselves as good citizens, in giving it on all occasions their effectual support.

"It would be inconsistent with the frankness of my character not to avow that I am pleased with your favorable opinion of my administration, and fervent wishes for my felicity.

"May the children of the Stock of Abraham, who dwell in this land, continue to merit and enjoy the good will of the other inhabitants, while every one shall sit in safety under his own vine and fig-tree, and there shall be none to make him afraid.

"May the Father of all mercies scatter light and not darkness in our paths, and make us all in our several vocations useful here, and in his own due time and way everlastingly happy.

G. Washington"

The original manuscript of this letter rests in the Library of Congress in Washington. It was placed on display on the "Freedom Train" that toured the country in 1947, for this is one of the priceless documents of American history.

EXERCISES

I. Answer each question in a complete sentence. (Review section 1, pages 207 to 209.)

1. What were the occupations of Jews in America at the time of the Revolution?
2. How did the Bible inspire American patriots?
3. In what way was Francis Salvador an outstanding patriot?
4. What was the attitude of Rabbi Gershom Seixas to the cause of the Revolution?
5. What happened to the sacred objects belonging to the *Shearith Israel* Synagogue during the Revolutionary War?

II. Match. (Review section 2, pages 209 to 212.)

Column A	Column B
Isaac Franks	1. Stayed at the home of a Jewish patriot during an epidemic
James Madison	2. Received financial assistance from a Jewish patriot
Haym Salomon	3. Served as Rabbi of the *Shearith Israel* Congregation
Gershom Seixas	4. Escaped from the British in a rowboat
George Washington	5. Helped finance the Revolution

III. Name the state. (Review section 3, pages 212 to 214.)

1. The first state to provide in its constitution for religious and civil equality for all groups
2. The state for which Thomas Jefferson wrote the statute for religious freedom
3. The state in which the *Mikveh Israel* Congregation is situated
4. The state where Thomas Kennedy fought for religious freedom
5. The last state to abolish political discrimination against religious groups

IV. Explain the following quotations from Washington's letter. (Review section 4, pages 214 to 216.)

1. "The reflection on the days of difficulty and danger which are past is rendered the more sweet from a consciousness that they are succeeded by days of uncommon prosperity and security."

2. "All possess alike liberty of conscience."

3. "It is now no more that toleration is spoken of."

4. "For happily the government of the United States, which gives to bigotry no sanction, to persecution no assistance, requires only that they who live under its protection should demean themselves as good citizens."

5. "May the children of the Stock of Abraham, who dwell in this land, continue to merit and enjoy the good will of the other inhabitants."

V. Questions for discussion:

1. What contributions did Jews make to the cause of the Revolution?

2. What was meant by the historian who wrote: "Hebraic mortar cemented the foundations of American democracy"?

3. Brotherhood Week is celebrated during the week in which Washington's birthday falls. Why is this an appropriate time for Brotherhood Week?

THINGS TO DO

1. *Play*—Act out a play dealing with one of the historic events mentioned in this chapter. The "Eternal Light," for example, broadcast a stirring dramatization called "Thomas Kennedy." Copies of this script may be obtained by writing to "Eternal Light," 3080 Broadway, New York.

2. *Brotherhood Week*—Arrange an appropriate assembly in honor of Washington's birthday. Read an excerpt from Washington's letter to the Hebrew Congregation of Newport. Classes might prepare for this assembly by discussing the question, "How can we promote brotherhood in our school and community?"

CHAPTER XVIII

PROUD JEWS AND
PATRIOTIC AMERICANS

I. PATRIOTS

D EVOTION to their religion and love of their country—those were the great ideals of American Jews. In 1800, an opponent of Thomas Jefferson published an insulting letter about Major Benjamin Nones saying that he was a Jew and that he believed in a republic rather than in a monarchy.

This was the reply of Major Nones:

"*I am a Jew.* I glory in belonging to that persuasion, . . . which has preserved its faith secure and undefiled, for near three thousand years."

As for the second charge he wrote:

"I have not been so proud or so prejudiced as to renounce the cause for which I have fought, as an American throughout the whole of the Revolutionary War. . . . For three and twenty years I felt no disposition to change my political any more than my religious principles."

He then adds that as a Jew he is grateful for the privileges extended by republics to Jews.

"In the monarchies of Europe, we are hunted from society. . . . Among the nations of Europe we are inhabitants everywhere, but citizens nowhere unless in republics. . . . In republics we have rights, in monarchies we live but to experience wrongs."

American Jews again fought bravely for their new country during the War of 1812. There were 30 Jews in the garrison of Fort McHenry whose gallant defense inspired "The Star-Spangled Banner." Haym Salomon's son was an officer. Two members of the Nones family were enrolled in the ranks. Joseph Phillips, another volunteer, was the son of Jonas Phillips, the patriot who had fought in the Revolutionary War and who had written an eloquent plea for religious freedom to the Constitutional Convention. David Seixas, son of the patriotic Rabbi Seixas, also fought in the War of 1812. Three other members of his family were officers.

One of the most daring Jews was Captain John Ordronaux. In one month of war he hauled in nine British ships. Once his men began to retreat when a British crew boarded his boat. He stopped the retreat by threatening to blow up the magazine with a lighted match which he held in his hand.

Uriah P. Levy was a sailing-master during the War of 1812. He was put in charge of a prize-ship he had captured, but was taken prisoner by the British. After the war Levy continued to rise in rank. He was often the victim of racial prejudice in the Navy. A proud Jew, he warned that prejudice was a threat to every group in America. Shortly before the Civil War he was made a Commodore. One of his greatest achievements was the abolition of flogging in the Navy. Commodore Levy was a great admirer of Thomas Jefferson. He purchased Jefferson's home Monticello in Virginia, and helped to preserve this memorial of one of America's founding fathers.

The inscription on Commodore Levy's tombstone reads:

"He was the father of the law for abolition of the barbarous practice of corporal punishment in the United States Navy."

2. JUDAH TOURO

Another heroic veteran of the War of 1812 was the great philanthropist, Judah Touro.

Judah's father, Rabbi Isaac Touro, was minister of the famous Newport Congregation at the time when the historic building was erected in 1763. Beneath the altar is a secret trapdoor and passage leading to the basement. It is believed that this sealed tunnel was a feature of Marrano synagogues, which were provided with a means of escape in case of discovery by officers of the Inquisition. A frequent visitor to the synagogue was Ezra Stiles, president of Yale College. He studied Hebrew with Rabbi Touro, and later made it a compulsory subject at Yale. He would deliver his commencement address in Hebrew.

Judah was born on June 16, 1775, the day after George Washington had been made Commander-in-Chief of the colonial forces, and the day before the battle of Bunker Hill. When the British captured Newport, the synagogue was temporarily converted into a hospital. The Touro family went to Jamaica in the West Indies where the Rabbi died after a few years. Judah later grew up in the home of his uncle in Boston.

Judah fell madly in love with his cousin, Catherine Hays. His uncle was violently opposed to their marriage believing that cousins should not marry. He sent Judah on a long journey to the Mediterranean, in the expectation that Judah would forget his love for Catherine. Judah's boat was attacked by a French privateer. Judah showed great courage, and succeeded in safely bringing his profitable cargo to Boston. Judah's hope that his uncle would now relent came to naught. He and Catherine were forced to separate, each one taking a vow never to marry—a vow which they never broke.

The disappointed lover sailed for New Orleans, then in French hands. A year later Jefferson bought Louisiana from Napoleon, and New Orleans became an American seaport. Judah engaged in commerce and prospered. When war broke out with England, Touro took part in the defense of the city under General Andrew Jackson.

Judah Touro volunteered on January 1, 1815 for the dangerous mission of bringing shells and ammunition from the magazine to the battery. The terrible cannonading by the British made this a hazardous task. While crawling over an ex-

posed strip of land, Touro was struck in the thigh by a twelve
pound shot which produced a ghastly wound. He would
probably have died from his wound were it not for his loyal
Christian friend, Rezin Shepherd, who searched the battle-
ground for his wounded comrade and dragged him back to
safety. For a year Touro lay in agony, but finally recovered.

Touro became extremely wealthy. Rezin Shepherd, for a
while, served as his agent and associate. Touro, unmarried, devoted much of his wealth to charity. The Bunker Hill Monument, for example, remained neglected and uncompleted despite the eloquent appeals of Daniel Webster. A citizen of
Boston named Amos Lawrence and Judah Touro supplied the
necessary funds. There was general rejoicing throughout the
country, and the donors were widely acclaimed.

Every Jewish cause was close to the heart of Judah Touro.
He built a synagogue for the Jewish community of New
Orleans, now known as the Touro Synagogue. A hospital,
called the Touro Infirmary, is one of the largest hospitals in
the South. He provided for the preservation of the historic
synagogue in Newport, now a national shrine, where his father once served as Rabbi. Impressed by the romantic story
of Warder Cresson, American Consul in Jerusalem who became a convert to Judaism, he sent funds to Cresson to establish a Jewish agricultural colony near Jerusalem. When it was
discovered that there was a colony of Chinese Jews in Kai-
feng Fu, China, Touro established a society to help these Jews
who had been isolated from their brethren for many centuries.

Touro's gifts were not confined to his own people. When
he heard that the First Congregational Church was in danger
of losing its house of worship because of financial difficulties,
he purchased the building and presented it to the church. He
was made a liberal offer for the property by a merchant but
replied, "There is not enough money in the world to buy it."
When the building later burnt down he purchased another
building for the use of the church.

Touro established the Touro Free Library of New Or-

THE NEWPORT SYNAGOGUE—A NATIONAL AMERICAN SHRINE

leans; he supported Tulane University; he helped build Touro
Park in Newport. In most cases the contributions were secret,
but after Touro's death his gifts became known and the institutions were named after him.

His generosity extended to many individuals. He owned
but one slave whom he set free after making sure of his future
security. He also freed the slaves in the Shepherd household
where he lived, and assisted them to a fresh start in life.

Touro died in 1854 at the age of 79. His will has become
famous. He left a large sum of money to the Jews of Jerusalem, naming Moses Montefiore as the agent. Montefiore
made a special visit to Jerusalem, and established the Touro
houses in memory of the philanthropist. A generous gift made
it possible for Mount Sinai Hospital in New York, now one of
the most famous hospitals in the world, to erect its first building. Every major congregation in the country was remembered. In all, 65 Jewish organizations were aided.

Rezin Shepherd was made one of the executors of the will.
Touro referred to him as "my dear, old and devoted friend
to whom, under Divine Providence, I was greatly indebted
for the preservation of my life when I was wounded on the
1st of January, 1815." Shepherd was designated the heir of
the residue after all the legacies were paid.

Nor did Touro forget Catherine Hays. He left a generous
gift to her "as an expression of the kind remembrance in
which that esteemed friend is held by me." It is believed that
a lovers' correspondence had been carried on between them
for over 50 years, although they never met after Touro's departure from Boston. Alas, Judah did not know that Catherine
Hays, who had never married, died in Richmond, Virginia
two weeks before he did. According to one writer, Touro in
delirium during his last illness "talked of walking in a beautiful garden with Catherine Hays, his first and only love."

Touro was buried in the old cemetery at Newport, near
the historic synagogue. The inscription on his tombstone reads
in part:

To the Memory of
Judah Touro
The last of his name
He inscribed it in the Book of
Philanthropy
To be remembered forever

3. MORDECAI NOAH—FIRST AMERICAN ZIONIST

One of the most colorful leaders of that period was Mordecai M. Noah. He was born in Philadelphia in 1785, a descendant of Dr. Samuel Nunez, the Marrano doctor who had escaped so dramatically from the Inquisition and who had helped found the colony of Georgia. Mordecai Noah's father served in the Revolutionary War under Washington. There is a family tradition that Washington attended the wedding of Mordecai's parents and signed the marriage contract as a witness.

Orphaned at an early age, Mordecai Noah was brought up in the home of his grandfather, the patriotic Jonas Phillips. For a time he attended the school in New York, maintained by the *Shearith Israel* Congregation and headed by Rabbi Seixas, where he studied both Hebrew and secular subjects.

A journalist, Noah became active in politics as a supporter of the party of Jefferson and Madison. One of his political enemies challenged him to a duel with pistols at ten paces because of an article Noah had written. Noah wounded his opponent in the leg; both duellists then rode home in the same carriage, now that their quarrel had been settled on the field of honor.

As a reward for his journalistic support, Mordecai Noah was appointed by President Madison, during the War of 1812, to serve as Consul in the Kingdom of Tunis. Noah set sail in May, 1813. His boat was captured by the British on July 4, 1813, and Noah was sent as a prisoner-of-war to London. He was finally released, and, after further adventures, he proceeded to Tunis where he gallantly defended the honor of the United States. Often his life was in danger. He succeeded in rescuing several Americans held prisoner in Algiers.

To his amazement Noah received a letter on July 30, 1815 from James Monroe, Secretary of State, which said:

"At the time of your appointment, as Consul at Tunis, it was not known that the religion which you profess would form any obstacle to the exercise of your Consular functions. Recent information, however, on which entire reliance may be placed, proves that it would produce a very unfavorable effect. In consequence of which, the President has deemed it expedient to revoke your commission."

Noah was stunned by this blow. After having defended his country, despite personal danger, to be dismissed because of prejudice!

"I find my own government," he wrote, "the only protector I can have . . . violating my rights, and insulting my feelings, and the religious feelings of a whole nation. O! shame, shame!"

When he returned to the United States, Noah demanded vindication. After a long inquiry, his course of action as Consul was found to be justified. Nothing was said about Noah's religion. James Madison, however, wrote to Noah:

"It was certain, that your religious profession was well known at the time you received your commission, and that in itself could not be a motive in your recall."

Major Noah later received other political appointments. In 1822 he was made sheriff of New York.

"Pity," said one opponent, "that Christians are to be hereafter hung by a Jew."

"Pretty Christians," answered Noah, "to require hanging at all."

When a yellow fever epidemic threatened, Mordecai Noah released the prisoners confined in debtors' jail. As a result he had to pay many of the debts due the creditors.

Mordecai Noah enjoyed a distinguished career as editor and

dramatist. Most of his plays dealt with patriotic themes. For a while he served on the bench as a judge.

During all this time he was a leading spokesman for the Jewish community. At the consecration of the new building of the *Shearith Israel* Congregation, Mordecai Noah hinted that the time might soon come when the Jews might wrest Palestine from the Turks and restore a Jewish government. Meanwhile, his travels in Europe and North Africa convinced him that something must be done immediately to aid in colonization of oppressed Jewish communities.

Noah decided on a grandiose scheme. He applied to New York State in 1820 for the purchase of Grand Island, near Niagara Falls, so that it might serve as an asylum for oppressed Jews. The request was not granted at first, but in 1825 Grand Island was declared open for public settlement. Noah persuaded a friend to purchase a large section of the island. He then made known his scheme for establishing a city of refuge, to be called Ararat. (Noah's ark in the Bible, rested on Ararat while the flood-waters receded.)

Mordecai Noah ordered an imposing cornerstone on which he inscribed *Shma Yisrael* in Hebrew. Below the Hebrew was the following inscription:

ARARat

A City of Refuge for the Jews

Founded by Mordecai Manuel Noah, in the Month Tizri 5586

Sept. 1825 & in the 50th year of American Independence.

On September 15, 1825, a day after Rosh Ha-Shanah, Noah arranged an impressive ceremony in nearby Buffalo. Soldiers in uniform and Masons in full regalia marched while the band played. Behind them came Mordecai Noah dressed in black as a Judge in Israel, wearing the judicial robes of crimson silk, trimmed with ermine and a richly embossed gold medal suspended from the neck. In an eloquent speech he declared that the Hebrew nation, oldest of nations, must some day regain its own land, its own country and government. Meanwhile, Ararat would serve as a haven of refuge to which Jews from all countries would come.

He also issued a "Proclamation to the Jews" in which he declared:

"I, Mordecai Manuel Noah, Citizen of the United States of America . . . and by the grace of God, Governor and Judge of Israel, have issued this my Proclamation, announcing to the Jews throughout the world, that an asylum is prepared and hereby offered to them, where they can enjoy that peace, comfort and happiness, which have been denied them through the intolerance and misgovernment of former ages."

Special mention was made of the Indians, whom he believed to be the Lost Ten Tribes. They were invited to reunite with their brethren at Ararat.

Major Noah's proclamation was ridiculed by Jewish leaders in Europe. Some of Noah's opponents claimed that the project was only a real-estate scheme. Noah soon abandoned the entire plan.

Mordecai Noah later emphasized the idea of the restoration of the Jews to Palestine. In 1844 he addressed a passionate plea to the Christians of America to help gain Palestine for the Jews.

"Here we can unfurl the standard, and say, 'God is with you; we are with you; in His name, and in the name of civil and religious liberty, go forth and repossess the land of your fathers. . . . The ports of the Mediterranean will be again opened to the busy hum of commerce; the fields will again bear the fruitful harvest, and Christian and Jew will together, on Mount Zion, raise their voices in praise of Him whose covenant with Abraham was to endure forever. . . . This is our destiny. Every attempt to colonize the Jews in other countries has failed: their eye has steadily rested on their own beloved Jerusalem, and they have said, 'The time will come, the promise will be fulfilled.' "

He returned again and again to this idea until his death in 1851.

Today we realize that Mordecai Noah was 50 years ahead of his time. Historians often call him, "The First American Zionist."

EXERCISES

I. True or false? (Review section 1, pages 219 to 220.)

   1. Major Benjamin Nones said that he was proud to be a Jew.

   2. Nones believed that Jews were better treated in monarchies than in republics.

   3. Captain John Ordronaux threatened to put his men in prison if they retreated.

   4. Uriah P. Levy rose in rank despite religious prejudice in the Navy.

   5. Uriah P. Levy helped abolish flogging in the Navy.

II. Choose the correct word or phrase. (Review section 2, pages 220 to 225.)

   1. Isaac Touro was Rabbi of the synagogue in _____. (New Orleans, Newport)

   2. Ezra Stiles delivered the graduation address at Yale in _____. (Greek, Hebrew)

   3. Catherine Hays was the cousin of _____. (Judah Touro, Rezin Shepherd)

   4. Judah Touro was wounded at _____. (the Battle of New Orleans, Fort McHenry)

   5. Touro contributed large sums of money to the Jews of _____. (Palestine, Russia)

   6. Touro is remembered as a _____. (philanthropist, scholar)

III. Complete each sentence. (Review section 3, pages 225 to 229.)
Ararat, Grand Island, New York City, Palestine, Philadelphia, Tunis

   1. Mordecai Noah was born in 1785 in _____.

   2. He helped rescue several Americans while he was Consul in _____.

   3. Noah served as sheriff of _____.

4. Noah asked New York State for permission to colonize Jews on _____.

5. Noah's haven of refuge was to be known as _____.

6. Noah is called "The First American Zionist" because he wanted Jews to form their own government in _____.

IV. Questions for discussion:

1. In what way were the people who are mentioned in this chapter, "proud Jews and patriotic Americans"?

2. Who was a greater man in your opinion—Judah Touro or Mordecai Noah?

3. What are the advantages of studying Hebrew in a public high school or college?

THINGS TO DO

1. *Hebrew in Colleges*—We have seen how Hebrew was taught in Harvard and Yale since Colonial days. Among the distinguished professors of Hebrew were men like William McGuffey, editor of the famous "McGuffey Readers," and Clement Moore, author of " 'Twas the Night Before Christmas."

Write to the college that you hope to attend and ask whether they will accept Hebrew for entrance credit, and whether they offer instruction in Hebrew.

2. *College Seals*—Several colleges use Hebrew words in their seals. Make a book-plate or book-mark using as a design the seal of one of these colleges. The Hebrew motto found on the Columbia College seal means "God is my light." The seal also contains "Lord" in Hebrew. Dartmouth's seal contains the Hebrew words meaning "God Almighty." Yale's seal consists of an open book with the words "Urim V' Tumim," meaning "Light and Truth."

3. *Original Story*—Little is known about Mordecai Noah's father, Manuel Noah. It is believed that he spent many years in Europe suffering from melancholia after his wife's death. There is a family tradition that when Mordecai Noah was in Paris he saw a man wearing a queue and dressed in a Continental uniform. This man turned out to be his father.

Write an original story about the disappearance and return of Manuel Noah.

CHAPTER XIX

GROWTH AND CONFLICT

I. GERMAN-JEWISH IMMIGRATION

THE LEADERS of the Jewish community in the Colonial era and in the early years of the republic were Sefardim. As we have seen, many of them were descendants of Marrano Jews who came to America via Amsterdam or London. The *Shearith Israel* Congregation, oldest in America, is often popularly known as "The Spanish-Portuguese Synagogue." Men like Rabbi Seixas and Judah Touro were of Sefardic origin.

It is a mistake to think that all of the early settlers were Sefardim. Asser Levy was of Ashkenazic extraction. Haym Salomon was born in Poland, but married the daughter of a prominent Sefardic Jew. The daughters of Rabbi Seixas, on the other hand, married Ashkenazic Jews.

German Jews now migrated to the United States in increasing numbers. So large was their influx, according to one Sefardic historian, that many of their German expressions became part of daily speech. Thus, even the Sefardim began to refer to a synagogue as "shule," or to greet one another on the Sabbath with the words, "Good Shabess." Sefardic housewives would honor the Sabbath by preparing "kugel" (pudding). The German Jews, likewise, learned the delights of *olmendigas* (meatballs) and of other Spanish foods.

Unfortunately, long-established families were sometimes intolerant and would look down upon newcomers. Because of this, and because their ritual was different, Ashkenazic Jews established their own congregations in the larger cities.

The German-Jewish immigrant was a hardy soul. Often, penniless on arrival, he would begin life in the new country as a peddler, going from farm to farm with his wares.

One immigrant wrote bitterly, "Here I must go peddling . . . sweat and carry my basket."

In the East new congregations were formed in cities such as Albany, Baltimore and Boston. Many of the immigrants pushed westward toward the frontier. They opened stores, became merchants and engaged in trade. In one Pennsylvania community there were Jewish tailors, milliners, cattle dealers, brewers, lens-grinders, watch-makers, a lawyer, a boatman and a mail agent.

Cincinnati was typical of the new communities that grew up in the first half of the 19th century. In 1817 Joseph Jonas, attracted by the descriptions he had read of the beauty of the Ohio Valley, came to Cincinnati. Jonas, an English Jew, had married Rachel Seixas, daughter of Rabbi Gershom Seixas. He was warned by a friend, "In the wilds of America, you will forget your religion and your God."

Jonas replied that maybe it was God's will "that a new resting-place for the scattered sons of Israel should be commenced, and that a sanctuary should be erected in the Great West, dedicated to the Lord of hosts."

Many of the inhabitants had never seen a Jew before. The story is told that people came to gaze at him, among them a Quaker woman eager to see "one of God's chosen people." She circled around him, examining him carefully, and finally said in disappointment, "Thee art no different to other people."

Jonas, who was a watchmaker and silversmith, prospered. The Jonas family was the only Jewish family in Cincinnati for two years. But then they were joined by other Jews from England and Germany, among them Abraham Jonas, brother of Joseph and also married to a daughter of Rabbi Seixas. In 1820 they celebrated Rosh Ha-Shanah with a public service attended by a *minyan* (quorum of ten). A congregation called "Sons of Israel" was organized in 1824, and met temporarily in a room. An appeal was circulated several years later among the older American congregations for assistance in erecting a synagogue building.

"Separated as we are," they wrote, "and scattered through the wilds of America as children of the same family and faith, we consider it as our duty to apply to you for assistance in the erection of a House to worship the God of our forefathers. . . . For the last four or five years, we have congregated where a few years before nothing was heard but the howling of wild beasts, and the more hideous cry of savage man."

Joseph Jonas records that among those who came to the assistance of the congregation were 52 Gentiles living in Cincinnati. He adds that the Jews in Cincinnati enjoyed the esteem of their neighbors as the group with the fewest drunkards, vagrants and violators of the law.

The synagogue was finally constructed in 1836. The dedication ceremonies were held three days before Rosh Ha-Shanah. It was an impressive sight. The leader of the procession marched before those holding the scrolls of the law. He knocked on the outer door saying in Hebrew, "Open unto me the gates of righteousness." The doors were opened from within, and the scrolls carried around the ark seven times. The torch-bearer lit the *Ner Tamid*, or Eternal Light, and the scrolls were placed within the ark as the choir sang.

Cincinnati was followed by many other communities. Cleveland, St. Louis, Louisville, Chicago, Milwaukee, Detroit, Indianapolis soon boasted organized Jewish communities. Jews settled in Texas and helped Sam Houston in the struggle for Texan independence. There were Jews with Davy Crockett at the Alamo. There were Jews among the Forty-niners when the gold rush began. In 1849 services were held during Yom Kippur in a tent in San Francisco. By 1850, there were two congregations—one of German Jews and one of Polish Jews.

The exciting events of 1848 in Europe gave new impetus to immigration. Revolutions broke out that year in France, Italy, Austria and Germany. The king of Prussia promised a constitution, and hopes for equal rights rose high in the hearts of the Jews. But the revolutions were crushed, and the disappointed victims turned in despair to the New World. Instead of hundreds, there were many thousands of Jews who came each year to the shores of America seeking new life and new hope.

At the time of the Revolutionary War there were about 2500 Jews in the colonies. By 1865 there were over 200,000 Jews in the United States. Jewry had increased a hundred-fold.

2. RELIGIOUS LEADERS

The most prominent religious leader in the pre-Civil War period was Isaac Leeser. Born in Germany in 1806, he came to America at the age of 18. He soon became known because of a series of articles by him defending Jews against anti-Jewish slanders. In 1829 he was invited to serve as Rabbi of the well-known *Mikveh Israel* Congregation in Philadelphia.

Rabbi Leeser was greatly concerned about Jewish education. Some of the congregations maintained schools where pupils received both an English and Hebrew education. Many Jews, however, obtained no religious education at all. With Rabbi Leeser's cooperation, Rebecca Gratz organized the first Sunday School for Jewish children. Rabbi Leeser wrote a text-book for the pupils in the form of a catechism (question and answer). Rebecca Gratz, a remarkable woman, was admired by many Americans because of her charm, wit and sterling character. It is believed that Sir Walter Scott modeled Rebecca, the heroine of the novel *Ivanhoe*, after Rebecca Gratz.

To promote an understanding of Jewish problems, Isaac Leeser began to publish a monthly magazine called *The Occident and Jewish Advocate* in 1843. Through this magazine, Rabbi Leeser combatted missionary efforts, opposed intermarriage, defended civil rights, promoted the formation of hospitals and charitable institutions and encouraged Jewish scholarship. The Jewish Publication Society, for example, owes its existence to the persistent efforts of Rabbi Leeser.

Congregations throughout the country looked to Rabbi Leeser for leadership. A vivid account of the formation of the Jewish community in Cincinnati was written by Joseph Jonas at the request of Rabbi Leeser, and published in *The Occident*. Judah Touro was in constant communication with Isaac Leeser when he planned the construction of a synagogue in New Orleans, and when he engaged a Rabbi to minister to the new congregation. Rabbi Leeser officiated at the consecration of the synagogue in New Orleans, as well as at the funeral of Judah Touro in Newport. Mordecai Noah, supported by Leeser, advanced a proposal for the formation of a Hebrew college in *The Occident*, and eloquently defended his ideas on the restoration of Zion in that magazine.

Rabbi Leeser saw that one of the great needs of Jews in America was unity. He was aided in these efforts by Rabbi Isaac M. Wise of Cincinnati who published a "Call to Israelites" in the pages of Leeser's magazine. Rabbi Wise pleaded for all Jews "to be united as one man."

To aid in unifying American Jewry, Rabbi Leeser became a "circuit rider." For sixteen weeks, in 1851, he traveled through the South and West visiting isolated Jewish communities. Upon his return he urged not only a closer tie among all congregations, but increased knowledge of Hebrew. He looked forward to the day when all worshipers would comprehend the Hebrew prayers, and when Hebrew "would cease to be a dead tongue, and take its rank among those called living languages." He dreamed of making America a center of Jewish learning.

Rabbi Leeser and Rabbi Wise cooperated in calling a conference of Rabbis in 1855. This attempt at unity failed, however, because of growing differences of opinion about the introduction of reforms in Jewish ritual and practice.

Together with Rabbi Samuel M. Isaacs of New York, Leeser helped to organize the Board of Delegates of American Israelites in 1859. This group was modeled after the Board of Deputies of British Jews, headed so brilliantly by Sir Moses Montefiore. Rabbi Isaacs became the first president of the new organization, and Rabbi Leeser served as its vice-president until his death in 1868. The Board of Delegates of American Israelites succeeded in defending Jewish rights throughout the Civil War and post-war periods.

One of Rabbi Leeser's most ambitious projects was the translation of the entire Bible into English. He felt that such a translation was needed since the King James Version of the Bible contained some Christian interpretations, and was also inaccurate in many places. He completed this giant task in 1853. It is an achievement for which he will long be remembered. His translation is still widely used. It was the standard Jewish version of the Bible until 1916 when the Jewish Publication Society translation was printed.

Rabbi Leeser had frequently urged the establishment of a school to train American Rabbis. In 1867, Maimonides College was opened for this purpose in Philadelphia with Leeser as president. Six years later, however, the school was forced to close its doors because of lack of means. In 1887 Leeser's successor as Rabbi of *Mikveh Israel*, Sabato Morais, created a new Rabbinical school called the Jewish Theological Seminary of America. The Seminary is now the nucleus for Conservative Judaism in America.

Meanwhile, Isaac M. Wise had become the leading advocate of Reform Judaism. He edited a magazine *The Israelite* to further his views. He compiled a prayer-book which became the basis for the order of prayers in Reform synagogues. In 1875, he founded the Hebrew Union College in Cincinnati and served as its president.

In 1896 the Rabbi Isaac Elchanan Yeshiva was founded in New York City for the training of Orthodox Rabbis. Later this school was expanded into Yeshiva University including a college, a graduate school, a medical school and other departments. Other Yeshivot were formed in various cities to encourage the study of Talmud and to train Rabbis.

Thus, the United States has become a center of Torah and of learning. Isaac Leeser's dream had come true.

3. THE SLAVERY ISSUE

Jews living in the United States, like other Americans, were divided on the question of slavery. Many Jews, however, were prominent in the cause of emancipation of the slaves.

The great French Jew, Adolphe Crémieux, appeared at an international antislavery convention in London in 1840. Speaking as a Jew he demanded freedom for all.

"I feel great pleasure in joining this Convention," he said, "because I am a descendant of those Hebrews who were first to proclaim the abolition of slavery; and I this day only repeat what the Jews have always admitted in principle. . . . The slavery of man by man is a perpetual crime against humanity."

Ernestine Rose, a Jewish immigrant and ardent advocate of women's rights, was an outspoken opponent of slavery. She referred to herself as "a daughter of the downtrodden and persecuted people called the Jews." Attacking slavery she said:

"Humanity recognizes no color, mind recognizes no color; pleasure or pain, happiness or misery, life or death recognizes no color."

Rabbi Sabato Morais, a native of Italy, came to minister to the *Mikveh Israel* Congregation in 1851 when Isaac Leeser resigned to devote himself to his literary work. From the moment he entered the pulpit until the outbreak of the Civil War, Rabbi Morais was a fiery opponent of slavery. Although many members of his congregation tried to silence him, Rabbi Morais preached what he felt to be right. It was he who later organized the Jewish Theological Seminary of America.

Rabbi David Einhorn of Baltimore was another ardent abolitionist. Preaching in a state where slavery was widespread, Rabbi Einhorn argued that all men, regardless of color, were made in the image of God. There were plots against the life of the Rabbi. On April 22, 1861 those in Baltimore in favor of secession began to riot. Friends warned Rabbi Einhorn that he was among those whom the mob intended to kill unless he displayed the rebel flag. A volunteer guard of young men from his congregation remained in his home ready to shield him against assault. At last, yielding to the pleas of the officers of the congregation, Rabbi Einhorn and his family fled to Philadelphia.

An anti-abolitionist was Rabbi Morris Raphall of New York who preached that slavery was not sinful, but that slave-owners must recognize that a slave is human and must be treated with kindness. Rabbi Raphall's anti-abolitionist views were violently opposed by Einhorn, Morais and others. Although an anti-abolitionist, Rabbi Raphall supported the Union. His son, Alfred, joined the Army, became a major and fought at Gettysburg where he was wounded and lost an arm.

When war came thousands of Jews were enrolled in the ranks, some wearing the blue and others the gray. Among those who championed the cause of the South was Judah P. Benjamin, confidential adviser to Jefferson Davis, who served as Secretary of War and Secretary of State for the Confederacy. He has been called "the brains of the Confederacy."

The attitude of Jews in the North, on the other hand, was eloquently expressed by Rabbi Samuel Isaacs who supported Lincoln's call for volunteers by publishing an editorial in *The Jewish Messenger* in which he wrote:

"Then stand by the flag! Whether native or foreign born, Christian or Israelite, stand by it, and you are doing your duty, and acting well your part on the side of liberty and justice!

"We know full well, that our young men, who have left their homes to respond to the call of their country, will . . . render a good account of themselves. We have no fears for their bravery and patriotism. Our prayers are with them. God speed them on the work which they have volunteered to perform!

"Let them, and all of us, renew our solemn oath that, whatever may betide, we will be true to the Union and Constitution, and *Stand By The Flag!*"

4. ABRAHAM LINCOLN AND THE JEWS

When Lincoln began his journey from Springfield, Illinois on February 11, 1861 he received a symbolic gift from a Jewish resident of Chicago named Abraham Kohn. The gift was a flag of the United States of America. Across the face of the flag was a Hebrew inscription from the Book of Joshua, *Cha-zak ve-e-matz*. This was the slogan used by Joshua when he led the Israelites into the promised land. It means, "Be strong and of good courage!"

Several months after the war began Congress passed a law providing for the appointment of chaplains. The law stated that the chaplain "must be a regular ordained minister of some Christian denomination." The Board of Delegates of American Israelites protested against this exclusion of Jewish chaplains. Rabbi Arnold Fischel of *Shearith Israel* was sent to Washington to request a change in the law. Rabbi Fischel was cordially received by President Lincoln who agreed that the complaint was a justified one, although the exclusion was probably unintentional.

Lincoln then sent Rabbi Fischel a letter in which he stated:

"I shall try to have a new law broad enough to cover what is desired by you in behalf of the Israelites."

Lincoln kept his promise. The law was changed in March, 1862 and several Rabbis were appointed to serve as chaplains.

Lincoln again showed his friendliness to Jews by seeking to prevent discrimination against American Jews in Switzerland. Although the Senate refused to ratify any treaty with Switzerland which excluded American Jews from the enjoyment of reciprocal rights, the Swiss continued to discriminate against Jews. Lincoln showed his feelings in the matter by purposely appointing a Jewish Consul to Zurich, Switzerland. It was not until 1873 that Switzerland finally granted all Jews full equality.

On December 17, 1862, Jews were shocked by an order issued by General Grant expelling all Jews from the Department of Tennessee of which he was in charge because of illegal cotton trade. Several merchants and peddlers had been trading in cotton with the Confederacy. Although some of the cotton speculators were Jewish, many were not. Condemning an entire group because of the sins of a few was a serious violation of justice.

The order, known as General Order No. 11, read:

"The Jews, as a class violating every regulation of trade established by the Treasury Department and also department orders, are hereby expelled from the department within twenty-four hours from the receipt of this order."

On January 3, 1863, the Jews of Kentucky, who were directly affected by the order, sent a delegation to Washington headed by a merchant named Cesar Kaskel. They obtained an immediate interview with President Lincoln.

After listening very patiently to their complaint, Lincoln said in a kindly manner, "And so the children of Israel were driven from the happy land of Canaan?"

Mr. Kaskel, bowing, replied, "Yes. They have come to Father Abraham's bosom to seek protection."

Father Abraham Lincoln replied, "And this protection they shall have."

He seated himself at his desk and drafted a note revoking Order No. 11.

A second delegation from Cincinnati which included Rabbi Isaac M. Wise and Rabbi Max Lilienthal arrived two days later. When they heard that the order had been revoked they requested an interview with President Lincoln to thank him for his understanding. Rabbi Wise records that Abraham Lincoln expressed surprise that General Grant should issue such an unfair order. (Grant later showed warm friendship toward Jews.)

President Lincoln then added: "To condemn a class is, to say the least, to wrong the good with the bad. I do not like to hear a class or nationality condemned on account of a few sinners."

Rabbi Wise in describing the interview wrote: "The President . . . convinced us that he knows of no distinction between Jew and Gentile, that he feels no prejudice against any nationality."

One of Abraham Lincoln's close friends was Abraham Jonas, son-in-law of Rabbi Seixas and one of the founders of the Jewish community of Cincinnati. Jonas had moved to Kentucky and later to Illinois where he studied law. Both Lincoln and Jonas served as legislators in Springfield, Illinois. Jonas was an ardent supporter of Lincoln and was appointed postmaster of Quincy by the President.

When the Civil War began, one of Jonas' sons fought for the Union and the others for the Confederacy. Charles H. Jonas, son of the postmaster, was taken prisoner by the Union Army. Abraham Jonas became critically ill toward the close of the war and kept asking for his son. Mrs. Jonas sent a telegram to their good friend, Abraham Lincoln, pleading that Charles be allowed to visit his dying father. Despite Army regulations, the kind President could not deny the wish of his sick friend. The official order read:

"Allow Charles H. Jonas now a prisoner of war at Johnson's Island a parole of three weeks to visit his dying father, Abraham Jonas, at Quincy, Illinois.

A. Lincoln"

Lincoln's death was a tragic blow to the entire country. The place he held in the hearts of American Jews can be judged from the tribute paid by Rabbi Max Lilienthal of Cincinnati.

Preaching in the Congregation "Sons of Israel," which Abraham Jonas had helped found, Rabbi Lilienthal said:

"We revered him, we loved him, we regarded him as a man of superior destiny, and entrusted willingly and thankfully to him the helm of our ship. . . . This man, with a smile for everyone and everything, with the welcoming grasp and winning word. . . . Yes, this man is Lincoln; behind this homely appearance beats a heart full of faith, love and charity. . . .

"We will forgive, as his example has taught us, the repentant sinner. Over the fresh grave of our hero, we will take him back to our heart, sharing with him our blessings and our rights. . . . We will stand firm to our Government and our flag, till the work thou hast so gloriously begun shall be brought to a still more glorious end. Smile on! thy name shall be as immortal as the truth of thy teaching. Abraham Lincoln, friend of the people, the poor and the slave, farewell! We will cherish and revere thy memory forever."

EXERCISES

I. Answer each question in a complete sentence. (Review section 1, pages 231 to 234.)

1. What are some German words or expression that became part of the daily speech of American Jews?

2. What occupations did the German-Jewish immigrants engage in?

3. Tell about the history of the first Jewish congregation in Cincinnati.

4. Describe the consecration of the first Cincinnati synagogue.

5. Why did many German Jews come to the United States after 1848?

II. Isaac Leeser or Isaac M. Wise? (Review section 2, pages 234 to 236.)

1. _____ was Rabbi of *Mikveh Israel* in Philadelphia.

2. _____ was an advocate of Reform Judaism.

3. _____ translated the Bible into English.

4. _____ was vice-president of the Board of Delegates of American Israelites.

5. _____ was founder of the Hebrew Union College in Cincinnati.

III. Match. (Review section 3, pages 237 to 238.)

Column A	*Column B*
Adolph Crémieux	1. Secretary of State for the Confederacy
Ernestine Rose	2. Author of editorial, "Stand By The Flag"

David Einhorn	3. Advocate of women's rights and abolition of slavery
Judah P. Benjamin	4. Rabbi who was forced to flee because of abolitionist views
Samuel Isaacs	5. French Jew who was delegate at anti-slavery convention

IV. Explain each quotation. (Review section 4, pages 239 to 242.)

1. "Be strong and of good courage!"
2. "They have come to Father Abraham's bosom to seek protection."
3. "I do not like to hear a class or nationality condemned on account of a few sinners."
4. "Allow Charles H. Jonas . . . a parole of three weeks."
5. "We will forgive, as his example has taught us, the repentant sinner."

V. Questions for discussion:

1. Compare the role of the Spanish Jews and of the German Jews in American Jewish history.
2. Rabbi Isaac Leeser was the outstanding religious leader of American Jewry in the pre-Civil War days. Show how this is true.
3. What was the attitude of American Jews to slavery?
4. How did Abraham Lincoln prove that he was a friend of the Jews?

THINGS TO DO

1. *Bible Translations*—a) Prepare a report on interesting Bible translations. Consult any standard encyclopedia.

b) Compare the King James translation, the Leeser translation and the Jewish Publication Society translation by studying typical Psalms such as Psalm 2 and Psalm 23. (All three versions can be readily found in any synagogue library.)

2. *Lincoln's Day Assembly*—Such an assembly might include a dramatization of "Lincoln and Jonas" or "Lincoln and Grant's Order No. 11." The reading of the excerpt from Rabbi Lilienthal's sermon would be appropriate. Brief talks might be given on a topic such as, "Lincoln—Friend of the Jews." Excellent material can be found in Philip Goodman's *Lincoln's Birthday*.

CHAPTER XX

"YOUR HUDDLED MASSES
YEARNING TO BREATHE FREE"

1. THE GOLDEN DOOR

WE HAVE already seen how the May Laws adopted by Russia in May, 1882 expelled Jews from the villages and forced them to crowd into cities within the Pale of Settlement. Entire communities were ruined. Whither could the Jew turn?

The magic word "America" gave the Jewish masses new hope. "In America Jews are treated like human beings," they heard. "America is the land of opportunity," people said. "We have heard," some would add, "that everybody in America is rich. They say that the streets are paved with gold."

America drew the immigrants to its shores like a magnet. A well-known poet, Joaquin Miller, expressed the feelings of the American people when he wrote:

"Rise up and come where Freedom waits
Within these White, wide ocean gates."

There were tearful scenes as the head of the family departed for Amerca. It might be years before he could save up enough money to buy steamship tickets for the other members of the family. Who knows whether the family would ever be united again? Often the immigrant would not be able to pay for the expenses of the journey, but organizations were formed in Germany, France, England and America to ease his path.

Upon his arrival in America the immigrant was dependent upon the mercy of relatives and *landsmen* (people from the same original community). Bewildered by a new language and new customs, the immigrant clung to his beloved "mama-loshn" ("mother-tongue"), Yiddish. A Yiddish press and Yiddish theater and Yiddish-speaking fraternal organizations helped the immigrant to retain his precious culture, and to adjust to the New World.

Immigrants fled not only from pogroms in Russia but from persecution in Roumania and from poverty in Galicia (the section of Poland absorbed by Austria). At first the immigrants arrived by the thousands, then by the tens of thousands and by the hundreds of thousands. In 1906 and 1907, 150,000 Jews a year came to the United States. Between 1880 and 1920, about two million Jews poured into the ports of America, chiefly New York.

The HIAS (Hebrew Immigrant Aid Society) is one of the major organizations which made these immigrants feel welcome. The files of the HIAS contain the following incident. On the day of his arrival an immigrant inquired, "Where is the police station in which we have to register?"

"You do not have to register with the police in America," he was told.

"Please, I don't want to get into trouble. Tell me where the police station is."

Finally when convinced that people were free to move about in America without police interference, the immigrant turned to his wife and said:

"Thank God, at last we have found a home."

Millions who in Eastern Europe knew nothing but poverty and persecution, discovered that at last they had found a real home in America.

As the boats neared New York harbor, the eager immigrants would strain to see the beacon light in the Statue of Liberty. On the base of the Statue of Liberty are inscribed the words written by a Jewish poetess, Emma Lazarus. Daughter of a Sefardic Jewish family, Emma Lazarus had devoted her early poems to themes not related to her people. Once, however, when she visited Ward's Island in the East River her heart

EMMA LAZARUS AND THE STATUE OF LIBERTY

was wrung by the sight of these unhappy creatures waiting for admission to the new land. She was inspired to sing the songs of her people.

In "The New Colossus," Emma Lazarus compares the new statue to the old statue Colossus which once stood in the harbors of Greece. Unlike the Colossus of old which stood for conquest, the new Statue of Liberty calls to the Old World, "Give me your tired, your poor, your huddled masses yearning to breathe free."

Here are the immortal words of this inspiring poem:

The New Colossus

Not like the brazen giant of Greek fame,
With conquering limbs astride from land to land;
Here at our sea-washed, sunset gates shall stand
A mighty woman with a torch, whose flame
Is the imprisoned lightning, and her name
Mother of Exiles. From her beacon-hand
Glows world-wide welcome; her mild eyes command
The air-bridged harbor that twin cities frame.

"Keep, ancient lands, your storied pomp!" cries she
With silent lips. "Give me your tired, your poor,
Your huddled masses yearning to breathe free,
The wretched refuse of your teeming shore.
Send these, the homeless, tempest-tost to me,
I lift my lamp beside the golden door!"

2. "BY THE SWEAT OF THY BROW"

The immigrant who expected to find the streets of America paved with gold, soon learned that the new country was not at all like the paradise he had dreamed about. He, like Adam, had to earn his daily bread by the sweat of his brow. Finding employment was not at all easy.

Many immigrants, like the German Jews before them, turned to peddling. But the peddler was no longer a traveling department store going from farm to farm. The peddler now carried small articles such as matches and pins; the day's profits were a matter of pennies. It was the hope of every peddler, after he had saved enough money to bring over the rest of his family, to open a little store or shop.

Some of the newcomers preferred industry to peddling. Swarms of immigrants worked in factories that manufactured leather, metal goods, cigars and other articles. Above all, the immigrants turned to the needle trades. For generations Jews in Europe had sewn their own clothing. This background became the basis for the tremendous role played by Jews in the garment industry.

Conditions in the regular factories were very bad; but in the "sweatshops" they were even worse. Contractors would take cloth or unfinished garments out of the regular factories and complete them in their unsanitary shops, usually located in a tenement flat, in an over-crowded basement, or in a dimly-lighted store. Wages in the 1890's ranged between $4 and $8 a week. During the busy season, workers were at their machines as much as 16 hours a day. During the "slack season," workers were unemployed and deprived of a livelihood.

This vicious system was finally overthrown through the efforts of the workers themselves who organized unions to improve labor conditions. Outstanding, for example, was the International Ladies Garment Workers Union, launched in 1900, which represented an industry where Jewish laborers were heavily concentrated. Gradually, hours were shortened, wages were raised and factory conditions were improved. A turning-point in this industry came with the crucial strike of 70,000 cloak-makers in 1910. This strike has become known as "The Great Revolt." It lasted two months and resulted in heavy losses for the manufacturers and severe suffering for the workers. The strike was finally settled by a great Jewish lawyer, Louis D. Brandeis, who served as mediator. A Board of Arbitration was organized to settle major disputes and a Committee on Grievances to solve minor issues. The agreement suggested by Brandeis served as a model for other industries.

Brandeis was greatly impressed by the willingness of both employers and workers, all of whom were Jewish, to cooperate in coming to a peaceful solution.

"What struck me most," he said, "was that each side had a great capacity for placing themselves in the other fellow's shoes. . . . They really understood each other. . . . They argued, but were willing to listen to argument."

Although a majority of the immigrants settled in New York, many moved to other cities such as Chicago, Philadelphia and Boston. The philanthropist, Jacob H. Schiff, initiated the Galveston Project, which arranged for steamship companies to bring immigrants to Galveston, Texas. In this way, it was hoped, the newcomers would spread out to the sparsely settled communities in the South and West. This project was only partially successful since it was natural for immigrants to settle near their relatives and friends.

Attempts were also made to settle Jews on the soil. The most successful of these colonies were in Carmel and Woodbine, New Jersey. Jewish youths were prepared for agriculture by the National Farm School in Daylestown, Pennsylvania, which was established by Rabbi Joseph Krauskopf. By 1954, there were over 100,000 Jews in America who earned a living from farming. The world's best known agricultural reformer was a Jew named David Lubin who organized the International Institute of Agriculture. Born in Galicia, he settled in California where he became a fruit-grower. After years of thinking about the problem, David Lubin became convinced that only through international cooperation could the farmer's lot be improved. As head of the International Institute of Agriculture, he organized help for the farmer on a world-wide basis. It has been said that Lubin will go down in history as one of the great benefactors of mankind.

3. THE TWENTIETH CENTURY

The history of the American Jew in the 20th century is really a study in itself requiring an entire volume. Only the bare outlines can be suggested here.

The Immigration Act of 1924 reduced the tidal wave to a mere ripple—only a few thousand Jews each year succeeded in gaining admittance to the United States. Immigrants sought new havens of refuge. Argentina, Latin America, Canada, Australia and South Africa attracted those fleeing the persecution and poverty of Europe. Palestine became once more the destination of the wanderers seeking a home and a homeland.

American Jews again and again displayed their ardent patriotism. 200,000 Jews served with the colors in World War I. Three times that number, 600,000 in all, served in World War II. They were on all the fighting fronts ranging from the torrid jungles of the Pacific to the frozen wastes of the Aleutians. 36,000 were cited for bravery. When the portrait of Meyer Levin, heroic bombardier in World War II, was unveiled in the Pentagon's Hall of Fame, the father tearfully said, "We gave something fine to our country." He spoke for all American Jews.

Jews gained distinction in many fields. In science there were men like Albert Einstein and Dr. Jonas Salk. In music there were composers like Ernest Bloch, George Gershwin and Leonard Bernstein. There were 2 Jewish members of the Cabinet, Oscar Straus, Secretary of Commerce and Labor under Theodore Roosevelt, and Henry Morgenthau Jr., Secretary of the Treasury under Franklin Roosevelt. Three Jews served as Judges of the Supreme Court, Louis D. Brandeis, Benjamin Cardozo and Felix Frankfurter. Herbert Lehman gained a national reputation as Governor of New York State and as a Senator in Washington. Presidential advisers like Bernard Baruch and Judge Samuel Rosenman helped with their wise counsel. Labor leaders like Samuel Gompers, Sidney Hillman and David Dubinsky were in the forefront in gaining better conditions for the workers of America. In art, sports, entertainment, industry and the professions Jews made valuable contributions.

By 1954 when American Jewry celebrated its 300th anniversary, the economic structure of Jews in America had changed in many ways. There were now 5 million Jews who had penetrated into every section of the country serving as merchants, salesmen, business executives, mechanics, workers, teachers, doctors, clerks and farmers. Jews were still prominent in the needle trades as manufacturers; the number of Jewish workers in these trades, however, had dwindled. There were but few peddlers; they and their children had succeeded in establishing themselves in trade or in light industries such as clothing and headwear, food, fur and printing. Eager for education children of immigrants had studied in colleges and universities and had entered professions such as medicine, law, pharmacy, teaching and civil service.

Jewish community life had prospered, always centering around the synagogue. Religious education, although attracting larger numbers, remained a serious problem. The Sunday School movement, founded by Isaac Leeser and Rebecca Gratz, had spread. Seeking to provide a more intensive education, many communities sponsored congregational weekday schools. The *Talmud Torah* in the early years was a school providing both secular and Hebrew education. This type of school was revived with the formation of the elementary Yeshiva or all-day school. The fact that many Jewish children received no religious education and that others discontinued their education at the time of *Bar Mitzvah* or confirmation was a matter for grave concern.

Anti-Semitism had by no means been eradicated. Nonetheless, the large majority of Americans followed the traditions of Washington and Jefferson and condemned bigotry and prejudice. New York State's Commission Against Discrimination served as a model for other states which aimed to eliminate bias through law and through education. Organizations like the American Jewish Committee and the American Jewish Congress protected Jewish civil rights. Jews were active in the interfaith movement, and helped organize groups such as the National Conference of Christians and Jews which sought to spread the ideals of good will and brotherhood.

American Jews never forgot their ties with Jews in other countries. Through the many organizations financed by the United Jewish Appeal large sums of money were raised to aid colonization in Israel and to provide overseas relief. Leaders like Justice Louis D. Brandeis and the eloquent Rabbi Stephen S. Wise gained support for the rebuilding of Zion both among Jews and Gentiles. The revered Henrietta Szold founded the Hadassah, the Women's Zionist Organization of America which promoted health and social welfare in Palestine. When the hour of decision came in 1947 and the United Nations debated the fate of Palestine, American Jews lent powerful support to the ideal of a new Jewish state.

4. 1654-1954

The 300th anniversary of the Jewish settlement in America was celebrated in 1954 with great enthusiasm. The Synagogue Council of America and the New York Board of Rabbis at a public gathering presented medals and citations to the 14 oldest congregations in the United States. (See page 311.)

Rabbi Abba Hillel Silver of Cleveland, addressing the American Zionist Council, listed the following as the outstanding achievements of American Jewry:

1—American Jews, as loyal and proud citizens of the United States, have made notable contributions to the welfare of the country in war and in peace.

2—American Jews have remained faithful to their religious heritage, and have built synagogues, schools and institutions of higher learning which teach the ideals of Judaism and the Jewish way of life.

3—American Jews have built noble institutions dedicated to human service and social welfare.

4—Amercan Jews have never failed to come to the aid of their brothers throughout the world in time of need.

5—American Jews rallied almost as one man to the task of building the State of Israel.

The Proclamation calling upon American Jews to join in

giving thanks for the blessings bestowed upon the Jewish community is indeed a stirring one:

To Our Jewish Brethren in the United States of America

PEACE BE WITH YOU AND YOUR NEIGHBORS

BE IT KNOWN UNTO YOU that in Elul 5714 (September 1954) the Jewish community of the United States will commemorate the 300th anniversary of Jewish settlement in this country.

BY THE GRACE OF GOD and under the protection of the Constitution of the United States, we have lived and prospered in this land. We have been an integral part of American life. We have worked with all other Americans in the never-ending search for the democratic way of life and for the light of faith. Our ancient prophetic ideals and the teachings of the sages have been foundation stones of this nation. Our work, our hopes, and above all, our living religion, have been among our proudest offerings to the American community.

IN SOME LANDS ACROSS THE SEAS our brethren have felt the searing flame of prejudice, persecution and death. We in America have had the sad yet inspiring opportunity to save the lives of scores of thousands—to bring comfort to the oppressed, to help in the making of a new and honored nation on the ancient soil of Israel, and to acquire a new recognition of our responsibility for human welfare in keeping with the ancient teachings of our faith. In some lands across the seas our brethren have been pressed to give up their religious beliefs and practices and to disappear in a well of namelessness.

BUT WITHIN THE HOME OF AMERICA we have succeeded in preserving the unique identity of the Jewish religion, worshipping in keeping with our historic tradition; and we have preserved our ancient teachings, our ethics, and our religious ideals in the free climate of our nation. Our religion is strong, as our American loyalty is strong.

MINDFUL OF THESE BLESSINGS and with deep gratitude in

our hearts to the God of Israel, who, in 1654, led our fathers to the shores of this great new land,

WE HEREBY PROCLAIM the period from Elul 5714 (September 1954) to the end of Sivan 5715 (May 1955) as one of thanksgiving, prayer, study and celebration of the American Jewish Tercentenary.

WE CALL ON ALL OUR BRETHREN throughout the nation to participate in the observance of this anniversary; to offer thanks unto the Lord for the blessings bestowed on us in America; to pray for the continued peace and prosperity of our country and all its inhabitants and to rededicate ourselves to the ideals of our faith within the freedom of American democracy.

EXERCISES

I. Choose the correct word or phrase. (Review section 1, pages 244 to 247.)

1. Jewish immigrants after 1882 came mostly from _____. (Germany, Russia)
2. The May Laws forced Jews to settle _____. (in cities, on farms)
3. *Mama-loshn* refers to _____. (Russian, Yiddish)
4. The "New Colossus" was a statue in the harbor of _____. (Greece, New York)
5. The Statue of Liberty pleads with the Old World to send those who are _____ to America. (poor, rich)

II. True or false? (Review section 2, pages 247 to 249.)

1. Many of the immigrants began life in America as peddlers.
2. Jews were prominent in the steel and coal industries.
3. Needle trades workers received high wages in 1890.
4. Louis D. Brandeis helped bring about peace in the garment industry in 1910.
5. Jacob H. Schiff helped organize the Galveston Project.
6. There are no Jewish farmers in America.
7. David Lubin helped farmers throughout the world by organizing the International Institute of Agriculture.

III. Identify each of the following. (Review section 3, pages 249 to 252.)

  1. Ernest Bloch 2. Louis D. Brandeis 3. Albert Einstein 4. Rebecca Gratz 5. Sidney Hillman 6. Herbert Lehman 7. Meyer Levin 8. Henry Morgenthau, Jr. 9. Oscar Straus 10. Stephen S. Wise

IV. Mention 4 great achievements of American Jewry. (Review section 4, pages 252 to 254.)

V. Questions for discussion:

  1. What was meant by Emma Lazarus when she wrote, "Give me your tired, your poor, your huddled masses yearning to breathe free."

  2. Compare the wave of immigration of Jews from Eastern Europe with the Spanish and German waves of immigration.

  3. What problems confronted the Russian-Jewish immigrants?

  4. What are some of the major problems of American Jewry today?

  5. What was meant by those who issued the Proclamation calling on Jews to celebrate the 300th anniversary of American-Jewish settlement when they wrote, "Our religion is strong, as our American loyalty is strong."?

THINGS TO DO

1. *Film*—Some interesting films dealing with Jews in America are:

  a) *Sons of Liberty*—The story of Haym Salomon

  b) *Of These Our People*—Contributions of Jews in America

  c) *With These Hands*—From the sweatshop to the modern factory as seen by a Jewish member of the International Ladies Garment Workers Union.

  d) *Music in America*—The contributions of outstanding Jewish musicians such as George Gershwin, Mischa Elman and others.

Information concerning these films as well as film-strips and recordings can be obtained by writing to the Jewish Education Film Library, 13 East 37, New York City.

2. *Project on American Jewish Life*—Committees might be formed to bring in reports on some of the following topics:

a) The Jew in Science
b) The Jew in Labor and Industry
c) The Jew in Sports
d) The Jew in Entertainment
e) The Jew in Music and Art
f) The Jew in Government
g) The Jew in World War II

3. *Family History*—Inquire of your parents and grandparents about your family history. Write a brief account describing the country in which they were born, how they came to America, hardships etc.

UNIT SIX
Israel

CHAPTER XXI

ZIONISM

THERE WERE many in Russia who reacted to the pogroms of 1881 and to the May Laws of 1882 by saying, "Let us return to Zion" (the Land of Israel). Dr. Leo Pinsker, author of *Auto-Emancipation*, headed an organization called *Hovevei Zion* ("Lovers of Zion").

"Let Jews return to their own land," they said. "Let them till the soil and rebuild the waste places. Only in Zion can Jews find freedom and emancipation."

The *Hovevei Zion* were very much interested in Moses Montefiore's proposal to form agricultural colonies in Palestine. There were many Jews who were eager to return to the soil. With help and under proper conditions they might succeed. Meanwhile, the Alliance Israélite Universelle had organized an agricultural school near Jaffa called *Mikveh Israel* ("Hope of Israel").

Within a few years there sprang up a series of agricultural colonies such as *Rishon Le-Zion* ("First of Zion") and *Petach Tikvah* ("Door of Hope"). The colonists, with zeal and fiery idealism, sought to plant and to build. Vines, olive-trees and citrus fruits soon rewarded the planters for their labor. But the hardships were many. Lack of water, disease, primitive conditions—all took a heavy toll. It was at this point that Baron Edmond de Rothschild of Paris became interested in the colonies. For many years he helped to finance the colonists until at last the mother-colonies of the new *Yishuv* (Settlement) became self-supporting.

259

2. BILU

Among the early pioneers were a group of students from Russia. When the riots broke out these students declared, "How can we look forward to careers in a country which destroys Jews? Let us rather rebuild our ancient homeland."

They adopted as their motto the Hebrew words, *"Bet Yaakov L'chu V'nelcha"* ("House of Jacob, come let us go forward!") They called themselves Bilu from the initials of the Hebrew words. Their experiences in Palestine read like an adventure story.

The first group of students left Europe during the summer of 1882. In the group were 13 boys and one girl. The leader was an idealistic student named Israel Belkind. When their boat anchored at Cyprus on the way to Palestine they were amazed to find a boatload of Jews returning from Palestine.

"What is wrong?" they asked.

"We were turned back at Jaffa," was the reply. "The Turkish government has decreed that no Jews may enter Palestine."

The students continued on their journey with heavy hearts. Perhaps this long voyage was all in vain. They rejoiced when they caught sight of the shores of the Holy Land, but anxiously waited to see what destiny lay in store for them. The Turkish officials who ascended their boat at Jaffa scanned their passports.

"You may go ahead," they said. "The Turkish government does not object to the entry of small groups."

Israel Belkind and his friends soon found work at the *Mikveh Israel* Agricultural School. They rented two rooms—the 13 boys occupying one room, the girl the other. Then they joyfully sent word to the other members of Bilu urging them to follow.

Their joy was short-lived, however, for their troubles had just begun. Convinced that the students were not strong enough for manual labor, Mr. Hirsch, the director of *Mikveh Israel*, gave them the hardest tasks to do. He expected in this manner to show them how mistaken they were in their ideas, and thus force them to leave Palestine. With pick, shovel and spade the students trudged to the field to perform back-breaking work. After a full day's toil under a merciless sun they would fall exhausted to the ground, every bone in their bodies aching. Two of the men contracted fever. One suffered from sunstroke.

But no matter what the hardships, the students remained true to their motto, "Let us go forward!" They refused to turn back. Dr. Charles Netter, secretary of the Alliance in Paris, visited Palestine and wept tears of joy when he saw the students at work and discussed their ideas with them.

"If only I were younger and had your strength, I would join you," he said.

Thanks to Dr. Netter the students were treated more kindly. Later, they were paid to help the colonists who had just bought farms in *Rishon Le-Zion*. Hirsch, however, never ceased urging the youths to go back to Europe, and even offered to pay their return fares.

The members of the Bilu dreamed of the day when they would settle on their own land. J. M. Pines, agent of the Montefiore Memorial Foundation, now came to their aid. He persuaded the *Hovevei Zion* to buy land in Gedera for the earnest students.

Here they encountered new difficulties. The ramshackle houses they moved into were not sufficient for the group, but the Turkish government would not grant a permit to put up new houses. There was nothing, however, to prevent them from constructing shelters for the animals. Since they owned but few animals, they themselves moved into the crude shel-ters. The Arab neighbors protested that the colonists had no right to build these structures. But there was a Turkish law which stated that once a building was completed nobody could destroy it. The shelters were allowed to remain. Ulti-mately, with the help of J. M. Pines, permission was obtained to put up permanent houses.

Turkey now decreed that no Jews at all could enter Palestine. But still the colonists arrived. One day a sack of potatoes was delivered to Gedera. When the bag was opened, out stepped a stowaway who had been taken from the boat with other pieces of cargo. Each shipment of lumber or furniture usually included one or two stowaways who came to join their friends in Palestine. The original group had been reinforced several times, the colony now containing about 20 families.

Lack of water was one of the most serious problems. The colonists were forced to pay the Arab peasants for the right to use an Arab well whose impure waters often contained worms and leeches. But again J. M. Pines secured the funds needed for digging a new well.

Protection against Arab thefts and violence also caused grave concern. Here the colonists depended on the strong arm of Israel Feinberg who was feared by the Arabs because of his strength and courage. They would refer to him as *Shaitan Lulu* ("Devil Lulu"). No matter how great the odds against him and his comrades, "Lulu" Feinberg would never turn his back in fear. He seemed to strike terror into the heart of every brigand, for as soon as he appeared on horseback all Arabs in sight would flee.

The neighboring Arabs learned to respect Feinberg and to call upon him for aid. Whenever passing Bedouins tried to steal cattle or horses, the village Arabs would shout, "Lulu, to the rescue! Lulu, to the rescue!"

On one occasion Feinberg caught a thief from the local village redhanded. Despite his protests of innocence, the thief was bound so that he could be turned over to the Turkish officials. That night the entire Arab village, under the cover of darkness, attacked the colony. Feinberg and his friends met the onslaught with whatever weapons they could muster.

Suddenly several Arabs could be seen running away.

"After them!" shouted one of the colonists.

"Wait," cautioned Feinberg. "It might be a ruse. They may be lying for us in ambush."

His suspicions were justified. The real attack came a few moments later. With the aid of the women colonists the attackers were driven off. Feinberg knew, however, that the attack would be renewed the following night. A messenger took his life in his hands and rode to *Rishon Le-Zion* for reinforcements. A group of colonists arrived before sunset on Friday just as the *shofar* was sounded to announce the coming of the Sabbath.

Secure against further attack the colonists now awaited the arrival of the Turkish soldiers from Jaffa. Escorted by the soldiers they descended to the Arab village to demand a cessation of hostilities. The Arabs placed the blame on a distant Arab tribe. The soldiers noticed, however, that nearly every villager was bruised or bandaged. Suspicious, they took the village leaders to Jaffa for further questioning. There was never another attack, thereafter.

Thus, overcoming these hardships one by one, the Bilu colonists became rooted in the land. Cypress, pine and fruit-trees blossomed where once there was sandy waste. The story of the pioneers spread far and wide and inspired others to settle in the old-new land of Israel.

3. THEODORE HERZL

Theodore Herzl changed the colonization efforts of *Hovevei Zionism* into the world-wide movement of political Zionism.

Herzl was born in the city of Budapest, Hungary in 1870. He received a Jewish as well as secular education. He was called to the Torah at his *Bar Mitzvah* and recited a portion from the prophets. He was always intensely proud of his Jewishness. At the age of 14 when a teacher in the *Realschule* insulted the Jews, Herzl proudly defended his people. He then turned around, walked out of the school, and never came back. As a law student in Vienna, he resigned from his fraternity when a motion was passed limiting the number of Jews to be accepted.

After practicing law for a short while, Herzl discovered

that there was little room for advancement for a Jew. He became a journalist and playwright, and was a brilliant success
in both fields. He drifted further and further from the Jewish
community although he still gave thought to the vexing problem of anti-Semitism and intolerance. In 1894 Herzl was sta-
tioned in Paris as a correspondent for a Viennese newspaper.
As a reporter he covered the famous Dreyfus spy trial. Alfred
Dreyfus was a Jewish captain in the French army who was
falsely accused of revealing military secrets. It soon became
clear that the army refused to clear Dreyfus, despite his innocence, because of prejudice and corruption. Poor Dreyfus was
sentenced to solitary confinement on Devil's Island. Some of
the leading writers and statesmen of France took up the struggle in behalf of Captain Dreyfus. But it was not until 12 years
later, after several stirring trials, that Dreyfus was acquitted
and restored to his former rank.

Herzl was present on January 5, 1895 when the public
degradation of Dreyfus took place. Captain Dreyfus was led
before a general seated on horseback who said: "Alfred Dreyfus, you are unworthy to bear arms. In the name of the French
Republic I degrade you from your rank. Let the sentence be
carried out."

At that moment the drums were beaten, and the officers tore
from the condemned man's uniform the buttons, cords and
decorations. Dreyfus lifted his right arm and called out: "I declare and solemnly swear that you are degrading an innocent
man."

As Dreyfus was led away the crowd shouted, "Death to the
traitor! Death to the Jews!"

Dreyfus replied to these constant shouts, "I am innocent!
Tell all France I am innocent!"

The cry, "Death to the Jews!" kept ringing in Herzl's ears.
Is it possible, he asked, for such a thing to happen in modern
France? Is it possible not only to condemn an innocent man,
but an entire people? If such prejudice existed in France, what
hope was there for the Jew in the rest of Europe?

Theodore Herzl was thrown into a mood of intense excitement. He began to see that European Jews had lived in a fool's paradise, for they believed that full emancipation would come to them if they were patient. Only a Jewish state, thought Herzl, can free the Jew. He wrote feverishly, putting his thoughts on paper. He called this book *The Jewish State.*

"We are a *people*, a people," wrote Herzl. "Everywhere we have tried honestly to disappear in the surrounding community, and to retain only the faith of our fathers. We are not permitted to do it. In vain do we show our loyalty, and in some places an exaggerated patriotism; in vain do we bring the same sacrifices of blood and gold as our fellow-citizens; in vain do we exert ourselves to increase the glory of our fatherlands by achievements in art and science."

The solution to the problem of the Jew is an independent Jewish state.

"In the long night of their history the Jews have never ceased to dream that kingly dream: 'Next year in Jerusalem.' It is an ancient saying among us. The task before us now is to prove that this dream can be transformed into a thought of the bright daylight."

Herzl carefully outlines his plan. A "Society of Jews" will negotiate for the land with the great powers. A "Jewish Company" will finance the building of the state. Colonization alone is not sufficient for without international recognition no state can come into existence. He proposes a flag for the new state. He also discusses the place of science and labor, for the Jewish state is not to be a state like all others but a model state based on progressive ideas.

He suggests that the Rabbis serve as the nucleus for each group that wishes to migrate.

"The Rabbis will also be the first to understand us, the first to be enthusiastic; from their pulpits they will spread their enthusiasm to others."

The book closes with an expression of profound faith in the future of the Jew.

"I believe that a race of wonderful Jews will grow out of the earth. The Maccabees will rise again! . . . The Jews who will it shall have their state. We shall at last live as free men on our own soil and die peacefully in our own homeland."

4. THE FIRST ZIONIST CONGRESS

Theodore Herzl's book came as a thunderbolt. It is true that many of Herzl's ideas were not new. Mordecai M. Noah, Moses Montefiore and Leo Pinsker had expressed similar ideas. But never had anybody combined such precise plans with such an eloquent plea to the Jewish people.

Herzl tried to interest Baron Edmond de Rothschild who was already helping many colonies in Palestine. But Baron Rothschild refused to support a political movement which aimed at the creation of a Jewish state. Others called Herzl a mad dreamer.

He did, however, win many supporters. In France there was Max Nordau, famous doctor and author. In Germany there was David Wolffsohn, designer of the Jewish flag. In America there was Stephen S. Wise. In Russia there were the members of the *Hovevei Zion*. In England there was Colonel Albert E. Goldsmith, son of baptized parents who brought up their child as a Christian without informing him of his Jewish origin. When, as an adult, Colonel Goldsmith learned of his Jewish ancestry he identified himself with the Jewish people.

"This is my life's idea," he said to Herzl. "We shall work for the liberation of Israel."

Those who believed in the establishment of a Jewish state and in the return of Jews to Zion came to be known as Zionists. Their movement was called Zionism. Herzl saw the need for uniting all Zionists. With this in mind he and Max Nordau issued a call for Zionists throughout the world to send delegates to the First World Zionist Congress which met in Basle, Switzerland in August, 1897.

It was a historic gathering. Delegates came from Palestine, from Russia, from Germany, from Austria-Hungary, from

Roumania, from France and England, from America and from many other countries. With great enthusiasm they sang a recently-composed song, *Hatikvah*, later to become the national anthem of Israel. The sessions took place in a concert hall decorated with a flag designed by David Wolffsohn: a white field with two blue stripes and the Star of David. Wolffsohn had chosen the colors of the ancient *tallit*, or prayer-shawl; white represented purity, blue represented lofty idealism and the Star of David represented courage. Each delegate carried a card with the two-fold symbol of the ancient Wailing Wall and the new Jewry of modern Palestine.

The Congress was opened with the recitation of the benediction: "Blessed art Thou, O Lord our God, King of the Universe, who has kept us alive, sustained us and has given us the privilege of witnessing this day." Then Herzl arose and walked to the speakers' platform. Here is the description by a Hebrew writer who attended the convention:

"Before us rose a marvelous and exalted figure, kingly in bearing and stature, with deep eyes in which could be read quiet majesty and unuttered sorrow. It is no longer the elegant Dr. Herzl of Vienna; it is a royal scion of the House of David, risen from among the dead, clothed in legend and fantasy and beauty. Everyone sat breathless, as if in the presence of a miracle. And in truth, was it not a miracle which we beheld? And then wild applause broke out; for fifteen minutes the delegates clapped, shouted and waved their handkerchiefs. The dream of two thousand years was on the point of realization."

Herzl immediately described the task of the Congress. "We are here," he said, "to lay the foundation stone of the house which is to shelter the Jewish nation."

Theodore Herzl was elected President and Max Nordau vice-president. Suggestions were made for establishing the Jewish National Fund, a bank, a Hebrew University, cooperatives and many other projects. Colonization was discussed, but it was pointed out that colonies without a state were not enough. It was agreed to encourage the immigration of laborers and agricultural workers, and to seek the support of various governments.

The official goal of the Zionist movement was described in these words: "Zionism seeks to secure for the Jewish people a publicly recognized, legally secured home in Palestine for the Jewish people." This came to be known as the Basle Program.

After the close of the First Zionist Congress, Herzl wrote in his diary, "If I were to sum up the Basle Congress in a single phrase, I would say: In Basle I created the Jewish State. Were I to say this aloud I would be greeted by universal laughter. But perhaps five years hence, in any case, certainly fifty years hence, everyone will perceive it."

Herzl's words were prophetic. 50 years later the State of Israel was officially proclaimed.

5. THEODORE HERZL—ZIONIST STATESMAN

Herzl bent all efforts toward obtaining a charter from the Turkish government permitting Jews to settle in Palestine. Knowing that the German Kaiser, Wilhelm II, had great influence with the Sultan he sought an audience with the Kaiser. He was received by Wilhelm II in Constantinople in October 1898 when the German ruler was en route to Palestine. Wilhelm II was very much interested in Zionism. He arranged for another interview with Herzl in Palestine, promising also to speak to the Sultan about the charter.

Herzl proceeded to Palestine with David Wolffsohn and other leading Zionists. He examined the colonies where he was received with great enthusiasm. In one colony he was welcomed by sixteen young men riding on horseback. As Theodore Herzl approached they shouted,

"Long live Theodore Herzl! Long live Theodore Herzl!"

Behind the youths on horseback was a delegation led by the elders of the colony carrying the scrolls of the law. As they blessed Herzl, tears appeared in the eyes of the Zionist leader.

Herzl met the Kaiser near *Mikveh Israel*. The German Emperor recognized Herzl from a distance and rode toward him. He held out his hand and said, "How are you?"

"I thank your Majesty," replied Herzl. "I am taking a look at the country. How has your Majesty's journey been till now?"

"Very hot. But the land has a future."

"For the moment it is still sick," said Herzl.

"It needs water," answered the Kaiser, "plenty of water."

"Yes, your Majesty, large scale irrigation."

"It is a land with a future," repeated the Kaiser.

He extended his hand again to Herzl, and then rode off. Herzl was received a few days later by Wilhelm II in Jerusalem where they discussed plans for developing the country. There was no reference, however, to the charter. Herzl gathered the impression that the Kaiser had spoken to the Sultan who was unfriendly to the idea.

Three years passed by before Herzl, after extended efforts, succeeded in gaining an audience with Sultan Abdul-Hamid. While in Palestine, Herzl was warned by his friends that the Turkish police had issued a secret warrant for his arrest, to be used if he stirred up any trouble. But now he was given a warm welcome by the Sultan. A special honor was conferred upon him, and he was presented with a tie-pin containing precious stones.

In the interview Herzl compared Turkey, which was saddled with heavy debts, to the lion that suffered from a thorn in its paw. The Jews of the world might remove this thorn by financing a loan for Turkey. Later, Herzl wrote to the Sultan's advisers stating that in return for helping Turkey, the Jews would expect a charter permitting them to settle in Palestine. Poor Herzl's hopes were doomed to disappointment. The rich Jews to whom he spoke were not interested in his scheme; furthermore, the Sultan was willing to allow

HERZL ON THE WAY TO THE LAND OF ISRAEL

Jews to scatter throughout his empire but not to gather in great numbers in Palestine.

6. "IF YOU WILL IT, THEN IT IS NO LEGEND"

Herzl continued his gigantic labors with undiminished zeal. Much of what he earned as correspondent and playwright he used to further Zionism. The bank, which was called the Jewish Colonial Trust, was formed. The Jewish National Fund was established to redeem the soil. Herzl sought interviews with the leading statesmen of England, Germany and Russia hoping to gain their support. He also appeared before the Pope and the King of Italy.

Inspired by his experiences in the Holy Land, Herzl wrote a novel describing the Palestine of the future. He called this novel *Altneuland* ("Old-new Land"), a name taken from the *Altneuschul* ("Old-new Synagogue") of Prague. The book tells of the visit to Palestine by two friends who see a barren wasteland. Twenty years later they return to find that the Jewish people have transformed the desert into a land flowing with milk and honey.

Haifa has become the greatest harbor in the Mediterranean. A canal connecting the Mediterranean and the Dead Sea provides the land with unlimited water and power. Cooperatives assure all groups a high standard of living. Women enjoy equal rights with men. Care is provided for the sick. All have the right and duty to work without discrimination. New Jerusalem has become a garden city. The Sabbath and Jewish festivals have become national holidays.

Herzl chose as the motto for his book, "If you will it, then it is no legend." But he closed the novel with this warning, "But if you do not will it, then what I have recited remains but a legend."

Meanwhile, time was running short. Riots in Kishineff, Russia claimed the lives of many Jewish victims in 1903 and 1904. Since Turkey was unwilling to grant a charter, Herzl turned to England with the request for a temporary homeland. The English government responded by offering Uganda, a territory in East Africa, as a "New Palestine" for the creation of a Jewish colony.

Herzl presented this plan to the Sixth Zionist Congress which met in Basle in 1904. He emphasized that there could never be any substitute for Palestine, but Uganda might serve as a lodging for the night. Many of the delegates were shocked by this action since they knew that there could never be any Jewish state outside of Palestine. The majority, interested in providing a temporary refuge for the persecuted masses of Russia, agreed to send a commission to Uganda to explore the possibilities.

Saddened by the division in the ranks, and worn out by his unceasing labors, Herzl's health took a turn for the worse. He had sacrificed everything for his people—his fortune, his health, his very life. On July 2, 1904 he said to one of his visitors:

"Tell them I have given my heart's blood for my people."

The next day he was dead. Thus passed away the greatest Jewish statesman since the days of the Maccabees.

At his grave his faithful lieutenant David Wolffsohn said, "We utter a solemn promise here before your final resting-place, to carry on faithfully and courageously the great work of the redemption of Israel which you have so well begun."

EXERCISES

I. Complete each sentence. (Review sections 1 and 2, pages 259 to 263.)

Bilu, Gedera, *Hovevei Zion, Mikveh Israel, Rishon Le-Zion*

1. Leo Pinsker headed an organization known as _____.
2. One of the first new colonies in Palestine was called _____.
3. The motto of the _____ was, "House of Jacob, come let us go forward!"
4. The Alliance Israélite Universelle supported an agricultural school named _____.

5. J. M. Pines helped secure land for the colonists at
_____.

II. True or false? (Review section 3, pages 263 to 266.)
1. Herzl received no Jewish education.
2. Captain Alfred Dreyfus was sent to Devil's Island even though he was innocent.
3. Herzl became interested in the Dreyfus trial because he was closely related to Captain Dreyfus.
4. Herzl wrote in *The Jewish State* that the Jewish problem can be solved only if the Jewish nation lives under its own government.
5. Herzl believed that science, labor and religion would play an important part in the new Jewish state.

III. Choose the correct word or phrase. (Review section 4, pages 266 to 268.)
1. The idea of a Jewish state was also expressed by _____. (Mordecai Noah, Judah Touro)
2. Herzl's idea of a Jewish state was supported in France by _____. (Baron Rothschild, Max Nordau)
3. The First World Zionist Congress met in _____. (Basle, Paris)
4. The colors of the flag used at the Zionist Congress were blue and _____. (red, white)
5. The goal of the Zionist movement was the establishment of _____. (a Jewish state in Palestine, new colonies in Palestine)

IV. Who am I? (Review section 5, pages 268 to 271.)
1. I was emperor of a great country. I was friendly to Zionism and met the leader of Zionism in Constantinople, in *Mikveh Israel* and in Jerusalem. I believed that Palestine could develop if it had more water.
2. I was the founder of political Zionism. I tried to obtain a charter permitting the Jews to settle in Palestine.
3. I was the designer of the flag used at the Zionist Congress. I accompanied the leader of Zionism to Palestine.
4. I wanted the Jews to help solve my country's financial problems. I was willing to allow Jews to settle in my

country, but refused to grant a charter for Jewish settlement in Palestine.

V. Answer each question in a complete sentence. (Review section 6, pages 271 to 272.)

1. What is the purpose of the Jewish National Fund?
2. What countries did Herzl visit to further Zionism?
3. What changes in Palestine did Herzl predict in his book *Altneuland?*
4. Explain the quotation, "If you will it, then it is no legend."
5. Why was Herzl willing to accept England's proposal to establish a Jewish colony in Uganda?
6. What promise did David Wolffsohn make at the grave of Herzl?

VI. Questions for discussion:

1. Compare the hardships of pioneers in Palestine and pioneers in America.
2. What was Herzl's greatest accomplishment?
3. What was the difference between the *Hovevei Zion* movement and the Zionist movement?
4. Was Herzl justified in accepting the British proposal to establish a Jewish colony in Uganda?
5. Compare the First Zionist Congress in Basle in 1897 and the meeting of the Grand Sanhedrin in Paris in 1807.

THINGS TO DO

1. *Pen-Pals*—Write a letter to a person your age in Israel. Addresses can be obtained through the Israeli Consul.

2. *Jewish National Fund*—Arrange an assembly dealing with the Jewish National Fund. Describe the work of the J.N.F. in redeeming the soil of Israel. Plant trees in honor of a member of your family or a friend through the purchase of a J.N.F. tree certificate.

3. *Model Congress*—Pretend you are delegates to the World Zionist Congress in Basle. Debate whether to send a commission to Uganda. Discuss other projects, such as the establishment of the Jewish National Fund, a bank, cooperatives and a Hebrew University.

CHAPTER XXII

REBIRTH

1. THE REVIVAL OF HEBREW

THE JEWS of Palestine had made many steps forward since the first *Aliya* (wave of immigration) in 1882. Their most notable achievement was the revival of Hebrew as a spoken language. This was the result of the fanatical enthusiasm of Eliezer Ben-Yehuda who resolved to devote his life to this cause. His motto was, "Speak Hebrew and you will be redeemed."

Ben-Yehuda's first step in this direction was to make his own family Hebrew-speaking. When his oldest son, Ittamar, was born in 1882 he made his wife vow never to allow the child to hear any language other than Hebrew. Unfortunately, the child was slow in speaking. Even Ben-Yehuda's friends such as J. M. Pines felt that Ben-Yehuda had made a serious error. They urged him to speak a European language to the child, but Ben-Yehuda had an iron will which could not be broken.

Later Ittamar gave the following description of the memorable day when he was finally blessed with the power of speech:

"Day after day and night after night, my father would stand near my bed beside my bewildered mother, wondering why my lips uttered no sound. The greatest author in the Jerusalem of that day, Jechiel Pines, would rebuke my mother. 'Why do you permit such folly? Unless you speak and sing to him in some other language, the child's mentality will be permanently affected!'

"But the vow my mother had made to her husband on the day of her marriage never to utter a word in their home in any language other than Hebrew, made it impossible for her to give heed to these rebukes. Each day she would whisper to her son:

" 'Speak, child, speak.'

"In vain.

"One day my father rode away on his donkey to *Rishon Le-Zion*. In his absence, my mother placed me on her knees and sang to me a Russian song by Lermontov. At that moment it began to snow, and the mountains of Jerusalem were clothed in white. Suddenly the door opened with a loud noise and my father entered covered from head to foot with snow-flakes— the donkey had refused to continue its journey in the bitter cold and my father was forced to turn homeward.

"His eyes burned with indignation. 'That is how you fulfill your vow—by singing Russian songs to our first born child?'

"Before my mother could reply, my father pounded with his first on the desk, upon which at night he would work on his dictionary, and smashed it to bits.

"And I remember, as clearly as if it all happened but yesterday, that I tore myself away from my mother's warm embrace, ran towards my father, my little fists waving in the air, and shouted: '*Aba!* (Father!)'

"It was the first word I had ever uttered."

The child was not allowed to play with the neighboring children, since they spoke no Hebrew and would spoil his speech. The poor lad's one companion was a dog, which he named *Mahir* (speedy.) But even this companionship did not last very long, for the pious neighbors thought they heard Ittamar call the dog "Meir." Scandalized at the thought that a dog was called by the name of a great sage, the neighbors forcibly removed the animal, and Ittamar was left without companionship.

But the experiment succeeded. Ittamar was the first child in modern times whose mother tongue was Hebrew. He was destined to be the instrument whereby a dead language became the living speech of a people reborn.

Other families introduced Hebrew into their homes. Ben-Yehuda was engaged to teach Hebrew in the Alliance school in Jerusalem. Israel Belkind, leader of the Bilu colonists, opened a school in Jaffa with Hebrew as the sole language of instruction. New words were coined by Ben-Yehuda. The magazine he edited helped spread a knowledge of modern Hebrew. For forty years he worked on a Hebrew dictionary which is a mine of information concerning the Hebrew language. Within a generation Hebrew had become the language of school and street, of farm and factory.

2. THE SECOND *Aliya*

After Herzl's death, his devoted follower David Wolffsohn was elected president of the World Zionist Organization. The question of Uganda was reconsidered and dropped. There were too many difficulties in the way. Above all, no land other than Palestine could serve as the basis for a national homeland. It was suspected that Herzl, himself, was really interested in using the Uganda offer to help give him bargaining power in his negotiations with the Sultan.

The pogroms in Kishineff and in other Russian cities in 1903-1904 stimulated the second *Aliya* (wave of immigration). The new colonists who came to Palestine were motivated by pioneer and labor ideals. They were shocked to see that most of the Palestinian farmers were plantation owners who served as overseers while the manual labor was performed by Arabs. The ideals of the Bilu had been forgotten. The new *haluzim* (pioneers) believed in the return to the soil, the establishment of a strong labor element among Jews and the building of a cooperative society. Women accepted the same pioneer duties as the men and received equal privileges.

Among those who came to Palestine during the second *Aliya* was David Ben-Gurion. Arriving in 1906 he worked as farmhand and *shomer* (watchman). A year later he helped found the *Poalei Zion*, a labor organization which he headed.

He was destined to become Israel's first Prime Minister in 1948.

In 1907, Dr. Chaim Weizmann, then a young chemist and active Zionist, paid his first visit to Palestine. He was impressed by signs of progress on all sides. Escorted by Arthur Ruppin who was in charge of colonization activity, Dr. Weizmann walked outside of Jaffa over the sand dunes to the north of the city.

Ankle-deep in sand, Arthur Ruppin paused and said, "Here we shall create a Jewish city."

Chaim Weizmann looked at him in dismay.

"Why should people come to live out in this wilderness where nothing would grow?" asked Dr. Weizmann.

Arthur Ruppin replied to his technical questions showing how all problems could be solved. Two years later, in 1909, the new garden city was actually founded. It was called Tel Aviv ("Hill of Spring"), for Ezekiel, prophet of hope, had once lived in a city by this name. Furthermore, Herzl's *Altneu-land* when translated into Hebrew was entitled *Tel Aviv*. Thus a great city, symbol of hope and spring, came into existence.

3. DEGANIA

Two years later, in 1911, Degania, the first *kvutza* (co-operative settlement), was founded under the leadership of Aaron D. Gordon. Believing that only labor could transform the Jews into a nation, A. D. Gordon preached "the religion of labor."

"If we do not till the soil with our own hands," he wrote, "it will not be ours. . . . Labor is not merely the factor which establishes man's contact with the land and his claim to the land; it is also the principal force in the building of a national civilization."

When Gordon, who formerly lived a life of comfort as manager of an estate in Russia, obtained work as a laborer in Jaffa, he exclaimed, "I feel like a newborn child."

The colony that he founded in Degania, at the point where

the Jordan River leaves the Sea of Galilee, established the basis for the many cooperative settlements in Israel. Private property was abolished. All members earned alike and shared alike. Meals were eaten in a common dining-room. Women were able to share in the pioneer work, since they were relieved of many of their parental duties by those in charge of the nursery and kindergarten.

There were many hardships that the colonists in Degania had to endure. But nothing could dampen their spirits. When a strong wind overturned the large tent in which most of them slept, they laughingly said, "It doesn't matter. We'll sleep in the fields."

Once one of the colonists became seriously ill. The nearest doctor was several miles away but it was dangerous to go to him since Arab bandits threatened the lives of all passersby. Mosheh Barsaki, a member of the group, volunteered to ride to the doctor. A few hours passed and still there was no sign of Barsaki or of the doctor. In the evening the horse returned —riderless. Fearing the worst, the colonists combed the woods. At last they found their comrade—dead, his body riddled with Arab bullets.

The colonists wrote to the boy's parents in Russia informing them of the sad news. The father wrote back:

"Our loss is indeed tragic. But do not lose courage. I hope that my son's memory will inspire you to continue to work and to build."

A few months later the younger brother of Mosheh Barsaki came to Degania to take the place of the fallen pioneer.

4. THE BALFOUR DECLARATION

The war years 1914-1918 were a nightmare for the Jews of Palestine. Turkey fought on the side of Germany and persecuted all who might sympathize with the Allies. Zionist flags and books were destroyed; Zionist groups were disbanded. Some Zionist leaders were arrested, others deported. Among those who sought refuge in the United States were Ben-

Yehuda and Ben-Gurion. The Jewish Legion, consisting of volunteers, fought bravely with British troops under General Allenby and helped in the liberation of the Middle East.

Meanwhile, Dr. Chaim Weizmann lost no opportunity to interest English statesmen in Zionist aspirations. In his biography, Dr. Weizmann records the following conversation with Lord Arthur Balfour who could not understand why Jews preferred Palestine to Uganda.

"Mr. Balfour," said Chaim Weizmann, "supposing I were to offer you Paris instead of London, would you take it?"

Balfour sat up, looked at Weizmann and replied: "But, Dr. Weizmann, we have London."

"That is true," replied Dr. Weizmann. "But we had Jerusalem when London was a marsh."

Balfour then asked, "Are there many Jews who think like you?"

Weizmann's answer was, "I believe I speak the mind of millions of Jews whom you will never see and who cannot speak for themselves."

"It is curious," said Lord Balfour. "The Jews I meet are quite different."

"Mr. Balfour," replied Dr. Weizmann, "you meet the wrong kind of Jews."

During the war the English government turned to Dr. Weizmann, then professor of chemistry at Manchester University, for help. The supply of acetone was running short and without acetone it was impossible to manufacture the ammunition needed for the naval guns.

Dr. Weizmann was ushered into the presence of Winston Churchill, First Lord of the Admiralty, who said: "Well, Dr. Weizmann, we need thirty thousand tons of acetone. Can you make it?"

Chaim Weizmann replied that he believed that acetone could be produced by a fermentation process. He promised to try if the government would supply him with the necessary assistance. He succeeded in his task, thus making a great contribution toward England's war effort. The English government offered Dr. Weizmann many lucrative awards which he refused to accept.

David Lloyd George, Winston Churchill, Arthur Balfour and other leading statesmen were favorably impressed by Dr. Weizmann's plea that England should favor the establishment of Palestine, after the war, as a Jewish National Homeland. Lovers of the Bible, they felt that the rebirth of a Jewish nation would be the fulfillment of the ancient prophecies. Their support of Zionism was strengthened by the warm approval of President Woodrow Wilson who had become interested in Zionism through the efforts of Justice Louis D. Brandeis.

On November 2, 1917, British Foreign Secretary Balfour with the approval of Prime Minister Lloyd George and the British Cabinet, issued the following declaration:

"His Majesty's Government view with favor the establishment in Palestine of a National Home for the Jewish people, and will use their best endeavors to facilitate the achievement of this object, it being clearly understood that nothing shall be done which may prejudice the civil and religious rights of the existing non-Jewish communities in Palestine or the rights and political status enjoyed by Jews in any other country."

The document was brought to Dr. Weizmann, who was waiting anxiously outside of the Cabinet office, by an important official who exclaimed, "Dr. Weizmann, it's a boy."

In a way, this was the charter for which Theodor Herzl had worked so zealously. The Balfour Declaration ushered in a new and important era in the history of the Jewish people.

EXERCISES

I. Which of the following statements concerning Ben-Yehuda are true? (Review section 1, pages 275 to 277.)

1. Ben-Yehuda helped revive Hebrew as a spoken language.
2. Ben-Yehuda was a pioneer in an agricultural settlement.
3. Ben-Yehuda insisted that only Hebrew be spoken by his family.

4. Ben-Yehuda organized a school in Jaffa in which Hebrew was the language of instruction.

5. Ben-Yehuda worked for 40 years on a Hebrew dictionary.

II. Match. (Review section 2, pages 277 to 278.)

Column A	Column B
David Ben-Gurion	1. Zionist and chemist
Theodor Herzl	2. Second president of the Zionist Organization
Arthur Ruppin	3. Founder of labor organization in Palestine
Chaim Weizmann	4. Director of colonization in Palestine
David Wolffsohn	5. Founder of World Zionist Organization

III. Write a sentence about each of the following. (Review section 3, pages 278 to 279.)

1. Degania 2. A. D. Gordon 3. "Religion of labor" 4. a *kvutza* 5. Mosheh Barsaki

IV. Fill in the missing name. (Review section 4, pages 279 to 281.)

1. —————, author of the Hebrew dictionary, left Palestine during World War I in order to escape Turkish persecution.

2. —————, First Lord of the Admiralty, invited Dr. Weizmann to experiment with a new process for the manufacture of acetone.

3. —————, prominent Zionist and chemist, persuaded England to issue a declaration favoring the establishment of a Jewish Homeland.

4. —————, British Foreign Secretary, issued a declaration in the name of the British government in favor of a Jewish National Homeland in Palestine.

5. —————, President of the United States, informed England that he was in favor of a Jewish National Homeland.

V. Questions for discussion:

1. Why was the revival of Hebrew so essential for the Jews of Palestine?

2. What were the achievements of the second *Aliya?*

3. Compare the Balfour Declaration and the proclamation of Cyrus in 536 B.C.E. permitting the Jews to return from Babylon to the Land of Israel.

THINGS TO DO

1. *Hebrew Greetings*—Make posters containing Hebrew greetings used in Israel today. Consult *Modern Hebrew* by Blumberg and Lewittes.

2. *Scrap-Book*—Compile a scrap-book including pictures of Israel, magazine and newspaper clippings etc.

CHAPTER XXIII
UNDER THE MANDATE

1. WAR AND PEACE

ON DECEMBER 11, 1917 General Allenby entered Jerusalem at the head of British troops, and received the surrender of the Turkish garrison. The Jews greeted the British with enthusiasm, and looked forward to the day when, in accordance with the Balfour Declaration, Palestine would become a Jewish National Home.

In July of the following year Dr. Chaim Weizmann, in the presence of General Allenby and his staff, laid the foundations of the Hebrew University on Mt. Scopus. In the distance could be heard the sound of guns on the northern front. The setting on Mt. Scopus was one of sublime beauty.

"The declining sun," writes Weizmann, "flooded the hills of Judea and Moab with golden light. . . . Below us lay Jerusalem, gleaming like a jewel."

The dedication of a University in the midst of war was like an act of faith. Out of the ashes of destruction would rise a new Jewish life, aided by science and learning.

After World War I, the League of Nations assigned Palestine to England under a "mandate" or order to administer the country until it was ready for independence. The Balfour Declaration was included as the basis of the mandate. Palestine east of the Jordan, much to the disappointment of the Zionists, was excluded from the Jewish National Home. Hebrew, Arabic and English were recognized as the three official languages.

Unfortunately, English officials often proved to be unfriendly, partly because of the Arab problem. Nonetheless, the *Yishuv* now grew by leaps and bounds. The third *Aliya*, after the War, brought thousands of eager youths from Russia ready to serve as pioneers in the rebuilding of the land. Men like Chaim Nachman Bialik, Hebrew national poet, fulfilled the dream of a lifetime and settled in Palestine. In 1924, there began a fourth wave of immigration as Polish Jews, ruined by excessive taxes and legal restrictions, turned to Palestine to begin a new life in the old-new land. In 1933, a new wave of immigration brought thousands of German Jews seeking to escape from Hitler's Germany.

The all-Jewish city of Tel Aviv became Palestine's largest city. Haifa became an important Mediterranean seaport. New industries sprang up. The waters of the Jordan were harnessed to provide electrical power. Factories were set up at the Dead Sea for the extraction of potash and bromine. Jaffa oranges were shipped to countries throughout the world. Health conditions improved with the aid of the Hadassah Medical Organization which was founded by the noble Henrietta Szold. The *Histadrut* or General Labor Federation promoted the economic, social and cultural welfare of the workers. Schools, newspapers, theaters and other cultural activities enriched the lives of the people.

The new agricultural settlements were the pride of the entire *Yishuv*. The Jewish National Fund succeeded in buying large tracts of land in the Emek (Valley of Jezreel) which became the scene of intensive colonization. Some of the new colonies followed the example of Degania which was organized as a *kvutza* (cooperative settlement). Other groups preferred the *moshav*. A *moshav* is a semi-collective colony where homes and farms are held individually, but machinery is owned collectively.

The experience of the colonists in Nahalal, an outstanding *moshav*, shows us the spirit of the *haluzim* (pioneers). The first colonists to visit Nahalal were depressed by the sight that greeted them. There were a few abandoned houses in the midst of fever-infested swamps.

"Who built these houses?" they asked of an old Arab who happened to pass by.

"German farmers—many years ago."

"Where are these Germans?"

"They died."

"Who lived here after the Germans died?"

"Arabs."

"Where are they now?"

"They died too."

"Why?"

"The water. Death comes from the water and the swamps."

The colonists sadly looked at one another.

"We have come here to live, not to die," said one of the men in despair.

"Nonsense," replied a second colonist. "We'll dry the swamps, we'll plant trees and build houses and plow the fields. We will live and not die!"

And so it was. The *haluzim* suffered many hardships, but finally conquered the disease-ridden swamps. Today Nahalal is one of Israel's most beautiful colonies. Its tall, stately trees and green fields are a tribute to the spirit of the pioneers.

2. WEIZMANN AND THE ARABS

Dr. Weizmann and other Zionist leaders did all they could to gain Arab cooperation. At the suggestion of General Allenby, Dr. Weizmann made a dangerous trip during the war to meet Feisal east of the Jordan River. Feisal, who had led an Arab revolt against Turkey, was the recognized leader of the Arabs and later became King of Iraq. Surrounded by the famous Lawrence of Arabia and his advisers, King Feisal listened carefully to Chaim Weizmann's ideas. Feisal heartily agreed that as partners Arabs and Jews could build a great civilization in Palestine. He endorsed the program of Zionism feeling that the Arab world stood to gain much from a Jewish Homeland in Palestine. Lawrence of Arabia, an Englishman who gained fame as one of the organizers of the Arab revolt, became Weizmann's warm friend and strongly approved of Arab-Jewish partnership.

At the Peace Conference in Paris in 1919 a meeting was

arranged between Felix Frankfurter, then a member of the American Zionist delegation, and King Feisal. Lawrence of Arabia was also present. Again King Feisal expressed his approval of the Balfour Declaration. On March 3, 1919, Feisal wrote the following letter:

"Dear Mr. Frankfurter:

"I want to take this opportunity of my first contact with American Zionists, to tell you what I have often been able to say to Dr. Weizmann in Arabia and Europe.

"We feel that the Arabs and Jews are cousins in race, suffering similar oppressions at the hands of powers stronger than themselves, and by a happy coincidence have been able to take the first step toward the attainment of their national ideals together.

"We Arabs, especially the educated among us, look with the deepest sympathy on the Zionist movement. Our deputation here in Paris is fully acquainted with the proposals submitted by the Zionist Organization to the Peace Conference, and we regard them as moderate and proper. We will do our best, in so far as we are concerned, to help them through; we will wish the Jews a most hearty welcome home.

"With the chiefs of your movement, especially with Dr. Weizmann, we have had, and continue to have the closest relations. He has been a great helper of our cause, and I hope the Arabs may soon be in a position to make the Jews some return for their kindness. We are working together for a reformed and revived Near East, and our two movements complete one another. . . . I think that neither can be a real success without the other. . . .

"I look forward, and my people with me look forward, to a future in which we will help you and you will help us, so that the countries in which we are mutually interested may once again take their place in the community of civilized peoples of the world.

Yours sincerely,
Feisal"

In addition, as head of the Arab delegation, Feisal entered into an agreement with Dr. Weizmann in which he officially approved the Balfour Declaration and all measures that would encourage large-scale Jewish immigration and intensive settlement on the land.

3. THE ARAB PROBLEM

The Arabs of Palestine, however, did not adopt the same point of view. During the war they were not consulted since they fought against England. After the war they expressed violent opposition to the Balfour Declaration. The appointment of Sir Herbert Samuel, an English Jew, as High Commissioner of Palestine caused further concern among the Arabs. Actually, Sir Herbert Samuel, although a believer in Zionism, did everything he could to appease the Arabs. He granted them government lands, limited Jewish immigration and helped draft the clauses of the mandate which excluded Eastern Palestine (Jordan) from the Jewish National Home.

The Arabs argued that Palestine was already overcrowded and that Jews were displacing Arabs. They also claimed that since Arabs were in the majority they had the right to govern as they pleased and to exclude Jews.

Dr. Weizmann and the Zionists replied that Palestine, as in ancient times, could absorb millions of people. Arabs were not being displaced. On the contrary, they were increasing, as large stretches of desert land were reclaimed and made fit for human habitation. No land was taken from Arabs. Instead, they were enriched by selling unused land for many times its real value. Jews helped raise the Arab standard of living, gave employment to Arabs, and helped them to fight disease. Within one generation the Arab span of life had increased by ten years because of the medical and scientific improvements introduced by Jews.

Jews also refuted the claim that Arabs had the right to govern as they pleased and to exclude Jews. Palestine had not belonged to the Arabs; it had been ruled by Turkey for hundreds of years. Palestine had been a Jewish country from the days of Abraham until the Roman conquest. Jews had religious claims on the Promised Land, and had always felt strong bonds of attachment to it. Although most Arabs had fought against the Allies, they were granted independence in Iraq, Syria, Lebanon and Jordan. They possessed more than a million square miles of land which they allowed to remain desert, yet insisted that Palestine too remain a wasteland. The Balfour Declaration and the mandate which was endorsed by 52 nations gave Jews the legal right to settle in Palestine and to cultivate the land.

Jews also pointed out how insincere the Arab agitators were. Many of those who protested loudest against Jewish immigration were among the first to sell land to Jews at exorbitant prices. The *effendi,* or rich landowners, did nothing for the *fellahin,* or peasants. They employed Arab workers for a few cents a day, and charged high interest rates when peasants and workers requested loans. Many of the *fellahin* were sharecroppers who shared with absentee landlords the meager crops they raised. Poverty, filth and disease were the lot of the Arab peasant.

The Arab reply to Jewish claims was—bloodshed. There were organized riots in 1920, 1921 and 1929. The large influx of German refugees after 1933 further angered the Arabs. In 1936 the Grand Mufti of Jerusalem organized a campaign of terrorism which continued for three years. The British ordered the arrest of the Mufti but he escaped to Lebanon, and continued to direct the terrorism in Palestine. Shocked by the failure of the British to protect the population, Jews formed their own army of self-defense called the *Haganah.* Despite Arab terrorism, the *Yishuv* continued to grow.

In 1937 the Peel Commission tried to solve the problem by recommending that Palestine be divided into two states—an Arab state and a Jewish state. This proposal only served to intensify Arab terrorism.

In 1939, eager to appease the Arabs, London published a

White Paper which announced a new policy. Seventy-five thousand Jews would be admitted during a period of 5 years. After that immigration would be curbed. Land could be sold to Jews only in restricted areas. This seemed to be a death-blow to all Jewish hopes. The League of Nations, to whom England was responsible, declared the White Paper a violation of the mandate.

All further debate was checked by the outbreak of war in 1939. Jews in Palestine loyally supported Britain and the Allies despite the White Paper. Their attitude was summed up by David Ben-Gurion who said:

"We will fight the war as if there were no White Paper, and we will fight the White Paper as if there were no war."

EXERCISES

I. Answer each question in a complete sentence. (Review section 1, pages 284 to 286.)

1. When did Weizmann lay the cornerstone of the Hebrew University?
2. What are some of the provisions of the mandate?
3. Describe the changes that took place in Palestine after World War I?
4. What is the difference between a *kvutza* and a *moshav?*
5. What hardships did the colonists encounter in Nahalal?

II. Explain and illustrate each of the following statments in Feisal's letter. (Review section 2, pages 286 to 288.)

1. "We feel that the Arabs and Jews are cousins in race."
2. "We Arabs, especially the educated among us, look with the deepest sympathy on the Zionist movement."
3. "Our deputation here in Paris is fully acquainted with the proposals submitted by the Zionist Organization to the Peace Conference, and we regard them as moderate and proper."
4. "With the chiefs of your movement, especially with Dr. Weizmann, we have had, and continue to have the closest relations."

5. "We are working together for a reformed and revived Near East, and our two movements complete one another."

III. Choose the correct word or phrase. (Review section 3, pages 288 to 290.)

  1. The first High Commissioner under the mandate was _____. (Herbert Samuel, Chaim Weizmann)

  2. Before World War I, Palestine was ruled by the _____. (Arabs, Turks)

  3. Arab span of life _____ after Jews began to rebuild Palestine. (decreased, increased)

  4. The purpose of the *Haganah* was to _____. (buy land, defend the Jews)

  5. The League of Nations declared the White Paper of 1939 to be _____ the mandate. (a violation of, in keeping with)

IV. Questions for discussion:

  1. Describe some of the achievements of the *Yishuv* after World War I.

  2. How did Weizmann try to obtain Arab cooperation?

  3. Were the Jews justified in asking for the right to enter Palestine?

THINGS TO DO

1. *Israel Exhibit*—Arrange for an exhibit of Israeli stamps, newspapers, books, records and art objects. Write to the Jewish National Fund or the United Jewish Appeal for an Israeli film to be shown on that occasion. There are many Israeli students studying in American universities. Arrangements might be made for an Israeli student to speak about life in Israel.

2. *Research*—Interesting reports can be made about important figures in Zionism or the history of modern Israel. Here are some suggested titles of books that might be consulted:

Bein, Alex—*Theodore Herzl*
Huebener, Theodore and Voss, Carl H.—*This is Israel*
Learsi, Rufus—*Fulfillment: The Epic Story of Zionism*
Lowenthal, Marvin—*Henrietta Szold: Life and Letters*

McDonald, James G.—*My Mission In Israel*
St. John, Robert—*Tongue of the Prophets: The Life Story of Eliezer Ben-Yehuda*
Stone, I. F.—*Underground to Palestine*
Syrkin, Marie—*Blessed is the Match: The Story of Jewish Resistance*
Weizmann, Chaim—*Trial and Error* (Autobiography)
Wise, Stephen S.—*Challenging Years* (Autobiography)

CHAPTER XXIV

WAR AND RESISTANCE

1. WORLD WAR II

JEWS fought valiantly in World War II. Six hundred thousand fought in the armed forces of the United States. Over 400,000 fought for Soviet Russia. There were 75,-000 Jews enrolled in the armies of the British Commonwealth of Nations. Jews played a prominent role in the resistance movement in France and Central Europe.

The tragic fate that met European Jewry cannot be described in words. Six million Jews were condemned by Adolf Hitler to the gas chambers of Maidanek and Treblinka.

Among those who have been added to the long list of Jewish heroes are the Jews of the Warsaw Ghetto.

"Whether we live or die is not important," they said, "but *how* we live and *how* we die."

Knowing full well that they were doomed the Jews in Warsaw treasured every aspect of Jewish and human culture. Classes were formed for the teaching of Hebrew. Hundreds of children's programs were secretly presented. Historians gathered archives so that history might know of the life within the ghetto. Lectures were given to make the people familiar with the writings of Peretz, Sholom Aleichem and Bialik. There were concerts and dramatic presentations and a symphony orchestra which was the pride of all.

A Jewish Fighting Organization was formed under the leadership of Mordecai Anilewitz and Zivia Lubetkin. Contacts were formed with the Polish underground. Every cart bringing potatoes or vegetables into the ghetto contained hidden rifles and bullets. Hand grenades were brought in through tunnels and sewers.

On April 19, 1943, on the eve of Passover, the Nazi Storm Troopers, little suspecting any interference, moved into the ghetto for the final deportation. Shots rang out and the Nazis were forced to retreat. A few minutes later a line of German tanks crept forward. A bottle of benzine was tossed at the first tank. It was a direct hit. Two hours later the Nazis brought up machine gun reinforcements. From 29 Zamenhof Street, which stood directly above the ghetto entrance, there was a sudden volley of hidden grenades which destroyed the machine guns.

At times could be heard the inspiring song:
"I believe . . .
I believe . . ."

The melody would grow louder and louder:
"I believe . . .
I believe . . .
I believe . . .
I believe in the coming of the Messiah!"

The heroes of the Warsaw Ghetto knew that they could not survive, yet they believed that their sacrifice was not in vain. They believed in the redemption of Israel, and had faith that the Jewish people could not be destroyed.

For 35 days the glorious resistance continued. The Storm Troopers, thoroughly defeated, were withdrawn. The German air force was sent in to subdue the resistance by means of incendiary bombs. Mordecai Anilewitz met a heroic death. Zivia Lubetkin and a few survivors crawled to safety through the sewers of Warsaw.

Word of the heroism of the Jews of Warsaw spread throughout Europe. All who fought against the Hitler terror were given renewed courage in their struggle for freedom.

2. "THE FORGOTTEN ALLY"

Despite the White Paper the Jews of Palestine fought bravely on the side of the Allies. The Jewish National Home

produced the only fighting contingent in the Middle East on
which the Allies could depend. One Gentile author who feels
that their brilliant war record has not been sufficiently recognized calls Palestinian Jewry "The Forgotten Ally."

On the day that war was declared Chaim Weizmann wrote
to Prime Minister Chamberlain:

"The Jews stand by Great Britain and will fight on the
side of the democracies. . . . The Jewish Agency is ready to
enter into immediate arrangements for utilizing Jewish man-
power, technical ability, resources etc."

Palestinian Jews were in the front lines in North Africa.
The "pipe line to victory" at El Alamein which helped turn
the tide of battle was the work of Brigadier General Herman
Kisch, chief engineer of the British Eighth Army and former
chairman of the Jewish Agency for Palestine. Kisch, although
51 years old when World War II broke out, was the first
Palestinian to volunteer for active duty. He fell in action in
North Africa in 1943.

Fifteen hundred Jews from Palestine served in the Royal
Air Force. Hundreds more served in the Royal Navy. Brave
Palestinian youths undertook dangerous missions which helped
defeat the pro-Germans in Syria and in Iraq.

After five years of fighting Winston Churchill announced
the formation of a Jewish Brigade in September, 1944. He
said then:

"I know that there are vast numbers of Jews serving with
our forces and the American forces throughout all the Allied
armies. But it seems to be indeed appropriate that a special
Jewish unit of that race which suffered indescribable torment
from the Nazis should be represented as a distinct formation
among the forces gathered for their final overthrow."

The Jewish Brigade saw action on the Italian front and in
Central Europe. They rendered great service not only to the
Allied forces but to many of the homeless Jewish victims of

Fascist terror. Their symbol was the *Magen David* (Shield of David) which was greeted with enthusiasm wherever they went.

The exploits of the 32 Palestinian parachutists are especially famous. Trained by the British they were given the task of establishing contact with Tito's partisans in Yugoslavia and the partisans in Hungary and Roumania. A special purpose of their mission was to help free the hundreds of fallen American and British aviators, who had been imprisoned in the Balkan countries, by supplying them with maps, documents etc. Many an American aviator owes his freedom to the brave Palestinians.

Among the parachutists was a girl named Hannah Senesch. She had come to Palestine from her native Hungary in 1939. After studying at an agricultural school in Nahalal, she entered a colony called *Sdot Yam*. Hannah was chosen for her dangerous mission partly because of her knowledge of Hungarian. She and the others agreed to parachute into Europe provided they would also be permitted to rescue Jews in these lands.

On March 13, 1944 Hannah and 4 men parachuted into Yugoslavia where they immediately established contact with Tito's partisans who greeted them with the words, "Death to fascism; freedom to the people." After completing her mission Hannah resolved to cross the border into Hungary in the hope of rescuing Jewish survivors.

Hannah Senesch compared her life to a match which kindles a flame. The match may be consumed, but the flame continues to burn brightly. This thought she expressed in a brief Hebrew poem of 4 lines which she penned while on her mission.

> Blessed is the match that is consumed while kindling
>   flames,
> Blessed is the flame which burns in the secret chambers
>   of our hearts,

Blessed are the hearts which, for honor's sake, will
    cease their beating,
Blessed is the match that is consumed while kindling
    flames.

Her words were prophetic. After crossing the border into
Hungary Hannah Senesch was betrayed by peasants. She was
executed because of her refusal to reveal the secret code of
the partisans.

Her life had been consumed so that the flame of freedom
might burn more brightly.

3. UNDERGROUND TO PALESTINE

Meanwhile, the gates of Palestine remained closed. Before
the outbreak of war the Jewish Agency asked for the immediate admission of 30,000 children from Poland and the Bal-
kans. The request was denied. The children were trapped,
and were later sent to extermination camps by the Germans.

Thousands of refugees who succeeded in escaping from
Europe were prevented by the British from entering Palestine.
The tragic story of the *Struma* in 1941 is an example of what
the White Paper meant to the helpless victims of persecution. Not permitted to land in Palestine the unseaworthy boat
foundered in the Black Sea and sank. Seven hundred and
sixty-eight refugees aboard the *Struma* were drowned.

After the war the Jewish survivors throughout Europe
pleaded, "Open the gates of Palestine."

Guided by agents of the *Haganah*, the refugees streamed
toward Mediterranean ports and crowded into whatever boats
could be found. Sometimes they were merely small motor-
boats or sailboats. Yet nothing could prevent the wanderers
from continuing toward their goal.

One of these small ships which set sail in the winter of
1945 was named the *Hannah Senesch*, in honor of the brave
parachutist. A terrible storm broke out as the boat approached
the shores of Palestine. The rowboats which were used to
land the immigrants capsized. Those waiting on the shore

COLONISTS IN ISRAEL

leaped into the waves and swam to the rowboats, each one returning with an immigrant on his back. A human chain was then formed and the remainder of those aboard were passed along until all had been saved. The British found the empty boat the next day capsized on a sand-bank. On the overturned ship was a blue and white flag and a declaration by the *Haganah* that Israel would return to its home.

Another ship which was intercepted by the British outside of Haifa flew a long banner over the deck which contained these words:

"We survived Hitler. Death is no stranger to us. Nothing can keep us from our Jewish homeland. The blood be on your head if you fire on this unarmed ship."

Soon the detention camps set up by the British in Palestine were filled to overflowing with those to whom Zion represented their one hope in life.

EXERCISES

I. True or false? (Review section 1, pages 293 to 294.)

1. Over one million Jews fought in the Allied armies in World War II.
2. The heroes of the Warsaw Ghetto expected to defeat the German army in Poland.
3. There were many cultural activities within the Warsaw Ghetto.
4. The heroes of the Warsaw Ghetto had faith in the future of the Jewish people.
5. Mordecai Anilewitz, leader of the Warsaw Ghetto, escaped through the sewers of Warsaw.

II. Complete each sentence. (Review section 2, pages 294 to 297.)

Winston Churchill, General Kisch, Hannah Senesch, Marshall Tito, Dr. Weizmann

1. _____ pledged the support of Palestinian Jewry and the Jewish Agency to Britain during World War II.

2. _____ helped win the Battle of El Alamein by planning the "pipe line to victory."

3. _____ gave English permission for the formation of a Jewish Brigade.

4. The parachutists had to establish contact with the partisans under the command of _____.

5. _____ was captured when she crossed the border into Hungary in the hope of saving Jewish lives.

III. Write a sentence about each of the following topics. (Review section 3, pages 297 to 299.)

1. *Struma* 2. The White Paper 3. *Haganah* 4. The *Hannah Senesch*

IV. Questions for discussion:

1. What contribution did Jews make to the war effort in World War II?

2. How did Palestinian Jewry carry out the policy set by David Ben-Gurion: "We will fight the war as if there were no White Paper, and we will fight the White Paper as if there were no war"?

3. Why have Jews been inspired by the resistance of those in the Warsaw Ghetto?

THINGS TO DO

1. *Songs*—The song of the Warsaw Ghetto, *Ani Maamin* ("I believe") has become famous. Learn one of the songs of the Jewish partisans in Europe or of the *Haganah* and the resistance movement in Palestine. These songs have been recorded and may also be found in song anthologies.

2. *Eternal Light*—Here are some "Eternal Light" scripts that can be dramatized or read in class:

"All These Barren Hills"—The story of *Kibbutz Buchenwald* where the survivors of a concentration camp prepare for life on the soil in Palestine

"The Battle of the Warsaw Ghetto"

"The Girl Without A Name"—The story of a survivor of a concentration camp

"The Lantern in the Inferno"—The story of Hannah Senesch

"Lifeline"—An American Jew helps refugees reach Palestine
"Little Sakiki"—A war-torn family is reunited
"On Wings of Eagles"—The Yemenite Jews return to Zion
"The Trees of Galilee"—A memorial forest is planted by the
children of America

CHAPTER XXV

AN INDEPENDENT JEWISH STATE

1. PARTITION

MOVED by the plight of the inmates of European concentration camps, President Harry Truman wrote to British Prime Minister Clement Attlee in 1945 urging that 100,000 certificates be issued immediately for Jewish immigration into Palestine. After long negotiations it was decided to send an Anglo-American Committee of Inquiry to investigate the possibilities of immigration. The 12 members of the Anglo-American Committee conducted an extended series of investigations. They then unanimously recommended the revocation of the White Paper. They advised that restrictions on land sales be dropped and that 100,000 Jews be permitted to enter Palestine immediately. Truman quickly endorsed these recommendations. To the astonishment of the world, however, Britain turned them down saying they could not be enforced.

Meanwhile, England decided on a harsher policy toward the refugees. They sent all whom they intercepted to the island of Cyprus where the immigrants were placed in detention camps behind barbed wires. When this did not deter the refugees the British forcibly returned those on the boat *Exodus: 1947* to Germany. The civilized world was shocked at the barbaric action of forcing helpless victims of Hitler to return to the country where they had suffered so deeply.

The Jews of Palestine now resorted to active resistance. There were serious incidents involving attacks, reprisals, imprisonment and hanging.

Unable any longer to maintain peace and order, England referred the Palestine question to the United Nations. Again, there was a committee of inquiry. This time the committee revived the partition proposal. Let Palestine be divided, they recommended, into two states—an Arab state and a Jewish state. Jerusalem would belong to neither state, but would be internationalized because of its holy places.

Chaim Weizmann appeared before a committee of the General Assembly of the United Nations to endorse the partition proposal. Only in this way, he believed, could there be peace between Arab and Jew.

"The independence of all Arab territories outside Palestine," he said, "has now been fulfilled. The realm of Arab independence stretches far and wide. Independence is not the exclusive right of the Arabs. We Jews have an equal claim to it."

The Arab nations were fiercely opposed to any such compromise. President Truman approved the partition resolution as a fair solution. Soviet Russia, too, agreed that a Jewish state be established in those sections of Palestine where the Jews were in a majority, and that the remainder of Palestine be set up as an Arab state. Since Russia had outlawed Zionism, her support came as a distinct surprise.

After a historic debate the United Nations General Assembly approved the partition resolution on November 29, 1947 by a vote of 33 to 13.

2. INDEPENDENCE

The United Nations had made no provision for enforcing the resolution. It was clear that there would be war between the Arabs and Jews as soon as the British evacuated Palestine on May 15, 1948.

On the eve of the British evacuation, on May 14, 1948, the Jews of Palestine announced the formation of a new Jewish state to be called Israel.

The Israeli Declaration of Independence proclaims:

"The land of Israel was the birthplace of the Jewish people. . . . Here they wrote and gave the Bible to the world.

"Exiled from Palestine, the Jewish people remained faithful to it in all the countries of their dispersion, never ceasing to pray and hope for their return and restoration of their national freedom.

"Impelled by this historic association, Jews strove throughout the centuries to go back to the land of their fathers and regain statehood. In recent decades they returned in their masses. They reclaimed a wilderness, revived their language, built cities and villages, and established a vigorous and ever-growing community, with its own economic and cultural life. They sought peace, yet were ever prepared to defend themselves. They brought blessings of progress to all inhabitants of the country.

"In the year 1897 the first Zionist Congress, inspired by Theodore Herzl's vision of a Jewish state, proclaimed the right of the Jewish people to a national revival in their own country.

"This right was acknowledged by the Balfour Declaration of November 2, 1917, and reaffirmed by the mandate of the League of Nations, which gave explicit international recognition to the historic connection of the Jewish people with Palestine and their right to reconstitute their national home.

"In the Second World War, the Jewish people in Palestine made a full contribution in the struggle of freedom-loving nations against the Nazi evil. . . .

"On November 29, 1947, the General Assembly of the United Nations adopted a resolution for re-establishment of an independent Jewish State in Palestine. . . . This recognition by the United Nations of the rights of the Jewish people to establish their independent state may not be revoked. . . .

"Accordingly we, the members of the National Council, representing the Jewish people in Palestine and the Zionist movement of the world, met together in solemn assembly by virtue of the natural and historic right of the Jewish people and the resolution of the General Assembly of the United Nations, hereby proclaim the establishment of the Jewish state in Palestine, to be called Israel."

3. THE NEW STATE

A provisional government was formed under the leadership of David Ben-Gurion. President Truman immediately recognized the new state in the name of the United States.

Seven Arab nations declared war against Israel as soon as the British departed. Egypt, Iraq, Jordan, Labanon, Saudi Arabia, Syria, and Yemen defied the United Nations and sent their armies to destroy the new state. The soldiers of the *Haganah*, now the army of Israel, fought like the Maccabees of old. To the amazement of the world the *Haganah* won a series of brilliant victories over the invading armies. Besieged by the Arab Legion, the new city of Jerusalem was, for a while, completely isolated from the rest of Israel. Although Jerusalem had been declared an international city no nation raised a finger in its defense. Jews, however, succeeded in building a Burma Road over the hills, and supplied the necessary provisions to the besieged population.

The Security Council of the United Nations twice demanded that there be an immediate truce. Israel readily agreed but the Arabs continued to wage war until they recognized that they were hopelessly beaten. At last they signed an armistice which put an end to the fighting.

Meanwhile, elections were conducted in Israel so that a permanent government could be formed. On February 14, 1949 the elected members of the *Knesset*, or parliament, met in Jerusalem. It was the traditional day for the planting of trees, and indeed in the hearts of the Jewish people there was springtime and the seeds of new hope.

On February 17, 1949 Dr. Chaim Weizmann was elected the first President of Israel. An honor guard led him to the platform as the *shofar* was sounded and *Hatikvah* was sung.

Dr. Weizmann then took the oath of office, "I, son of Ozer and Rachel Weizmann, undertake as President of the state to maintain allegiance to the State of Israel and its laws."

Dr. Weizmann chose David Ben-Gurion as the first Prime Minister of the new state.

On May 11, 1949 Israel became the 59th member of the United Nations.

From all corners of the world Jews now turned toward Zion. First came the displaced persons of Europe. They were followed by the Jews of Yemen, Iraq and Iran who were brought by airplane since land and water routes were closed to them. This project was appropriately named "Operation Magic Carpet." The Jews of North Africa came next. Within three years the population of Israel had more than doubled.

There were many problems confronting the new state. Arab nations were still hostile; immigrants had to be absorbed; the desert waited to be reclaimed. It was a long and hard road that the Jews of Israel had to traverse. Yet there was rejoicing in the heart of every Jew. The words of the prophet Jeremiah had at last come true:

"Refrain thy voice from weeping,
And thine eyes from tears;
For thy work shall be rewarded, saith the Lord;
And they shall come back from the land of the enemy.
And there is hope for thy future, saith the Lord;
And thy children shall return to their own border."

EXERCISES

I. Choose the correct word or phrase. (Review section 1, pages 302 to 303.)

1. _____ recommended admission of 100,000 Jews to Palestine. (President Truman, Prime Minister Attlee)

2. The Anglo-American Committee of Inquiry advised that the sale of land to Jews throughout Palestine be _____. (permitted, prohibited)

3. England forced the refugees on the _____ to return to Germany. (*Exodus: 1947, Hannah Senesch*)

4. The proposal that Palestine be divided between an Arab State and a Jewish State was approved by the _____. (Arabs, Jews)

5. The United Nations _____ partition by a vote of 33 to 13. (approved, rejected)

II. Explain the importance of each of these dates in Jewish history. (Review section 2, pages 303 to 304.)

1. 1897 2. November 2, 1917 3. November 29, 1947 4. May 14, 1948

III. Match. (Review section 3, pages 305 to 306.)

Column A	Column B
David Ben-Gurion	1. Recognized the new state of Israel
Haganah	2. First Prime Minister of Israel
Knesset	3. Defense army of Israel
Harry Truman	4. First President of Israel
Chaim Weizmann	5. Parliament of Israel

IV. Questions for discussion:

1. What are some of the problems confronting Israel today?
2. One proposal made before the partition of Palestine was a bi-national state where Jews and Arabs would enjoy equal rights. Do you think such a solution would have succeeded?
3. Was England successful in carrying out the mandate?
4. How has the United States helped in establishing a Jewish State?

REVIEW QUESTIONS

for Units Five and Six (pages 205 to 307)

1. Mention the contribution of each of the following Jews to American life: Francis Salvador, Gershom Seixas, Haym Salomon, Isaac Franks, Uriah P. Levy, Emma Lazarus, Louis D. Brandeis, Jonas Salk.
2. Tell why each of the following is important in Jewish history: Judah Touro, Mordecai Noah, Isaac Leeser, Theodore Herzl, Eliezer Ben-Yehuda, Chaim Weizmann, David Ben-Gurion.
3. Tell how each of the following American presidents helped the Jewish people: Washington, Jefferson, Lincoln, Truman.
4. Discuss each of the following quotations:
    a. "Proclaim liberty throughout all the land unto all the inhabitants thereof."

    b. "Give me your tired, your poor, your huddled masses yearning to breathe free."

    c. "If you will it, then it is no legend."

    d. "Blessed is the match that is consumed while kindling flames."

5. Identify:

Joseph Jonas, Isaac M. Wise, David Lubin, Henrietta Szold, Stephen S. Wise, Albert Einstein, David Wolff-sohn, Baron Rothschild, A. D. Gordon, Herman Kisch, Hannah Senesch.

6. Tell why each of the following is important in the history of Zionism: *Hovevei Zion*, Bilu, Basle Program, Balfour Declaration, League of Nations Mandate, United Nations Partition Resolution, May 14, 1948.

7. Mention 4 great achievements of American Jewry.

8. Discuss each of the following topics:

    a. Jews As American Patriots

    b. The Main Waves of Jewish Immigration to the United States

    c. Herzl's *Jewish State* and *Altneuland*

    d. Palestine Under the British Mandate

    e. Jews in World War II

    f. The Arab Problem

9. Discuss the importance of each of the following places in Israel: *Rishon Le-Zion, Mikveh Israel,* Tel Aviv, Degania, Nahalal, Haifa, Jerusalem.

10. Explain each of the following: *Aliya, kvutza, moshav, Yishuv, haluzim, Haganah, Knesset, Magen David.*

TEST

on Units Five and Six

I. Match. (20 points)

Column A	Column B
Emma Lazarus	1. Parachutist who wrote poem, "Blessed is the Match"
Isaac Leeser	2. Poet who wrote, "New Colossus"

Baron Rothschild   3. Financier who aided American Revolution

Haym Salomon   4. Rabbi who translated Bible into English

Hannah Senesch   5. Financier who aided colonies in Palestine

II. Who am I? (20 points)

1. I wrote a letter to the Jews of Newport, Rhode Island stating that the United States gives "to bigotry no sanction," and extends equal rights to all of its citizens.

2. I served my country at the Battle of New Orleans. I was known for my generous gifts. I helped to provide the funds for the Bunker Hill Monument. I supported synagogues, hospitals, libraries, schools, Palestine and many other worthy causes.

3. I was known as the first American Zionist. I tried to establish a Jewish colony called Ararat at Grand Island, New York. I served as American Consul in Tunis, North Africa.

4. I was a correspondent who witnessed the Dreyfus trial in France. I founded the World Zionist Congress in Basle in 1897 and negotiated with the Sultan of Turkey for a charter to Palestine.

5. I was a chemist who discovered a new method for producing acetone. I persuaded England to issue the Balfour Declaration in 1917, and was elected first president of Israel in 1949.

III. Choose the correct word or phrase. (20 points)

1. "Proclaim liberty throughout all the land unto all the inhabitants thereof," is found on the _____. (Liberty Bell, Statue of Liberty)

2. The man who did the most for the revival of Hebrew as a spoken language was _____. (David Ben-Gurion, Eliezer Ben-Yehuda)

3. The name of the novel by Theodore Herzl telling of Palestine's glorious future is _____. (*Altneuland*, *The Jewish State*)

4. The partition resolution establishing a Jewish state was

approved by a vote of 33 to 13 by the General Assembly of the _____. (League of Nations, United Nations)

5. The Israeli Parliament is called _____. (*Knesset, Yishuv*)

IV. Complete each sentence. (20 points)
Degania, Jerusalem, *Mikveh Israel*, Nahalal, Tel Aviv

1. An agricultural school was established at _____ by the Alliance. The Bilu colonists obtained work here. It was also the scene of a meeting between Theodore Herzl and the German Emperor.

2. _____ was established in the sand dunes north of Jaffa. It became Israel's largest city.

3. _____ is a *moshav* or semi-collective. It was established by *haluzim* in the Emek on land purchased by the Jewish National Fund. The colonists had to dry the swamps which were a source of sickness.

4. _____ is a *kvutza* or collective. It was established in 1911 by A. D. Gordon and others who believed in the "religion of labor."

5. _____ was the capital of David's kingdom. Weizmann laid the cornerstone of the Hebrew University on Mt. Scopus near this city in 1918. According to the partition resolution it was supposed to be an international city, but the Jews have governed the newer section of the city since the nations of the world failed to defend its population against Arab attack in the Israeli War for Independence.

V. Discuss fully any *2* of the following topics. (20 points)
1. The Main Achievements of American Jewry
2. Jews as American Patriots
3. Palestine under the British
4. Jews in World War II

OLDEST CONGREGATIONS IN THE UNITED STATES

Name	City	Year
Shearith Israel ("Remnant of Israel")	New York City, N. Y.	1654
Jeshuat Israel ("Salvation of Israel")	Newport, Rhode Island	1658
Mikveh Israel ("Hope of Israel")	Savannah, Georgia	1733
Mikveh Israel	Philadelphia, Pennsylvania	1740
Beth Elohim ("House of God")	Charleston, South Carolina	1750
Beth Ahabah ("House of Love")	Richmond, Virginia	1789
Rodeph Shalom ("Pursuer of Peace")	Philadelphia	1800
Baltimore Hebrew Congregation	Baltimore, Maryland	1823
B'nai Israel ("Sons of Israel")	Cincinnati, Ohio	1824
B'nai Jeshurun ("Sons of Righteousness")	New York City	1825
Touro Synagogue	New Orleans, Louisiana	1828
Adath Israel ("Congregation of Israel")	Louisville, Kentucky	1836
Shaarei Zedek ("Gates of Righteousness")	New York City	1837
Beth Emeth ("House of Truth")	Albany, N. Y.	1840

IMMIGRATION TO ISRAEL, 1948-1956

Country	Number
Iraq	123,179
Roumania	123,118
Morocco, Tunis and Algiers	114,074
Poland	104,723
Yemen	45,894
Bulgaria	38,477
Turkey	35,250
Libya	32,150
Iran	31,645
Other North African Countries	20,798
Czechoslovakia	18,323
Hungary	14,414
Germany	9,215
Yugoslavia	7,714
India	5,199
Russia, Latvia and Lithuania	5,012
France	4,677
Other Asiatic Countries	4,608
Aden	3,267
Austria	3,169
England	2,813
Argentina	2,705
United States	2,585
China	2,506
Greece	2,150
Italy	1,615
South American Countries	1,579
Holland	1,431
Belgium	1,270
Other Countries	31,930
Total	**795,392**

WORLD JEWISH POPULATION (1955)

United States	5,200,000
Soviet Russia	2,000,000
Israel	1,488,470
England	450,000
Argentina	360,000
France	300,000
Morocco	255,000
Canada	230,000
Roumania	225,000
Algeria	140,000
Hungary	140,000
Brazil	120,000
Union South Africa	110,000
Tunisia	105,000
Iran	80,000
Australia	53,750
Turkey	50,000
Poland	45,000
Belgium	40,000
Chile	40,000
Egypt	40,000
Uruguay	40,000
Italy	34,400
Holland	25,000
India	25,000
Mexico	25,000
Other Countries	245,000
Total	11,866,620

IMPORTANT DATES IN
JEWISH HISTORY

1215   Rabbi Meir of Rothenburg was born. He died in 1293.

1242   The Talmud was burned in Paris.

1264   Jews of Poland received a charter of privileges.

1290   Jews were expelled from England.

1394   Jews were expelled from France.

1437   Don Isaac Abravanel was born in Lisbon. He died in Venice in 1508.

1480   The Inquisition was established in Spain. It was introduced into Portugal in 1536.

1492   Abravanel led the exodus of Jews from Spain.

1492   Jews helped Columbus in the discovery of America.

1516   Turkey gained control of Palestine. In 1561 Turkey granted Joseph Nasi permission to rebuild Tiberias.

1524   David Reubeni was acclaimed in Rome as an ambassador of the Lost Ten Tribes.

1555   Joseph Karo completed the *Shulchan Aruk*, code of Jewish laws, in Palestine.

1593   Marrano Jews established the first Jewish community in Amsterdam.

1630   Jews settled in Pernambuco, Brazil.

1648   Chmelnitzki destroyed many Jewish communities in Poland.

1654   Twenty-three Jews from Brazil landed in New Amsterdam.

1655   Menasseh ben Israel helped reestablish a Jewish community in England.

1666   Sabbatai Zevi, the false Messiah, was imprisoned by the Sultan.

1700   Israel Baal Shem Tov, founder of *Hasidism*, was born. He died in 1760.

1776   The Declaration of Independence ushered in an era of equality for Jews in the New World.

1786   Moses Mendelssohn died.

1791   Jews of France were granted full equality.

1795   The final partition of Poland took place. Over a million Jews became subject to the Russian Czar.

1798   The Vilna Gaon died.

1807   Napoleon called together the Grand Sanhedrin in Paris.

1840   Moses Montefiore succeeded in freeing the Jews of Damascus from the blood accusation.

1848   Political unrest in Germany caused many Jews to migrate to the United States.

1858   English Jewry achieved full political emancipation.

1881   Eliezer ben Yehuda began his campaign for the revival of Hebrew as a spoken language.

1882   The May Laws in Russia caused mass immigration of Jews from Eastern Europe to the United States.

1882   Members of the Bilu student organization began the first *Aliya* (wave of immigration) to Palestine.

1897   Theodore Herzl presided at the first World Zionist Congress in Basle, Switzerland.

1909   Tel Aviv was founded.

1917   The Balfour Declaration was issued by the British Government on November 2.

1933   Hitler's rise to power meant ruin for German Jewry.

1943   The Jews of the Warsaw Ghetto put up a heroic resistance against the Nazis.

1947   On November 29 the United Nations approved the partition plan which provided for the establishment of a Jewish state.

1948   On May 14 the new State of Israel came into existence.

1949   Israel became the 59th member of the United Nations.

1954   American Jewry celebrated its 300th anniversary.

INDEX

KEY

ärm, hăt, āte, ēat, ĕnd, thêy, înk, īce, ĭll, ōld, nŏt, môre, rūle, ŭp

A-bō'ab, 95-96
A-brä-va-nel', Isaac, 37-43, 61-62, 91
A-brä-va-nel', Samuel, 36-38
Alexander II, 196-197
Alexander III, 197
Ä-lî-yä', 277, 284
Amsterdam, 80-89, 97-99
Arabs, 72, 286-289, 305
Auto-Emancipation, 198

Bä'-äl Shem Tôv, 132-139
Băl' foūr, 279-281
Bay Psalm Book, 102
Ben-Gū-rî-on', 277-278, 290, 305
Ben-Ye-hu-da',275-277
Berlin, 157-166
Bible, 14, 20, 39, 54, 86, 117, 134, 165,
  198, 207, 236, 306
Bî-lū', 260-263
Black Plague, 30
Bōle' släv, 112
Brandeis, 248-252
Brazil, 93-96

Chä-nu-kah', 13, 118
Chmel-nïtz' ki, 123-124, 127
Columbus, 91-93
Con-stan-ti-nō'ple, 67, 127, 268
Cŏs'sacks, 123-125
Council of the Four Lands, 113-116,
  128
Cré-mieux', 183-184, 237
Cresques (crĕsk), 35
Cromwell, 86-88
Crusades, 17, 19, 26, 71, 111

Da-măs'cus, 183-184
De-gän'ia, 278-279
Drêy' fus, 264

Ein'steïn, 250
Emancipation, 160-164, 169-177, 180-
  191
England, 25-29, 180-190, 279-303
Fer'di-nänd, 39-46
France, 17-19, 169-177
Fran'kel, 157
Franks, 211-212
Frederick, 159-161
Fur-tä'do, 172-176

Germany, 17, 19-22, 47-49, 155-166,
  285, 293
ghĕt'to, 155-156, 293-294
Gordon, 278
Gra-nä'da, 40-41

Hä-gä-näh', 289, 297, 299, 305
Haï'fa, 271, 285, 299
hä-lū-zim', 285-286
Hä-me-äs-sĕf', 164-165
Häs'i-dism, 132-139, 146-147
Häs-kä-läh', 164-166, 198
Hebrew, 35, 198-199, 230, 275-277
Hebrew Union College, 236
Hebrew University, 284
hê'der, 116, 132, 157
Herzl, 263-272
Holland, 80-89, 94-101
Hope of Israel, 84-86
Hō-ve-vāi' Zion, 259, 261

Ïbn Ĕz'ra, 34, 92
Ïn-qui-śi'tion, 40, 45-55
Isaac El-chä-nän' Yeshiva, 236
Ïś-a-bĕl'la, 39-46, 91-92
Israel, Land of, 71-78, 147, 187-190,
  259-305, 312
Italy, 50-52, 61-68

317

Jefferson, 207, 210, 212-213
Je-ru'sa-lem, 13, 126, 187-190, 284, 305
Jewish Theological Seminary, 236-237
Jō'nas, 232-233
Jō'seph of Rōs'heim, 47-50, 53

Käb-bä-läh', 73-74, 125, 132
Kăr'ō, 76-78
ke-hĭl-läh', 113, 149
Kisch, 295
Knĕs'set, 305
kvü-tzä', 278, 285

La-dî'nō, 67, 112
Lăz'a-rus, 245-247
League of Nations, 284, 290
Lēe'ser, 234-236
Les'sing, 158-163
Lē'vī ben Gersh'on, 36
Lē'vy, Ăs-ser, 95-101
Levy, Urī'ah, 220
Lincoln, 239-242
Lith-u-a'ni-a, 144-150
London, 25-29, 80, 180-190
Longfellow, 103-104
Love of Zion, 198-199
Lū'bin, 249
Lûb-lîn', 114-116, 122
Lū'ri-a, 73-74
Lū-si-ťa'nus, 63, 68-69

Mä-gen' Dä-vid', 296
Mä-pū', 198
Mar-rä'nos, 45-55, 80-88, 91-94, 180
Mär-ti-nĕz', 36-37
May Laws, 197,244
Mĕdz'î-buz, 134
Mê-îr' of Rŏ'then-burg, 17-24
Me-năs'seh ben Israel, 82-89
Men'dels-sohn, 155-166
Mĕs-sī'ah, 51, 62, 125-128
Mik-vêh' Israel, 260, 269
Mir-a-beau', 169-171
Mŏl'cho, 51-53
Mon-te-fi-ô're, 180-190
mô-shäv', 285

Nä-hä-läl', 285-286
Napoleon, 172-177
Nä-sī', Grä'ci-a, 65-72

Nä-sî', Joseph, 66-73
Nathan the Wise, 162-164
Nĕm'i-rov, 124
New Amsterdam, 96-101
Newport, 103-104
New York, 96-101, 245-249
Nicholas I, 184-185, 194-196
Noah, 225-230
Nū'nez, Maria, 80-82
Nū'nez, Samuel, 55

Ŏk'up, 132

Paris, 17-18, 171-175
Passover, 13, 46-49, 118, 195
Pĕr'etz, 195-196, 199-200
Per-nam-bu'-co, 94-96
Perpetual Almanac, 94
Pĕt'äch Tik-väh', 259
Pinsker, 198, 259
Poland, 111-150
Portugal, 35, 38-39, 46-55, 93-96
Purim, 13, 118

Räm-bäm', 17, 27, 35, 119, 157, 166
Räsh'î, 14, 64, 117
Rĕm'brändt, 82-85
Rĕn-ai-ssäncе', 62-64
Reū-bê'ni, 50-53
Richard the Lion-Hearted, 26-27, 32
Rī-shôn' Le-Zion, 259, 261, 263
Rŏth'en-burg, 19
Rothschild, Edmond de, 259, 266
Rothschild, Lionel de, 182
Roumania, 186-187
Russia, 148-150, 184-185, 194-200

Săb'ba-taī Ze-vî', 125-128
Săf'ed, 73-78
Salk, 250
Săl'o-mon, Haym, 209-212
Săl'va-dor, 207-208
Săn-hĕd'rin, 77, 173-176
Santangel, 91-93
Seixas (Sä'shis), 208-212, 220
Sĕn'esch, 296-297
Se-vîlle', 36, 91
Shakespeare, 29, 64, 80, 193
Shä-vū-ôt', 13, 116-117
She-ā-rith' Israel, 55, 99, 208-209
Shul-chän' Ä-rūk', 77

Sinz'heim, 172-175
Spain, 34-50
Spin-ō'za, 85, 166
Stuyvesant, 96-101
Suk-kôt', 13, 102
Syria, 183-184
Szōld, 252

Täl'mud, 14, 115, 119, 146, 148, 236
Tĕl A-vîv', 278
Tĭ-bē'ri-as, 71-73
Ti-rä'dō, 80-82
Tôr-que-mä'da, 40-46
Tŏr'res, 92-93
Toū'ro, 220-225
Trū'man, 302-303, 305
Turkey, 65-73, 125-128, 184, 269

United Nations, 302-303, 306
United States, 207-254

Venice, 61-66
Victoria, 181, 184, 185
Vil'na Gä-ôn', 144-150
Vō-lŏzh'in, 146-148

Warsaw, 149, 293-294
Washington, 212, 214-216
Weiz'mann, 278-284, 286-288, 305
Williams, Roger, 102
Wise, Isaac M., 235-236
Wise, Stephen S., 252, 266, 292
Wolff'sohn, 266-268, 272
World War II, 293-297

Ye-shî-vä', 119, 148, 236
Yiddish, 112, 199-200, 244
Yish-ūv', 259, 284, 289
Yôm-Kip-pur', 46, 81-82, 134, 136

Zä-cū'tō, 36, 92-94
Zionism, 259-271

Cyprus

Damascus

Mediterranean
Sea

Beth-El

Jerusalem

Hebron

Beersheba

Goshen

Egypt

Nile River

Red Sea